STRATEGIC CHALLENGES
in the BALTIC SEA REGION

STRATEGIC CHALLENGES
in the BALTIC SEA REGION
RUSSIA, DETERRENCE, *and* REASSURANCE

ANN-SOFIE DAHL, *Editor*
Foreword by ANDERS FOGH RASMUSSEN

Georgetown University Press
Washington, DC

The publisher is not responsible for third-party websites or their content. URL links were active at time of publication.

Library of Congress Cataloging-in-Publication Data

Names: Dahl, Ann-Sofie, editor.
Title: Strategic challenges in the Baltic Sea region : Russia, deterrence, and reassurance / Ann-Sofie Dahl, editor.
Description: Washington, D.C. : Georgetown University Press, 2018.
Identifiers: LCCN 2017036327| ISBN 9781626165700 (hardcover : alk. paper) | ISBN 9781626165717 (pbk. : alk. paper) | ISBN 9781626165724 (ebook)
Subjects: LCSH: Baltic Sea Region—Strategic aspects. | North Atlantic Treaty Organization—Baltic States. | Scandinavia—Strategic aspects. | North Atlantic Treaty Organization—Scandinavia. | Europe, Northern—Strategic aspects. | Russia (Federation)—Relations—Baltic Sea Region. | Baltic Sea Region—Relations—Russia (Federation) | North Atlantic Treaty Organization—United States.
Classification: LCC UA646.53 .S77 2018 | DDC 355/.0330485—dc23
LC record available at https://lccn.loc.gov/2017036327

♾ This book is printed on acid-free paper meeting the requirements of the American National Standard for Permanence in Paper for Printed Library Materials.

19 18   9 8 7 6 5 4 3 2   First printing

Printed in the United States of America

Cover design by Jeremy John Parker.

CONTENTS

FOREWORD

The security of the Baltic Sea region is a topic more pertinent now than ever before in our post–Cold War history. At the same time, it has been rather understudied. A comprehensive compilation of state-of-the-art analyses on various topics about the region by some of the top experts in the field, this book is a welcome contribution to public debate.

Ultimately, the Baltic Sea region is becoming a theater of increased geopolitical tensions. What is becoming ever more evident is that it has become a new front line in tensions with Russia. As a result, to calm tensions along this fragile border, the West must display more resolve and unity.

Russia seeks to play a role in the Baltic region, and that should be respected as long as the interests are exercised in accordance with international law and principles. The region constitutes the most densely populated area in Russia and is a main choke point for Russian exports of goods and oil. Russian ports on the Baltic Sea handle 53 percent of Russia's total container throughput—twice as much as the second-largest area, the Far East. With Nord Stream 1 and the planned Nord Stream 2 gas pipeline projects, the region has become a vital part of Russia's energy policy.

Nonetheless, Russia should play the role of a constructive partner in the region rather than seeking to escalate tensions to divert attention away from its deteriorating domestic situation and economy. Unfortunately, we are now experiencing quite the opposite. We have seen a rapid worsening of the relationship between the West and Russia in recent years. Russia has illegally occupied parts of Ukraine, Russian fighter jets and submarines are displaying aggressive behavior in the Baltic Sea, and Russia has been increasing its military presence on shared borders. Despite previous assurances of the opposite, Russia has deployed Iskander-M short-range ballistic missiles to Kaliningrad, effectively exposing the North Atlantic Treaty Organization's most critical areas of the Baltic Sea. The Kremlin's decision to deploy the missiles has altered the strategic landscape and rightly so set warning bells ringing in Estonia, Latvia, Lithuania, and Poland.

Our end-goal should be normalization with Russia. But we will not get there by division and weakness. The West has been slow off the mark. We failed to respond with unity and resolve when Russia seized gas supplies to Ukraine in 2006 and 2009 and when it invaded Georgia in 2008.

The 2014 invasion of Ukraine was an eye-opener for the Western community and helped to pave the way for the decision made at the 2014 NATO summit in Wales in which NATO member states decided to create a spearhead force of five thousand troops, maintained on high alert. Two years later at the 2016 summit in Warsaw, NATO additionally decided to deploy four multinational battle groups totaling five thousand troops to Poland and the Baltic countries, as well as to tailor a forward presence in Southeastern Europe as part of NATO's Enhanced Forward Presence. The recent reinforcements are the largest of their kind since the end of the Cold War and should be perceived as a clear signal to President Vladimir Putin that a Russian military invasion of any NATO Ally would trigger a response from the Alliance.

NATO's deterrence on land has improved in recent years but is far from perfect, and there are still significant gaps in its overall deterrence posture. NATO's naval presence in the Baltic Sea is inadequate. In the case of a military confrontation, Russia's Baltic fleet currently has the upper hand. If we are to deter further Russian aggression, we must be able to control the Danish Straits and step up our maritime antiaccess and area-denial capabilities. At the Warsaw Summit, NATO recognized cyber as a domain along with air, sea, and land. Acknowledging the threat image was important, but NATO is still not fully prepared to respond to cyberattacks, "little green men" (the masked soldiers in green uniforms who appeared with Russian arms on Ukrainian territory), and Russian disinformation. The Kremlin should be allowed no wiggle room to deploy these alternative weapons.

The emerging threats are not simply a matter of capabilities, however. Responding to a resurgent Russia requires bold leadership. For the United States, this means reaffirming America's unequivocal commitment to NATO's Article 5. On the European side, it means shouldering more of the responsibility and spending more on defense. Both need to do their part. The US must express explicit support for Article 5, and Europe should assume more responsibility for its own security.

Thus far the tensions in the Baltic Sea region have not escalated to the level of military confrontation, but the situation could easily spiral out of control if the Western world fails to demonstrate and communicate its unity and resolve. I hope this book will animate discussion on the topic and breathe new life into the debate about the security of the region.

Anders Fogh Rasmussen
Prime Minister of Denmark, 2001–9
Secretary-General of NATO, 2009–14

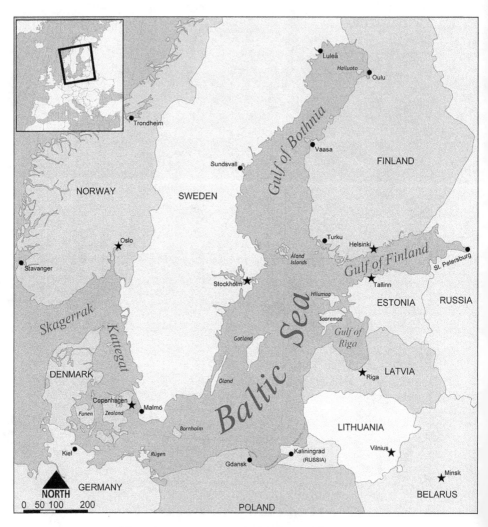

Map of the Baltic Sea region. *Norman Einstein, Wikimedia Commons*

Introduction

ANN-SOFIE DAHL

The arrival of troops from all around the North Atlantic Treaty Organization in the three Baltic states and Poland to take part in the Alliance's new Enhanced Forward Presence (EFP) in the spring of 2017 was a strong illustration of NATO's return to the original core task of collective defense. The photos of multinational troops setting up shop on NATO's eastern flank were loaded with symbolism, forceful demonstrations of the decisive turnaround undertaken by NATO in the wake of Russia's aggression in Ukraine and its illegal annexation of the Crimean Peninsula in early 2014. In addition, a US brigade combat team was cheered as it arrived in Poland and spread out to deploy across Eastern Europe as part of the European Reassurance Initiative, initiated by the United States in early 2016 with $1 billion and extended with $4.8 billion in 2017—comforting news to those who feared that the Donald Trump presidency was in the process of leaving Europe to its own destiny after seven decades of transatlantic alliance.

At the NATO summit in Wales in September 2014, a host of reassurance measures had been agreed on by the Allies in response to the Russian use of its modernized military against its neighbors. They were implemented and followed by a number of deterrence initiatives—among them the EFP—at the next summit in Warsaw in the summer of 2016.[1]

In the course of only a handful of years, the Baltic Sea region had thus made a dramatic return to the strategic front line as a result of the aggressive Russian behavior at sea, on land, and in the air. Simulated missile raids, reckless flying, incursions into the territorial waters of the countries bordering the sea, and much more, including various forms of cyber warfare, had at that point become a regular feature to the countries in the region. Added to this was a heavy military buildup, with deployment of state-of-the-art missile systems and an antiaccess/area-denial (A2/AD) challenge emerging out of the Russian enclave of Kaliningrad, including

1

Iskander missiles capable of carrying nuclear warheads and reaching targets within a hundred miles—thereby covering most, if not all, the capitals in the Baltic Sea region.[2]

Russian aggression put Baltic Sea security back at the top of NATO's strategic agenda for the first time since the Cold War and reintroduced the old, familiar concepts of deterrence and reassurance. With NATO's measures agreed on at the two summits to counter Russian revanchism and assist the vulnerable frontline states, collective defense made a forceful comeback after decades of out-of-area operations, with a focus on crisis management and collective security.

A few years after Russia shocked the world by its brutal attack on Ukraine, it is beyond dispute that the aggression emanating from Moscow is long-term and that it goes far beyond the territory of Ukraine or the Baltic Sea region. Rather, it amounts to a grand-scale challenge to the existing world order as we know it—or knew it until the annexation of Crimea. What we are seeing is a struggle for control of the entire international system, with the Baltic Sea region at the very heart of this strategic contest. By aptly exploiting the weaknesses in the West and using a range of instruments to deepen the split among and between the democratic societies and the transatlantic community, Russia has for the last decade or more consistently been seeking to undermine the role of the United States—in Europe and globally—in order to bring American global power and what remains of the unipolar system to a definite end.

In spite of the many strategic challenges confronting the West in the Baltic Sea region, there is, however, an obvious risk that regional security will gradually drop from the position as a top priority.[3] One reason for this concern is the broad spectrum of threats that we are confronted with today. While the barbaric plans of the so-called Islamic State (IS) to spread its medieval caliphate in the Middle East and beyond have successfully been halted by a US-led international coalition, Islamist terrorism has instead been brought to Europe. A historic refugee crisis, stemming from seemingly never-ending chaos in Syria and instability in Northern Africa and the Middle East, also continues to send shock waves through Europe. At a time with such daunting challenges, Baltic Sea security might not seem quite as urgent to everyone as only a short while ago when the war in Ukraine was still making headlines and Russian bombers practiced nuclear attacks in the Baltic Sea region on a more regular basis.[4]

The current global situation, with a full plate of crises, conflicts, and worries, indeed offers plenty of distractions with the ability to remove the strategic focus from the Baltic Sea region. For the countries in the region there is, however, no doubt that the Russian aggression—including the presence of tactical nuclear weapons, which according to Moscow could be used to "de-escalate" a regional conflict—has in no way slowed down. On the contrary, the deteriorated security situation caused by Russian aggression has, in a much-cited phrase used by the

Nordic defense ministers, become "the new normal" for the countries in the region.[5]

A number of factors further complicate the picture from a Western—and, in particular, a Nordic-Baltic—perspective. One, previously quite unexpected, is the scenario of a new and friendly phase in the US-Russian relationship that emerged with the election of the forty-fifth president of the United States. The prospect of a potential US strategic alignment with Russia is a disturbing notion to the actors in the Baltic Sea region and brings back memories in Europe of periods of superpower condominium during the Cold War. Though such cooperation has its declared focus on the joint struggle against IS, it could have potentially severe consequences for security in the Baltic Sea region. That would especially be the case if it were combined with a brand-new US approach to NATO's security guarantees, whereby America's support for its European Allies would be evaluated on a case-by-case basis and dependent on the level of national defense spending, as has at times been suggested by the White House. The uncertainties that keep surrounding the US commitment to NATO have added a new and disconcerting dilemma to the already complex picture of Baltic Sea security, where the EFP measures, though welcomed and appreciated by the frontline Allies themselves, are criticized by some experts for amounting to not more than a "trip wire."[6]

Another factor is Russia's expert use of untraditional methods such as hybrid warfare—"the *deliberate* 'blurring and blending'" of forces, weaponry, and tactics directed at different targets, which range from an adversary's military to the international legal order to domestic audiences.[7] Hybrid warfare, with cyber technology as a key part, makes it increasingly hard to determine, and for all Allies to agree on, when and where an attack demanding an Article 5 response has actually occurred. Such difficulties still remain, also now that cyber has been declared a domain by NATO and a cyberattack thus would constitute grounds for invoking an Article 5 response.

The fact that two of the countries of the Baltic Sea region are only NATO partners, not members, also complicates regional security and the implementation of reassurance and deterrence measures. These countries, Sweden and Finland, occupy a substantial portion of the shoreline and also possess the Åland Islands and the island of Gotland as strategic gems in the sea. Although part of NATO's exclusive group of Enhanced Opportunities Partners (EOP), nonaligned Sweden and Finland remain outside the collective-defense mechanisms of the Alliance and thereby put a strict limit to the extent and depth of military integration and joint planning in the region.

All of the above has an impact on the Baltic Sea region and needs to be taken into account when analyzing the security there. With this in mind how, then, should and could the countries in the region and their Allies meet the strategic challenges posed by an openly aggressive and expansionist Russia? What can be done to strengthen and enhance regional cooperation, and how can we make sure security in the region stays at the top of the strategic agenda at a time when other threats and challenges abound, at the same time that a split seems to be emerging within the transatlantic community between those countries in the south that see Islamic terrorism and migration as the prime causes of instability and those in the northeast confronted by Russian aggression? What are the views and perceptions of the present strategic challenges among the countries bordering the Baltic Sea, how do they differ, and why? On the following pages, these and other key aspects of Baltic Sea security today are discussed and analyzed from the expert perspectives of the authors of this volume.

This anthology is divided into three parts, with the first section assuming a broader perspective. How should Russian aggression—evident in the region already years before the Russian intervention in Ukraine—be interpreted? Are we facing a new Cold War, how has NATO responded, and what is the US perspective on security in the Baltic Sea region? This first part opens with a chapter analyzing the role of the United States—"Still the Indispensable Power"—by Robert Lieber, followed by a close look at Russian strategic thinking by Gudrun Persson. Jamie Shea provides a detailed analysis of NATO's response to the Russian aggression since 2014. Last but not least, Christopher Coker examines the West's ability to respond effectively to the challenges at hand.

The second part of this volume addresses security in the Baltic Sea region from the perspectives and responses of a number of regional Allies, which diverge in some ways but to a great extent display the converging trend that we have seen since the outbreak of hostilities in Ukraine in February 2014. While Andres Kasekamp makes the case that the Baltic states are not next in line after Ukraine, Mikkel Vedby Rasmussen takes a closer look at the ability of both Russia and the West to apply an A2/AD strategy in the region. From a Polish perspective, Justyna Got-kowska argues the need to further strengthen NATO's deterrence posture in the Baltic Sea region. Claudia Major and Alicia von Voss analyze the double-track policies of Germany, until now "the silent country" in the Baltic Sea region. And finally in this second part of the volume, Håkon Lunde Saxi concludes that Norway, a Nordic country not actually bordering on the Baltic Sea, nevertheless has vital security interests there.

The final part turns to NATO's two Nordic partners. Johan Raeder examines the role of Gotland, with a key strategic location in the Baltic Sea. Next, Ann-Sofie Dahl analyzes how the fact that two of the countries in the Baltic Sea region will be excluded for the foreseeable future from the Article 5 collective defense measures affects security in the region. In the final chapter, Karoliina Honkanen focuses on Russia's nonaligned neighbor—and NATO partner—Finland and the implications of NATO's return to collective defense on the security policy for that country.

This volume originally started as a project at the Centre for Military Studies in Copenhagen and has been sponsored by NATO Public Diplomacy.

Notes

1. For an analysis of the Wales and Warsaw Summits, see Karsten Friis, ed., *NATO and Collective Defence in the 21st Century: An Assessment of the Warsaw Summit* (London: Routledge, 2017).

2. See Gudrun Persson, Fredrik Westerlund, et al., *Russian Military Capability in a Ten-Year Perspective 2016* (Stockholm: FOI, 2016). For a presentation of the Russian weapon systems deployed in Kaliningrad, see "These Maps Show How Russia Has Europe Spooked," *Washington Post*, November 23, 2016.

3. Ann-Sofie Dahl, ed., *Baltic Sea Security: How Can Allies and Partners Meet the New Challenges in the Region?* (Copenhagen: Centre for Military Studies, January 2016).

4. Ann-Sofie Dahl, *A Continent in Chaos: The Security Implications of the European Migrant Crisis* (College Station: Scowcroft Institute, Bush School of Government, Texas A&M University, June 2016).

5. The phrase was used in an op-ed published simultaneously on April 10, 2015, in *Dagens Nyheter* (Sweden), *Aftenposten* (Norway), *JyllandsPosten* (Denmark), and *Hufvudstadsbladet* (Finland).

6. Friis, *NATO and Collective Defence*, 3.

7. Martin Murphy, Frank G. Hoffman, and Gary Schaub Jr., *Hybrid Maritime Warfare and the Baltic Sea Region* (Copenhagen: Centre for Military Studies, November 2016), 3.

PART I

The West, Russia, *and* Baltic Sea Security

1

Still the Indispensable Power

The United States and Baltic Sea Security

ROBERT J. LIEBER

For seven decades, the United States has served as the guarantor of security and stability in Europe. Yet for a time it appeared that this role was no longer so essential. The end of the Cold War, the breakup of the Soviet Union, the liberalization and democratization of Eastern Europe, and the successful independence of the Baltic states marked a profound transformation on the continent. Alongside these events, the enlargement of NATO, the expansion and deepening of the European Union (EU), and steps toward a working relationship with a much-diminished Russia through NATO's Partnership for Peace (1994) and the NATO-Russia Founding Act (1997) suggested that Ronald Reagan's vision of a Europe whole and free was at last at hand.

Under these circumstances, it was not surprising that Washington could undertake a sweeping drawdown of American forces in Europe. Already well under way in the 1990s when the focus for NATO seemed to be shifting and its challenge one of going-out-of-area or out of business, de-emphasis of the European theater accelerated after the terrorist attacks on New York and Washington on September 11, 2001. The US military soon found itself immersed in the Afghanistan and Iraq Wars, both of which became grinding conflicts after stunning initial successes. By the latter part of the decade, an American president elected with a mandate to bring the troops home now spoke of a pivot to Asia.

European Reassertion and Its Limits

Many Europeans too entertained the vision of a strong, prosperous, and self-confident Europe able to hold its own in world affairs, not divorced from America but now on a much more equal footing. This was evident as early as 1991 with the outbreak of conflict in the former Yugoslavia. Representing the then European Community (the EU's precursor), Luxembourg's foreign minister, Jacques Poos, could proclaim, "The Hour of Europe has dawned."[1] But four years, two hundred thousand deaths in Bosnia, and the Srebrenica massacre of July 1995 made painfully clear the painful limits to Europe's aspiration and finally brought the United States back in, as Washington led the NATO effort in achieving an uneasy end to the Bosnian conflict.

Sentiment for Europe's reassertion regained momentum in the following decade. The formal enlargement and deepening of the EU, the creation of the Eurozone, and the promise of a common European Defense and Foreign Policy seemed to signal that a prosperous and unified Europe of five hundred million people really was ready to assert itself.

Then came Iraq. In 2003 and 2004, France, Germany, Belgium, and others emerged as strident critics and political antagonists of the George W. Bush administration's fateful intervention against Saddam Hussein. To be sure, some two-thirds of the EU- and NATO-member governments had initially endorsed the war, either signing the Blair-Aznar letter or a similar statement of support by the Vilnius Group.[2] In the midst of a rancorous Atlantic debate, the then secretary of defense, Donald Rumsfeld, could favorably contrast support from Eastern European and Baltic countries, the "new Europe," with the "old Europe." In any case, events and growing public disenchantment during this period widened the sense of distance between Washington and key European capitals.

But that was then. The twenty-first century also saw change in Russia. Vladimir Putin succeeded the faltering Boris Yeltsin in 1999 and in the following years gradually reconsolidated state power, rebuilt the military, reined in the regions, and eviscerated the nascent Russian democracy. Emboldened in the mid-to-late 2000s by an explosive run-up in world oil prices and the almost limitless financial resources they seemed to provide, Putin began to pull back from Russia's growing engagement with the West. The process was by no means linear. Alternating the presidency and the prime ministry with the relatively more moderate Dmitri Medvedev, Putin nonetheless signaled a desire to reassert influence over Russia's former republics wherever the opportunity beckoned.

Moscow's covert and then overt interventions in the breakaway regions of Abkhazia and South Ossetia and its invasion of the Republic of Georgia in 2008 were the most conspicuous, but there was also Russia's role in the Transnistria region of Moldova and its heavy-handed influence in the internal politics and factional, regional, and ethnic conflicts of the former Central Asian republics of the

USSR. In addition, manipulation of natural gas supplies to Ukraine and Poland became a form of energy blackmail against Russia's neighbors.

Putin's return to the Russian presidency in 2011 and large-scale public protests against election rigging and repression were followed by a clampdown on domestic media and opposition groups. This was coupled with a growing and deliberately orchestrated antagonism toward Western values, increasingly explicit threats to Russia's neighbors, and a campaign of Soviet-style disinformation (*dezinformatsia*) against the United States and Western Europe.

Russia and Ukraine

Unwilling to see Kiev engage more fully with the EU and what it represented as a compelling alterative to a Moscow-dominated "Eurasian Community," Putin seized on the Maidan protests of early 2014 and the subsequent flight of Ukraine's president, Viktor Yanukovych, as a pretext to intervene. In doing so, he employed the tools of hybrid warfare. These included the arming, manipulation, and direction of local and not-so-local opponents of the Ukraine government in Crimea and then in the Donbas region of Ukraine, as well as the provision of well-armed military personnel whose uniforms and armored vehicles mysteriously lacked identifying military insignia (the notorious "little green men"). Accompanying these phenomena, there was propaganda, manipulation of the media, a rigged referendum on annexation of Crimea, and then overt intervention by Russian "volunteers" and military units.

Some, even many, of these measures had been foreshadowed by Putin's previous actions, but the scale of military intervention and the outright annexation of Crimea marked a shift in order of magnitude. Moreover, Moscow's actions in breaching a post-1945 border by force broke the rules of the European order that had been in effect since the end of World War II. This is no mere quibble about international norms and niceties: Putin transgressed agreements and treaties to which the Soviet Union and Russia had long been committed. These include the provisions of the United Nations Charter, the Helsinki Agreement of 1975, the Budapest Memorandum of 1994 (by which Ukraine surrendered its nuclear weapons in exchange for guarantees of sovereignty and nonintervention), and other signed accords, such as the Treaty on Conventional Forces in Europe.

Baltic and European Security beyond Ukraine

The meaning of these events and of Russia's actions is profound, though it remains disputed by some American advocates of offshore balancing and disengagement as well as by those in Europe who would rationalize Moscow's behavior as a reaction to Western provocation. But timing is everything. The enlargement of NATO and of the EU took place long before Putin's return to the presidency and did not then engender a fierce Russian reaction.

It is well to remember, after all, the Russian president's notorious remark that the breakup of the Soviet Union was the greatest catastrophe of the twentieth century. Putin's actions represent deliberate, willful measures to reassert Russian power.[3] In doing so, he has employed multiple methods from the Russian diplomatic, political, military toolbox. Among these has been political and financial support to populist parties in Europe that aim to weaken or fragment the EU, as was the case with a €9 million loan to Marine Le Pen's French populist party, the National Front. In addition, Moscow has employed an increasingly sophisticated information apparatus, broadcasting and distributing Kremlin propaganda and conspiracy theories across multiple media platforms.

Moreover, Russian policies in the Syria conflict have exacerbated refugee inflows to Europe, where the surge has contributed to disarray within the EU and to rising populist opposition to beleaguered European governments.

Still the Indispensable Power

Notwithstanding the more than seven decades that have passed since the end of World War II, the US role remains crucial. US commitments have a catalytic effect. They provide, as Michael Howard wrote during the Cold War, not only deterrence and defense but also *reassurance*.[4] No other Western country or group of countries comes close to possessing the overall capabilities of the United States. The fact that Europe has a larger population is beside the point because on security matters there exists no overall European entity that can be much more than the sum of its parts. As a result, NATO member countries require the tangible guarantee of Washington's support to galvanize their own collective efforts within the Alliance. Increases in American defense spending for Eastern Europe and the Baltic Sea region thus take on both practical and symbolic importance.

Though the measures taken were modest—a 2016 increase of $2.4 billion from military contingency funds rather than the base defense budget itself and an additional brigade of three to five thousand US troops to be rotated through the Baltics and Poland rather than permanently stationed in one place—they signaled that years of retrenchment in commitments to European defense were being reversed.

The importance of American engagement and evidence of what happens when it is not credibly present is telling. Two examples make this painfully clear. In the case of the 1994 Budapest Memorandum, the agreement had been signed by the United States, Russia, Ukraine, Britain, France, and China—that is, the five permanent members of the UN Security Council. Yet when the agreement was egregiously violated by Russia's actions in February 2014, it went unenforced. None of the other signatories were able or willing to step forward, and the one country that might have made a difference, the United States, responded to initial Ukraine pleas for defensive weapons by providing not body armor, night-vision goggles, or anti-tank weapons but military field rations.

A year later, in February 2015, an accord meant to halt the fighting in Eastern Ukraine (the Minsk II Agreement) was signed by the foreign ministers of France, Germany, Russia, and Ukraine and embodied terms promoted by the Russian government. Conspicuously absent from the negotiations was the United States. Not surprisingly, despite providing lip service to the agreement, Moscow and its proxies continued to violate its provisions without concern that the US might play a role in its enforcement.

In sum, Russian actions and explicit threats to the Baltic countries provide a reminder that the long-standing realities of international affairs have not been superseded in the twenty-first-century world. The United States thus remains critical for providing the military and diplomatic presence to deter Russia and the reassurance and leadership required for the European members of the Alliance to play their part in a coherent and effective partnership.

The Trump Phenomenon

The stunning surprise of Donald Trump's election as president of the United States and the contradictory signals sent by his words and appointments of senior foreign- and security-policy officials have stoked an atmosphere of uncertainty and even disarray in transatlantic relations. Defining a Trump foreign policy, let alone a Trump doctrine, is unrealistic, but, based on the foreign policy impulses that seemed to underlie his presidential campaigning and early phases of his presidency, he can best be understood as Jacksonian in his understanding of America's role at home and abroad.

This approach, as defined by Walter Russell Mead, is nationalist and populist. In Mead's words, a *"Jacksonian* believes that the most important goal of the U.S. government in both foreign and domestic policy should be the physical security and the economic well-being of the American people. . . . Jacksonians believe that the United States should not seek out foreign quarrels, but when other nations start wars with the United States, Jacksonian opinion agrees with Gen. Douglas MacArthur that 'There is no substitute for victory.'"[5]

Trump himself has left many Europeans unsettled, for example, in his contradictory statements about NATO, initially describing it as obsolete but subsequently expressing support. In addition, his "America First" slogan evokes comparisons with the reprehensible isolationist movement of the late 1930s, as do his complaints that America "never wins" in its negotiations and that existing bargains ought to be reevaluated.

European reaction has been negative and sometimes quite hyperbolic, replete with references to Benito Mussolini and to Weimar Germany.[6] A sense of distancing and alarm is evident, for example, in a widely circulated essay by the editor of Germany's *Der Spiegel Online*, which called for Germany to lead an international coalition, together with Asian and African partners, against the United States.[7]

A more nuanced, American perspective comes from the editor of the influential foreign policy journal *The National Interest*. He suggests that the Pax Americana could come to be replaced by a Pax Germania, adding that "[Chancellor] Merkel could oversee a truly consequential change in foreign affairs.... The role of guardian of the 'liberal world order'—tamping down national egoism, promoting peace— isn't one Germany has sought, but it may be one it can't avoid."[8] Another caution comes from former CIA director and general David Petraeus, who points to America's essential role in maintaining world order and to the fundamental importance of the United States and the major European democracies in defending Europe and its institutions:

> Americans should not take the current international order for granted. It did not will itself into existence. We created it. Likewise, it is not naturally self-sustaining. We have sustained it. If we stop doing so, it will fray and, eventually, collapse. This is precisely what some of our adversaries seek to encourage. President Putin, for instance, understands that, while conventional aggression may occasionally enable Russia to grab a bit of land on its periphery, the real center of gravity is the political will of major democratic powers to defend Euro-Atlantic institutions like NATO and the EU.[9]

How then should we understand America's European policies under a Trump presidency? Despite Trump's rhetoric often implying a go-it-alone approach, the United States simply cannot be a free rider. Others can do so, but without Washington's indispensable role in extended deterrence and in leading NATO, the security, economic interests, and values of the US would be at risk as well.[10]

Trump is justified in pointing to the deficiencies in European burden-sharing, though these have been a perennial problem since the height of the Cold War, when many member countries failed to meet NATO's annual defense spending target of 3 percent of gross domestic product. To the extent that his blunt language stimulates Europeans to step up their collective efforts, it may be useful, but there is a risk that his rhetoric could trigger serious disarray within the Alliance and embolden the Russians to become more assertive and risk-acceptant. Though mutual recriminations exist not only across the Atlantic but within Europe itself, it is worth recalling the words of Winston Churchill, who remarked about alliances that the only thing worse than fighting with allies is fighting without them.

Trade policy is another realm in which transatlantic relations have become deeply unsettled. Even before Trump's election, the proposed Transatlantic Trade and Investment Partnership between the United States and the EU was facing serious obstacles as protectionist attitudes became increasingly evident on both sides of the Atlantic. Trump's rejection of the proposed US-Asian Trans-Pacific Partnership, which both major Democratic Party candidates, Hillary Rodham Clinton and Bernie Sanders, had disavowed during the 2016 presidential campaign, is a signal that political support for free trade is in short supply. The reasons include not only the increased populist sentiment evident in Europe and the US but also the consequences of previous trade agreements. It is a truism in economics to note that free trade provides real benefits but that these are diffuse, while the costs are often focused on specific groups and communities. To be sure, technology accounts for a substantial part of the decline of traditional manufacturing centers, but the impact of competition with developing countries, and especially the predatory practices by China since its admission to the World Trade Organization in 2001, has intensified these phenomena and contributed to their political impact.

Despite the Trump presidency and emergent populist pressures in both Europe and the United States, it is far too soon to write the epitaph for NATO and the transatlantic relationship. The institutions are fundamental to regional security and stability, are deeply embedded, have weathered serious crises in the past, and continue to play a vital role. Thus the conspicuous deployment of Western military equipment to the Baltic countries and Poland, along with the rotation of four battalions of troops through the region and the rhetoric of Alliance solidarity, has been aimed at deterring Moscow and reassuring NATO member countries most at risk. All the same, there are good reasons to avoid complacency. Notwithstanding President Trump's combative demeanor and rhetoric, his policies could presage less of a departure from his predecessor's retrenchment in foreign policy than a continuation or even intensification of that approach. If so, this could undermine not only the regional and global order that America did so much to establish and sustain but also the long-term prosperity and security of the United States itself.

Notes

1. Quoted in Dusko Doder and Louise Branson, *Milosevic: Portrait of a Tyrant* (New York: Free Press, 1999), 109.

2. The Blair-Aznar letter was signed by the leaders of the Czech Republic, Denmark, Hungary, Italy, Poland, and Portugal and published in the *Times* (London), "Europe and America Must Stand United," January 30, 2003. The Vilnius Group included Albania, Bulgaria, Croatia, Estonia, Latvia, Lithuania, Macedonia, Romania, Slovakia, and Slovenia. See "Eastern Europe: Vilnius Group Supports U.S. on Iraq," Radio Free Europe, Radio Liberty, February 6, 2003, http://www.rferl.org/content/article/1102148.html.

3. On the causes of Russian behavior, see especially Kathryn Stoner and Michael McFaul, "Who Lost Russia (This Time)? Vladimir Putin," *Washington Quarterly* 38, no. 2 (Summer 2015): 167–87.

4. Michael Howard, "Deterrence and Reassurance," *Foreign Affairs* (Winter 1982/83).

5. Walter Russell Mead, *Special Providence: American Foreign Policy and How It Changed the World* (New York: Routledge, 2002), xvii.

6. For a more sober and informed view, see Tom Nichols, "Chill, America: Not Every Trump Outrage Is Outrageous," *Washington Post*, February 2, 2017.

7. Klaus Brinkbäumer, "Europe Must Defend Itself against a Dangerous President: The United States President Is Becoming a Danger to the World. It Is Time for Germany and Europe to Prepare their Political and Economic Defenses." *Spiegel* Online, February 5, 2017, http://www.spiegel.de/international/world/a-1133177-amp.html.

8. Jacob Heilbrunn, "Will Pax Germania Replace Pax Americana?" *Los Angeles Times*, February 9, 2017.

9. Testimony to the House Armed Services Committee, February 1, 2017.

10. I elaborate on the indispensability of the US role and the disruptive consequences of retrenchment in Robert J. Lieber, *Retreat and Its Consequences: American Foreign Policy and the Problem of World Order* (New York: Cambridge University Press, 2016).

2

Russia and Baltic Sea Security

A Background

GUDRUN PERSSON

The contemporary military-political situation
of the Baltic Sea is characterized, on the one hand, by efforts
of the imperialistic circles to turn the
Baltic Sea into a bridgehead for NATO, and, on the other,
by efforts of the progressive forces
to turn the Baltic Sea into a zone of peace.

Great Soviet Encyclopedia

In the twenty-first century
the line between
a state of war and peace is
getting more and more blurred.

Valerii Gerasimov, chief of the Russian General Staff

"Vladimir Vladimirovich, will there be a war?" asked television journalist Vladimir Soloviev of the Russian president at the end of 2015. Putin replied, "You mean a global war? I hope not. Anyway, under today's circumstances, it would mean a planetary catastrophe."[1] The fact that the Russian president received this question,

17

and answered it, in a well-produced documentary broadcast on TV clearly shows how the issue of war and peace has become a matter of broad discussion in Russia. During the past twenty years, Russian military theorists have had to rethink whether the art of war has in fact changed. What is war? When does it start? When does the military element get engaged in today's conflicts? Russian theorists are not alone in this. Military thinkers all over the world are concerned with these issues.

The Russian annexation of Crimea in 2014 and the use of Russian armed forces in Donetsk and Luhansk sent a wakeup call throughout Europe. The Russian snap exercises before and in connection with the annexation and aggression surprised and worried Europe, and again the Baltic Sea area was in focus as tensions rose. Recent developments and the Russian challenge to the West raise a number of important questions for the West and future Western policies. The Western reaction has been, to a large degree, characterized by a lack of insight into the developments of Russian military thinking in the last few years. From a Russian standpoint, the conflict has already started. Therefore, Russia's challenge to the contemporary Euro-Atlantic security architecture is possibly even greater than generally understood. When studying the Russian view of national security and security policy and the Russian military thinking about future wars, it becomes apparent that the Russian challenge reaches far beyond Ukraine.

In the West, the label "hybrid war" was quickly placed on Russia's behavior in Ukraine, as if Russia's actions were a new kind of warfare.[2] However, a closer study of Russian military doctrinal thinking shows that there is no developed doctrinal thinking on hybrid war. When Russian military theorists write about hybrid war, it is mentioned as a foreign, Western capability.[3] Fyodor Lukyanov, chairman of the Council on Foreign and Defense Policy, has formulated the Russian view. He notes that the interpretation of "war" is changing in Russia: "The war takes other shapes, supported by America, when it is conducted by UAVs, by sanctions or operations in cyber space."[4]

What seemed to surprise many Western observers was Russia's ability to combine military and nonmilitary means—that is, special troops, information operations, deception, and diplomatic, economic, and political means.[5] The Russian terms for this are "nonlinear (*nelineinaia voina*) warfare" or "asymmetrical (*asimmetrichnaia voina*) warfare." In addition, the official rhetoric on nuclear weapons—and the increased number of exercises involving both strategic and tactical (substrategic) nuclear weapons—has surprised observers, not only in the West but also in Russia. In terms of military activity we have seen a much more active Russian behavior over the past years in the Baltic Sea region. This has involved military exercises as well as border transgressions.[6] Much of this is a reminder of times past, and much is not necessarily new—although it takes place in a different environment and with other technological means.

In order to understand the Russian challenge to the West, it is, however, necessary to take a broader approach. Military capability can be assessed on three different levels: the conceptual level (in other words, doctrines and military thinking), the structural level (that is, the organization), and the personnel level (which refers to education, motivation, and the social situation). This chapter is focused on the conceptual level.

The View of the West and a New Security Order

The Russian definition of "national security" is very broad. The National Security Strategy, signed on December 31, 2015, encompasses nine different areas: (1) national defense, (2) security of the state and society, (3) higher living standards for Russian citizens, (4) economic growth, (5) science, technology, and education, (6) health care, (7) culture (including history), (8) ecology, and (9) strategic stability and strategic partnership.[7] The law "On Security" (article 4:1) defines security policy as part of both domestic and foreign policy. It involves a whole range of measures: political, organizational, socioeconomic, military, judicial, informational, special, and others.[8] Consequently, it is clear that national security from a Russian perspective entails much more than "just" defense and foreign policy.

At the strategic level, the Russian political and military leadership sees an encircled Russia. At the policy level, Russia chose the path of strategic solitude years ago, with an increased anti-Western stance and a focus on a Russian *Sonderweg* ("special path") in a globalized world. The Russian political leadership increasingly viewed the European Union (EU) with apprehension and as closely associated with NATO. Furthermore, Europe was considered weak and decadent, as it had failed to play a dominant role in the world.[9] Russia's actions in Ukraine can be said to be the mirror image of its perceptions of Western behavior in Iraq, Afghanistan, and North Africa. For the Russian political and military leadership, the conflict has already started, and Russia has the right to defend itself.

The revised National Security Strategy of December 31, 2015, is the most outspokenly anti-Western of all strategic documents published since 1997. Apart from the United States and NATO, which had been described as hostile toward Russia in earlier documents, the EU also belongs to this category.

According to the strategy (§§12–13), the United States and its allies are putting pressure (*davlenie*) on Russia politically, economically, militarily, and in terms of information. The US and the EU are held directly responsible for the developments in Ukraine since they supported an "anticonstitutional coup." The "deep social economic crisis brings Ukraine—in a long-term perspective—to a hearth of instability in Europe—at the very border of Russia" (§17).

In addition, the strategy notes that "certain countries use information and communication technologies to reach their geopolitical goals—for example, the manipulation of the public opinion (*soznanie*) and the falsification of history" (§21). This wording is noteworthy since it was precisely the use of information and communication technologies that Russia used when it annexed the Crimean

Peninsula and continued its military aggression in Donetsk and Luhansk.[10] NATO's enlargement and its advance toward Russia's borders is now said to be a threat against Russian national security (§15). This concern has become sharper since the 2009 security strategy, when NATO's "increased military infrastructure at Russia's borders" was described as "unacceptable."[11]

The Russian political leadership has been dissatisfied with the current security order in the world for a long time. Suffice it to recollect Vladimir Putin's 2007 speech in Munich, where he made it clear that Russia wanted a new world order.[12] In the Military Doctrine 2014, it is stated that "the current architecture (system) for international security does not provide equal security for all states" (§10).[13] This is the same wording as in the Military Doctrine 2010. To make this point even more explicit, the National Security Strategy states that "the regional security system in the Euro-Atlantic region, built on NATO and the EU as a foundation, is untenable" (§16).

In practice this means a world order where a few great powers divide the world into different spheres of interest. The room for small states to act independently in such a world order is very limited. This is a world order that echoes the agreements of the 1815 Congress of Vienna and the 1945 Yalta Conference, and Putin has pointed several times at these agreements as examples to follow.[14] In fact, it goes even further back in time, to the Westphalian world order of the mid-seventeenth century. Foreign Minister Sergei Lavrov recently emphasized the importance of this treaty and highlighted its significance in today's world.[15]

Modern Conflicts: A View from Moscow

The National Security Strategy notes that the role of violence in international relations is not diminishing (§14). According to the Military Doctrine, there is a difference between a military conflict and an armed conflict (§8). A military conflict is described as a type of solution for interstate or intrastate tensions through the use of military force. A military conflict encompasses all kinds of armed confrontation, including large-scale, regional, or local war and armed conflicts. An armed conflict, according to the doctrine, is an armed clash of limited scale between states or opposing sides within the territory of a single state.

Three different kinds of war are listed: local, regional, and large-scale (§8). A local war is said to have limited military political objectives and involves mainly the states that are opposing each other. A regional war involves several states in a region and is conducted with national armed forces or with a coalition of armed forces. Each party is striving for important military political objectives. A large-scale war is conducted between coalitions of states or between the great powers of the world. It could be the result of an escalating armed conflict, a local war, or a regional war, and requires mobilization of the country's total material and spiritual resources.

Current military conflicts are characterized by the Military Doctrine as an "integrated use of military force, and by political, economic, informational, or other means of a nonmilitary character through a wide use of the population's protest potential or of special operations troops." In addition, the doctrine mentions the use of "irregular armed forces and private military companies" in military operations and "indirect and asymmetrical methods." It also points to the belief that "political forces and civic movements that are financed and controlled from abroad" (§15) are used in contemporary conflicts.

It is clear that the Russian military political leadership paints a picture of contemporary warfare that includes not only military means but also all kinds of other means. The most important difference from the previous doctrine is the view that a protesting population is seen as a part of contemporary conflicts.[16] Political and other organizations are seen as part of the war. Some of this reflects the official rhetoric of the Russian political leadership on Ukraine, where Russia is said to be exposed to this kind of warfare by the West.[17]

This view has wide implications for the West in general and for the Baltic Sea region in particular. Since the view is now a part of the Russian military doctrine, it means that Russia can apply these power instruments in its military operations. One example of this was the Russian use of private military companies in Syria, long before the air campaign was launched on September 30, 2015.[18]

This line of thinking in the Russian military doctrine is not entirely new. Parts of it were included in the 2010 Military Doctrine, but this time the thinking is more detailed and elaborated. The head of the General Staff, Valerii Gerasimov, talked about this earlier and pointed out that the "Arab Spring" might be an example of wars in the twenty-first century and that there are important lessons to be learned from the recent conflicts in North Africa and the Middle East. Gerasimov noted that the rules of war have changed dramatically.[19] In his view, the use of political, economic, information, humanitarian, and other nonmilitary means have influenced the "conflict potential of the population." The lessons from North Africa and the Middle East have demonstrated that "fully functional states in a short period of time can be transformed into an area of an embittered, armed conflict, become the victim of foreign intervention, and end up as a chaotic swamp of humanitarian catastrophe and civil war." Nonmilitary means, according to Gerasimov, are now much more effective than the power of the gun in achieving political and strategic objectives. This line of thinking is apparently built on the assumption that the Arab Spring was created by the West.

With regard to defense policy, it is noteworthy that the Military Doctrine states that one of the responsibilities for defense policy is to "support the mobilization preparedness of the economy" (§21)—that is, to put the economy on a war footing. In addition, the defense policy should "increase the effectiveness within military patriotic education for the citizens of the Russian federation and their military service" (§21). Add to this that a fundamental domestic military danger is said to be "information operations to influence—above all—the younger part of the population in order to undermine historical, spiritual, and patriotic traditions within the defense of the Fatherland."[20]

Russia is, in other words, seen as being under attack from a hostile West, and the Russian armed forces will defend Russia's historical and spiritual traditions. This development ties in nicely with the many government programs on military-patriotic education and patriotic education, state-run efforts that clearly target the younger generation in Russia.[21] Before examining the importance of history in this regard, it is vital to address the Russian view of soft power, controlled chaos, and color revolutions, which is central to the understanding of how the Russian view of modern conflicts has evolved.

Soft Power, Controlled Chaos, and Color Revolutions

During the last couple of years, in particular after the Russian military aggression against Ukraine, a number of new topics have appeared in Russian military thinking. One distinct feature is the view and use of soft power, which is a new factor in international politics, according to Russia's Foreign Policy Concept 2013.[22] On the one hand, soft power can be used as a complement to classic diplomacy. On the other, there is a risk of soft power being used as a tool to intrude into the domestic affairs of states, "among other things to finance humanitarian projects and projects relating to human rights abroad" (§20). In the updated Foreign Policy Concept 2016, soft power is already described as an instrument that is an "integral part of modern international politics" (§9).[23] Clearly, the definition of soft power used here is not the traditional one of increasing the country's power of attraction but a rather different one.[24] Putin defines it as "instruments and methods to achieve foreign policy objectives without the use of weapons—information and other levers of influence."[25] This reflects a militarized view, where soft power is seen as an instrument of statecraft. The view of the Internet as a threat to national security has also affected Russian efforts to reach an international convention for information security.[26]

In the theoretical military debate, it is apparent that soft power is seen as one weapon among others. Makhmut Gareev, an influential military theorist and a veteran of the Second World War, links the annexation of Crimea with soft power and strategic deterrence. It is, according to him, necessary to learn from Crimea in order to "perfect our soft power, political and diplomatic means, and information tools, and thus increase the effectiveness in the system for strategic deterrence."[27]

It is noteworthy that "soft power," in this line of thinking, is put at the same level as strategic deterrence—a level usually associated with nuclear weapons and high-precision, long-range conventional weapons. It is clear that this view of soft power has little to do with increasing the attractiveness of a country—and is therefore worth taking into account, not least when it comes to the Baltic Sea region.

Another term used in the Russian theoretical military debate is "controlled chaos" (*upravliaemyi khaos*), which is sometimes used in connection with a discussion of soft power. Gareev considers the two as equal.[28] In connection with the Russian annexation of Crimea and the aggression in Donetsk and Luhansk, several articles in journals of military theory are devoted to controlled chaos and to color revolutions.[29] The former term was used by Putin in his preelection article on defense in 2012.[30] It means that Russia was under attack from the West, which, by various methods—political as well as economic—destabilized and undermined Russia's neighbors and ultimately Russia itself. The term "color revolution" is included in the National Security Strategy for the first time and is described as a threat to Russia's state security (§43).

According to this line of thinking, both these terms are seen as tools in the hands of the West and are used to attack Russia. Fyodor Lukyanov states that color revolutions are clear examples of what happens when "soft" and "hard" forms of influence start to interact and clash with each other.[31]

Thoughts on color revolutions existed in Russian military strategic writing long before any actual color revolutions occurred.[32] They result from the fact that the dissolution of the Soviet Union is seen as incomprehensible to the current political leadership in Russia, as when President Putin described the fall of the Soviet Union as "*the* great geopolitical catastrophe of the century. For the Russian people it was a true drama."[33]

The Importance of History for National Security

The use of history has become increasingly important for Russia's national security during Putin's time in power. The victory of the Great Patriotic War (1941–45) has been given an exceptional place in contemporary Russian history. Over the past decade, the Russian political leadership has taken active steps to use history in connection with its armed forces.

The Russian Military-Historical Society was originally founded in 1907, disbanded in 1917, and then refounded in March 2013. The historical names of the Preobrazhenskii and Semenovskii Regiments have been added to modern military units.[34] The first official Russian monument for the "heroes" of the First World War has been erected, and a special unit has been created within the armed forces to combat "falsification of history."[35] And in April 2016, the Russian president put the Rosarkhiv, the Russian federal archives, under direct presidential control.[36] As a consequence, the Rosarkhiv is now one of the so-called power ministries. There are a total of thirteen federal ministries, services, and agencies that are directly subordinated to the president. One might wonder why the political leadership is paying so much attention to Russia's historical past. After all, both the Foreign Policy Concept of 2013 and 2016 explicitly state that one of Russia's objectives is to "contribute to the depoliticization of historical discussions."[37]

However, this objective does not stop the political leadership from making statements on historical matters. In more recent times, the Russian president has, on a number of occasions, given his view on certain historical events. To understand the significance of these statements with regard to the Baltic Sea region, it is important to consider that in a controversial 2013 statement Putin claimed that the Soviet Union launched the Winter War with Finland in order to "correct mistakes" made when Finland gained its independence in 1917.[38] Another example concerns the Molotov-Ribbentrop Pact and the secret protocol, with all its implications for the Baltic Sea region. In the Russian president's current view, Poland fell victim to its own policy in the prewar years—a statement he has repeated several times.[39] The illegal annexation of Crimea was framed in the same language, as a way to correct historical injustices.

These statements speak volumes about the current political leadership's use of history to achieve security policy goals. Furthermore, by engaging in issues related to the past, the current political leadership tries to create a national identity for the country and its armed forces. Without a clear objective, armies rarely win wars. This effort is a normative process that is politically controlled.

History has a distinct place in the National Security Strategy. Attempts to falsify history are seen as threats to Russia's national interests within the cultural sphere, according to both the new and previous strategy. As noted above, the subjects of history, as well as Russian spiritual and moral values, are to be defended by the armed forces. The issue of exactly what the Russian spiritual and moral traditions consist of has been a topic of discussion in Russia and has also been addressed by Putin himself. At the Valdai Discussion Club meeting in 2013, Putin devoted his speech to elaborate on his thinking on the Russian national identity.[40] Its specific features are now specified in the National Security Strategy, including "priority for the spiritual over the material; collectivism; the historical unity among Russia's people; our Fatherland's historical heritage" (§78).

This corresponds to Putin's view of what it means to be Russian. In the "Direct Line with the President" (an annual television program with questions and answers broadcast live by all major Russian state television networks) on April 17, 2014, he claimed that people who live in a certain territory and share a common culture and history—and even climate—develop certain traits. A Russian, according to Putin, is characterized by not focusing on himself but on the greater good. "We are spiritually more generous," he claimed, and therefore different from Westerners. He said that, in the "Russian world," death is beautiful and that to die for one's friends, one's people, the Fatherland is beautiful. This is one of the foundations of Russian patriotism, he stated.[41] By including this in a strategic document, the Russian political leadership has narrowed its room for maneuver in the future. The possibilities to change the policy to a more Western-friendly approach have been erased. This confirms that the policy choice made in 2012, that Russia should turn away from the West and seek its own path through "strategic solitude," will remain for years to come.[42]

Nuclear Weapons

Strategic deterrence, with an emphasis on nuclear deterrence, is still a pillar in Russian military strategic thinking. However, in recent years Russia has increased its aggressive behavior with nuclear weapons in and around the Baltic Sea, with a loud official nuclear rhetoric attached. Just a few examples: In March 2015, the Russian ambassador to Copenhagen threatened to use Russian nuclear missiles should Denmark join NATO's missile defense.[43] At a meeting with the so-called Elbe Group in March 2015, the Russian envoys allegedly said that Russia would use nuclear weapons in the event of a NATO buildup in the Baltic states.[44] Such aggressive rhetoric is remarkable, not least because it comes from one of the permanent members of the UN Security Council.

In addition to the official rhetoric, the number of exercises involving both strategic and tactical (substrategic) nuclear weapons has increased in recent years. In the first week of September 2015, the Russian strategic missile forces conducted a large-scale exercise, and, if such behavior was disturbing news to outsiders, it also seemed to cause concern in Russia. An anonymous editorial titled "Russia Prepares for Victory in a Nuclear War" in the newspaper *Nezavisimaia gazeta* asked, with reference to the exercise, whether "the military no longer considers the use of weapons of mass destruction to be the end of the human race? And if so, please tell us straight out."[45]

The role of nuclear weapons in Russian security policy is traditionally defined in the Military Doctrine, in nuclear deterrence policy documents, and in key speeches and declarations by the political leadership. At the doctrinal level there has been no change in the Russian nuclear position. The newly revised Military Doctrine 2014 has the same wording as was previously used to explain Russia's policy with respect to the use of nuclear weapons. Section 27 states: "The Russian Federation reserves the right to utilize nuclear weapons in response to the utilization of nuclear and other types of weapons of mass destruction against it and (or) its allies, and also in the event of aggression against the Russian Federation involving the use of conventional weapons when the very existence of the state is under threat. The decision to utilize nuclear weapons is made by the President of the Russian Federation."[46]

According to the new National Security Strategy, "strategic deterrence and prevention of military conflicts are reached by upholding nuclear deterrence at a sufficient high level" (§36). This is slightly sharper wording than in the previous National Security Strategy, where the "importance of keeping the potential of the strategic nuclear forces" was emphasized. However, it should be noted that the wording is actually comparatively cautious compared to the official nuclear rhetoric during the last few years. In December 2015, for instance, President Putin said that Russia would "perfect its nuclear weapons as a deterrence factor."[47]

In addition to the latest public declarations and the increase in nuclear exercises for the last few years (both in size and duration), there is an ongoing debate in military newspapers and journals regarding the use of nuclear weapons to de-escalate a conflict, which needs to be highlighted. According to the Russian researcher Andrei Zagorski, nuclear de-escalation has been a part of Russia's nuclear deterrence policy since 2000.[48] Nuclear de-escalation means the use of tactical (substrategic) nuclear weapons when a local war is escalating into a regional war. The use of nuclear weapons would, according to this line of thought, scare the enemy away and de-escalate the conflict. In the military debate over the past few years, these ideas have become more frequent. Konstantin Sivkov, a well-known hard-liner at the Academy for Geopolitical Problems, argued in March 2014 (before the revision of the Military Doctrine had been completed) that a preventive strike with tactical nuclear arms against an enemy would not only be possible but also right.[49] He and others argued for a change in the official doctrine that would explicitly regulate Russia's possible use of a preventive nuclear strike. Makhmut Gareev has stated that the destruction of Russia's intermediate-range ballistic missiles in the late 1980s and 1990s was a mistake and that "now also the highest leadership of the Russian Federation recognizes this mistake."[50]

It would be too easy to write off this line of thought as something coming from a group of self-proclaimed experts—or to trivialize it by claiming that it is the task of every military staff to make plans for any conceivable event. But it is more sinister than that. The advocates of a preventive nuclear strike are challenging another school of thought that emphasizes the importance of a nonnuclear strategic deterrence for Russia. Andrei Kokoshin, one of Russia's leading strategic thinkers, has been arguing for years that Russia should look beyond nuclear weapons to other modern, high-precision weapon systems. "Excessive confidence in nuclear deterrence in national security policy is detrimental and even dangerous for Russia," he wrote in 2011.[51] Also, although the revised Military Doctrine contains the phrase "nonnuclear deterrence" (§21 l), it does not seem to have gained any broader acceptance within the armed forces and society at large.

So, how can the recent nuclear frenzy be explained? The official nuclear posturing is obviously a part of Russian strategic deterrence, as Aleksei Arbatov, a well-known nuclear expert, has observed. It is a political signal to the West not to interfere in Ukraine or anywhere else that the Russian political leadership considers within Russia's sphere of influence.[52]

But the nuclear posturing does not occur in a vacuum. It is taking place against the background of a surge of nationalism in Russia in the wake of the annexation of Crimea and the military intervention in Syria. In addition, the latest Military Doctrine emphasizes increased tensions and a growing rivalry between values and development models (§9), whereas the 2010 doctrine described a world of weakening ideological confrontation (§7). In other words, tensions are rising, and Russia is prepared to defend its interests with all means—military and nonmilitary—at its disposal. The Russian strategy is neither static nor fixed but is very flexible.

Conclusions

To sum up, recent world developments and the Russian challenge to the West are quite formidable and pose questions for the West and future policies. Russia claims that the post–Cold War situation does not provide security for Russia; the goal now is to create a global order run by the great powers. The Vienna Congress of 1815 or Yalta in 1945 are good examples to follow, according to the Russian president. The Holy Alliance resulting from the Concert of Europe provides the model where the great powers divided the continent into different spheres of interests and together controlled entire peoples, such as the Poles and Hungarians. At Yalta, the leaders of the Soviet Union, the United Kingdom, and the United States formulated the principles of the post–World War II global order. Today, such a system would mean that an authoritarian or totalitarian political system is recognized as equal to the Western democracies. This, in turn, implies that the sovereignty of small countries is subordinate to interests of a great power.

The Russian view of "war" and "national security" is broadly defined and includes not only the use of nuclear weapons but also Russian history and religious traditions. What does it mean for Russia and the West that Russian military thinkers and policymakers take into account areas not normally associated with warfare?

Finally, several Russian military thinkers entertain thoughts of a future "war of civilizations." Many of them have produced lengthy texts about such a war between ideas and cultures. Gen. Aleksandr I. Vladimirov, for instance, notes that Russia needs to rally the country around the "nationally vital resources": the faith (Russian Orthodox Church), the people (Russian, *russkii*), the state (Russia), the idea (Russian culture), and the language (Russian).[53] This echoes the past—though not as eloquently formulated as the catchphrase from czarist times, "Autocracy, Orthodoxy, Nationality." The Russian objective is very clear. It is often said that Putin does not have a strategy but is a brilliant tactician. That may be, but the long-term objective of his action is well-defined.

What is the response of a post-modern West to this challenge? A Russian sphere of interest should be acknowledged: Ukraine is definitely part of it, as are, for instance, Georgia, Moldova, and other former Soviet republics. But the challenge goes further. The Euro-Atlantic security order is to be rewritten. The political scientist Dmitry Suslov is explicit: "In this context, for Moscow the change of the political and foreign policy status quo in Ukraine is not only a matter of protection of interests in a neighboring state and in the post-Soviet space as a whole, it is, first and foremost, a matter of international status and position of Russia, a matter of international order."[54] This alone is a serious challenge to the West.

According to a saying usually attributed to Otto von Bismarck, "Russia is never as strong—or as weak—as she seems." The course of Russian history shows that—eventually, when the empire has overstretched—reforms will come. But until then, the West needs to recognize the scope of the current challenge and work out a long-term response.

Notes

Epigraphs: *Bolshaia Sovetskaia Entsiklopediia* (Great Soviet Encyclopedia), vol. 2, 3rd ed., ed. A. M. Prochorov (Moscow: Sovetskaia enstiklopedia, 1970), 587; Valerii Gerasimov, "Tsennost nauki i predvidenii: 'Novyje vyzovy trebuiut pereosmyslit formy i sposoby vedeniia boevych deistvii,'" [The value of science and predictions: New challenges demands new thinking on forms and methods for combat operations] *Voenno-promyshlennyi kurer*, no. 8 (February 2013).

1. *Miroporiiadok* [The world order], television documentary, December 20, 2015, https://www.youtube.com/watch?v=ZNhYzYUo42g.

2. The number of articles and analyses on "hybrid war" is extensive. For a good introduction, see András Rácz, *Russia's Hybrid War in Ukraine: Breaking the Enemy's Ability to Resist*, FIIA Report 43 (Helsinki: Finnish Institute of International Affairs, 2015); and Peter Pomerantsev, "Brave New War," *Atlantic*, December 29, 2015.

3. Ruslan Puchov, "Mif o 'gibridnoi voine'" [The myth of "hybrid war"], *Nezavisimoe voennoe obozrenie*, May 29, 2015. See also Roger McDermott, "Does Russia's 'Hybrid War' Really Exist?," *Eurasia Daily Monitor* 12, no. 103 (June 3, 2015).

4. Fyodor Lukyanov, "Sila miagkost lomit: V chem slabost v vneshnei politiki Rossii" [Strength breaks softness: On weakness in Russian Foreign Policy], *Forbes*, August 26, 2015.

5. Johan Norberg, Ulrik Franke, and Fredrik Westerlund, "The Crimea Operation: Implications for Future Russian Military Interventions," in *A Rude Awakening: Ramifications of Russian Aggression towards Ukraine*, ed. Niklas Granholm et al., FOI-R--3892--SE (Stockholm: Totalförsvarets forskningsinstitut, June, 2014), 41–49.

6. Richard Milne, Sam Jones, and Kathrin Hille, "Russian Air Incursions Rattle Baltic States," *Financial Times*, September 24, 2014; Richard Milne and Neil Buckley, "Baltic Security: Tensions on the Frontier," *Financial Times*, October 20, 2014; and Justyna Gotkowska, "Russian War Games in the Baltic Sea Region: The Swedish Case," OSW, October 22, 2014.

7. *Strategiia natsionalnoi bezopasnosti Rossiiskoi Federatsii* [The National Security Strategy of the Russian Federation], December 31, 2015, http://www.scrf.gov.ru/security/docs/document133/.

8. *Federalnyi zakon ot 28.12.2010 g. No 390-FZ, O bezopasnosti* [Federal law, 28.12.2010, no. 390, on security], http://kremlin.ru/acts/bank/32417.

9. Gudrun Persson and Carolina Vendil Pallin, "Setting the Scene: The View from Russia," in Granholm, *Rude Awakening*, 25–34.

10. See, for instance, Peter Pomerantsev and Michael Weiss, "The Menace of Unreality: How the Kremlin Weaponizes Information, Culture, and Money," *Interpreter*, Institute of Modern Russia, New York, 2014.

11. *O strategii natsionalnoi bezopasnosti Rossiiskoi Federatsii do 2020 g.* [On the National Security Strategy of the Russian Federation until 2020], May 12, 2009, §17, http://www.rg.ru/2009/05/19/strategia-dok.html.

12. President of Russia, "Speech and the Following Discussion at the Munich Conference on Security Policy," February 10, 2007, http://en.kremlin.ru/events/president/transcripts/24034.

13. *Voennaia doktrina Rossiiskoi Federatsii* [The Military Doctrine of the Russian Federation], December 25, 2014, http://www.scrf.gov.ru/security/military/document129/.

14. President of Russia, "Meeting of the Valdai International Discussion Club," September 19, 2013, http://en.kremlin.ru/events/president/news/19243, and "Meeting of the Valdai International Discussion Club," October 22, 2015, http://en.kremlin.ru/events/president/news /50548.

15. Sergei Lavrov, "Russia's Foreign Policy in a Historical Perspective," *Russia in Global Affairs*, no. 2, March 30, 2016 .

16. In the previous doctrine, contemporary military conflicts were characterized by, for instance, an integrated use of military force and nonmilitary means, as well as an increased role of information warfare. *Voennaia doktrina Rossiiskoi Federatsii*, February 5, 2010, §12, http:// www.rg.ru/2010/02/10/doktrina-dok.html.

17. See Vladimir Putin's speech when Crimea and Sevastopol were annexed to the Russian Federation, "Obrashchenie Prezidenta Rossiiskoi Federatsii" [The address by the president of the Russian Federation], March 18, 2014, http://kremlin.ru/events/president/news/20603.

18. Iliia Volzhskii, "Pesok im pukhom" [May you rest in sand], *Novoe vremia*, no. 40 (November 30, 2015): 16–19.

19. Valerii Gerasimov, "Tsennost nauki i predvidenii: 'Novyje vyzovy trebuiut pereosmyslit formy i sposoby vedeniia boevych deistvii'" [The value of science and predictions: "New challenges demand new thinking on forms and methods for combat operations"], *Voenno-promyshlennyi kurer*, no. 8 (February 27, 2013). See also Gudrun Persson, "Security Policy and Military Strategic Thinking," in *Russian Military Capability in a Ten-Year Perspective: 2013*, ed. Jakob Hedenskog and Carolina Vendil Pallin, FOI-R--3734--SE (Stockholm: Totalförsvarets forskningsinstitut, December, 2013), 71–88.

20. *Voennaia doktrina* 2014, §13c.

21. See, for instance, Gudrun Persson, "Patriotism och utrikespolitik i Ryssland: Kampen om historien" [Patriotism and foreign policy in Russia: The struggle over history], *Världspolitikens dagsfrågor*, December 2014; Gudrun Persson, "Vilka är vi? Rysk identitet och den nationella säkerheten" [Who are we? Russian identity and national security], *Nordisk Østforum* 3, no. 28 (2014): 199–214.

22. *Kontseptsiia vneshnei politiki Rossiiskoi Federatsii* [Foreign policy concept of the Russian Federation], signed by the President of Russia on February 12, 2013, http://www.mid.ru /foreign_policy/official_documents/-/asset_publisher/CptICkB6BZ29/content/id/122186.

23. *Kontseptsiia vneshnei politiki Rossiiskoi Federatsii* [Foreign Policy Concept of the Russian Federation], signed by the President of Russia on November 30, 2016, http://www.mid.ru /foreign_policy/news/-/asset_publisher/cKNonkJE02Bw/content/id/2542248.

24. Joseph Nye, *Soft Power: The Means to Success in World Politics* (New York: Public-Affairs, 2004). See also Gudrun Persson, "Russian Influence and Soft Power in the Baltic States: The View from Moscow," in *Tools of Destabilization: Russian Soft Power and Non-military Influence in the Baltic States*, ed. Mike Winnerstig, FOI-R--3990--SE (Stockholm: Totalförsvarets forskningsinstitut, December, 2014), 17–29.

25. Vladimir Putin, "Rossiia i meniaiuchshiisia mir" [Russia and the changing world], *Moskovskie novosti*, February 27, 2012.

26. Keir Giles, "Internet Use and Cyber Security in Russia," *Russian Analytical Digest*, no. 134 (July 30, 2013): 2–4; and Ulrik Franke and Carolina Vendil Pallin, *Russian Politics and the Internet in 2012*, FOI-R--3590--SE (Stockholm: Totalförsvarets forskningsinstitut, December, 2012).

27. M. A. Gareev, "Velikaia pobeda i sobytiia na Ukraine" [The great victory and what happened in Ukraine], *Vestnik Akademii Voennych nauk* 2, no. 47 (2014): 10.

28. Makhmut Gareev, "Na 'miagkuiu silu' naidutsia zhestkiie otvety" [Against "soft power" hard answers will be found], *Voenno-promyshlennyi kurer*, no. 47 (December 4, 2013).

29. Not only in Russia. See, for instance, Dave Johnson, "Russia's Approach to Conflict: Implications for NATO's Deterrence and Defence," Research Paper no. 111 (April 2015), NATO Defense College.

30. Vladimir Putin, "Byt silnymi: Garantii natsionalnoi bezopasnosti dlia Rossii" [To be strong: Guarantees for Russia's national security], *Rossiskaia gazeta*, February 20, 2012.

31. Lukyanov, "Sila miagkost lomit."

32. Gudrun Persson, "Mellan krig och fred: Militärstrategiskt tänkande i Ryssland" [Between war and peace: Military strategic thinking in Russia], in *Örnen, Björnen och Draken: Militärt tänkande i tre stormakter* [The eagle, the bear, and the dragon: Military thinking in three great powers], ed. Robert Dalsjö et al., FOI-R--4103--SE (Stockholm: Totalförsvarets forskningsinstitut, September, 2015), 46–64.

33. President of Russia, "Poslanie Prezidenta Federalnomy Sobraniiu Rossiiskaia Federatsiia" [Presidential address to the Federal Assembly of the Russian Federation], April 25, 2005, http://rg.ru/2005/04/25/poslanie-text.html.

34. Persson, "Security Policy and Military Strategic Thinking," 77.

35. "Russian Military Unit to Combat 'History Falsification,'" RIA Novosti, July 10, 2013.

36. *O Federalnom arkhivnom agenstve, Ukaz Prezidenta RF* [On the Federal Archive Agency, presidential decree], no. 151, April 4, 2016, http://www.kremlin.ru/acts/bank/40660.

37. *Kontseptsiia vneshnei politiki*, 2013, §39; and *Kontseptsiia vneshnei politiki*, 2016, §39.

38. President of Russia, "Vstrecha s uchastnikami uchreditelnogo s'ezda Rossiiskogo voenno-istoricheskogo obshchestva" [Meeting with the participants in the constituent congress of the Russian Military-Historical Society], March 14, 2013, http://kremlin.ru/events/president/news/17677.

39. President of Russia, "Vstrecha s molodymi uchenymi i prepodovateliami istorii" [Meeting with young scholars and teachers of history], November 5, 2014, http://kremlin.ru/events/president/news/46951. See also the transcript of the press conference that followed Putin's meeting with German chancellor Angela Merkel on May 10, 2015, http://kremlin.ru/events/president/transcripts/49455.

40. President of Russia, "Meeting of Valdai International Discussion Club," 2013.

41. President of Russia, "Priamaia liniia s Vladimirom Putinym" [Direct line with Vladimir Putin], http://kremlin.ru/events/president/news/20796.

42. Persson, "Security Policy and Military Strategic Thinking," 83.

43. Richard Milne, "Russia Delivers Nuclear Warning to Denmark," *Financial Times*, March 22, 2015.

44. Ian Johnston, "Russia Threatens to Use 'Nuclear Force' over Crimea and the Baltic States," *Independent*, April 2, 2015.

45. "Rossiia gotovitsia k pobede v iadernoi voine" [Russia prepares for victory in a nuclear war], *Nezavisimaia gazeta*, September 7, 2015, http://www.ng.ru/editorial/2015-09-07/2_red.html.

46. *Voennaia doktrina* 2014, §27.

47. "Putin: RF budet sovershenstovat iadernoe oruzhhie kak faktor sderzhivaniia" [Putin: RF will perfect nuclear weapons as deterrence factor], RIA Novosti, December 20, 2015, http:// ria.ru/defense_safety/20151220/1345657421.html.

48. Andrei Zagorski, "Russia's Tactical Nuclear Weapons: Posture, Politics and Arms Control," *Hamburger Beiträge Friedensforschung und Sicherheitspolitik, Heft 156* (February 2011). For a deeper discussion, see also Fredrik Westerlund, *Rysk kärnvapendoktrin 2010: Utformning och drivkrafter* [Russian nuclear doctrine 2010: Formation and driving forces], FOI-R--3397--SE (Stockholm: Totalförsvarets forskningsinstitut, January 2012).

49. Konstantin Sivkov, "Pravo na udar" [The right to strike], *Voenno-promyshlennyi kurer*, no. 8 (March 5, 2014).

50. Makhmut Gareev, "Eshche raz o sisteme znanii o sovremennoi voine" [Again about the knowledge system of contemporary war], *Voenno-promyshlennyi kurer*, no. 29 (July 31, 2013).

51. Andrei Kokoshin, "Ensuring Strategic Stability in the Past and Present: Theoretical and Applied Questions," paper, Belfer Center for Science and International Affairs, Harvard Kennedy School, June 2011.

52. Aleksei Arbatov, "Zachem Rossiia ugrozhaet Zapadu iadernym oruzhiem" [Why Russia threatens the West with nuclear weapons], April 22, 2015, http://carnegie.ru/2015 /04/22/ru-59866/ik4a.

53. Aleksandr I. Vladimirov, *Osnovy obshchej teorii vojny* [The principles for a general theory of war], *Chast I, Osnovy teorii vojny* [Part 1, the principles for a theory of war] (Moscow: Universitet Sinergiia, 2013), 477–94.

54. Dmitry Suslov, "'Normandy Four': The Best Possible Format," Valdai Discussion Club, *Expert Opinions*, October 2, 2015.

3

NATO's Role in Baltic Sea Security

Reestablishing Deterrence,
Projecting Stability

JAMIE SHEA

NATO's strategy for responding to the challenges from the East, and particularly in the Baltic Sea region, is rooted in the decisions taken by its leaders at their summit in Warsaw in July 2016. Although the NATO Allies held a short meeting with the new US president, Donald Trump, in May 2017, this was mainly focused on the age-old issue of burden-sharing and in no way changed the far more significant decisions taken the year before in Warsaw. Summits are often overblown with hype and media spin far ahead of actual concrete results. Yet at a time when the international security environment is deteriorating rapidly with instability along all of NATO's borders to the east and to the south, the Alliance can no longer afford the luxury of unproductive summits. This is a time when our publics (and, if President Trump is to be believed, our leaders also) no longer take international organizations for granted but judge them by their capacity to devise real answers to the challenges and their resolve to actually implement them—as Elvis Presley once put it, "a little less conversation, a little more action."

By this new, more demanding standard, the Warsaw Summit was the West's most coherent response thus far to the pressures Europe is facing from instability on the outside and a more fragmented, nationalist, and "me first" public opinion on the inside. Taken together, the Warsaw decisions aim to restabilize Europe and help it to regain an internal cohesion that has been under severe strain since Russia annexed Crimea in March 2014 and the group Islamic State reared its ugly head in

Syria and Iraq. Whereas summits, even the successful ones, often tackle only one problem at a time, the Warsaw gathering took actions on a whole raft of challenges and with regard to all the regions on Europe's periphery. As 2016, the year of decision, gave way to 2017, the year of implementation, let us look at the key deliverables and at some of the longer-term implications they raise, focusing on the east and the Baltic Sea region.

Less Conversation, More Action

In the first place, NATO's leaders announced that the Readiness Action Plan (RAP), adopted at the previous NATO summit in Wales in September 2014, is being substantially implemented. The security vacuum in Central and Eastern Europe exposed by a resurgent, revisionist Russia is being filled. In 2016, NATO and its member states held over three hundred exercises, many of which sent land, air, and naval forces to Poland and the Baltic states to demonstrate NATO's solidarity and resolve. The NATO Response Force (NRF) has been tripled in size to become a pool of forty thousand troops that can be configured in a number of ways to conduct land, air, and naval operations as either a spearhead or follow-on force.

NATO's Very High Readiness Joint Task Force, which is the spearhead element of the NRF, can be deployed in as little as forty-eight hours to support local forces and establish a NATO foothold to cope with a breaking crisis. Subject to annual rotations in national command, it will be exercised regularly to ensure that it is certified both for speed and combat capability. To support the rapid staging of reinforcement forces, NATO has also established eight Force Integration Units in its eastern member states to provide the incoming forces with training logistics, prepositioned equipment, and host-nation support. Eight capability packages have been prepared to utilize NATO common funding for the strategic lift, command and control, logistics, and communications to sustain this level of rapid reinforcement. The former German-Polish-Danish headquarters at Szczecin, Poland, has been upgraded to a Multinational Corps Headquarters Northeast to serve as a potential operational command center, able to coordinate combined arms operations in a way that NATO has not had to do, at a level of a division or above, since the end of the Cold War. In autumn 2015, the Trident Juncture exercise in Spain, Portugal, and Italy, with over thirty thousand participating troops, tested the Alliance's ability to deploy and exercise a much broader spectrum of forces in a more intense and contested combat environment than NATO ever had to do in Bosnia, Libya, Kosovo, or Afghanistan. This combined-forces exercise also tested NATO's ability to reengineer its forces for rapid reinforcement and has been followed by others, such as Anaconda in Poland in 2016 and Sabre Strike in the Baltic states in the summer of 2017.

All of this costs money, and, as NATO realizes that an assertive, even adventurist Russia in the east and jihadists able to acquire missiles and chemical weapons in the south are part of the "new normal," it will not be able to deter, let alone defend, without increased defense budgets. The Wales Summit in September 2014 adopted a defense investment pledge to raise the defense spending of Allies to 2 percent of gross domestic product (GDP) and to devote 20 percent of the budget to modernization and investment. Unsurprisingly, and in the light of the hard-pressed European economies, this pledge was greeted with some skepticism at the time. Indeed, two years later those countries meeting the 2 percent target have remained largely the same: the United States, the United Kingdom, Greece, Estonia, and, more recently, Poland. But the pledge has proven to be a good forcing mechanism. Seventeen Allies have increased defense spending since 2014, and collectively NATO's defense budgets have gone up for the first time since 2009. The 3.8 percent increase overall in 2016 produced €10 billion more for NATO's collective defense. Nine Allies have presented concrete plans to reach 2 percent within a decade, and Latvia, Lithuania, and Romania should reach this target in 2017. The number meeting the 20 percent investment target has also increased from five to ten.

Significantly, the Baltic states, Poland, and Romania have recognized that their calls for NATO solidarity will be more compelling if they improve their own national and reserve forces as the first line of defense. Germany has hovered around the mark of 1.2 percent of GDP despite a buoyant economy but has launched a new white paper and an investment program of €130 billion over fifteen years that should enable the Bundeswehr to reacquire some of its former heavy-armor capability, as well as seven thousand extra soldiers, immediately. France has also rescinded a cut of eleven thousand soldiers, although, in truth, this is due as much to the needs of internal security in the wake of the November 2015 terrorist attacks as to commitments in the Sahel or in the east. Before the recent French presidential election, the former prime minister, Manuel Valls, announced to the French Parliament an intention to increase defense spending to 2 percent of GDP by the end of this decade. Despite carrying out a onetime defense budget cut in 2017 to balance the state's finances, the French president, Emmanuel Macron, has not deviated from this long-term plan, which is designed as much to boost the European Union (EU) common foreign and defense policy as NATO.

This effort and others by Allies have become even more urgent in the wake of the arrival of Donald Trump in the White House. Some of the rhetoric from his election campaign questioned the relevance of NATO and the US commitment to its Article 5 obligation to defend its Allies in the event of an attack. Thankfully, this view has not become the official policy of the new administration. President Trump indeed has given a number of assurances regarding his commitment to the Alliance, particularly in his bilateral conversations with European leaders and NATO's secretary-general, but he has mixed these reassurances with a good deal of criticism of NATO's performance against terrorism and his insistence that the Allies have to take the 2 percent pledge seriously and not use the US NATO commitment as a default option for a lack of defense efforts at home. This was his key public and private message when he attended the NATO meeting with fellow Alliance leaders in May 2017.

So, before the next NATO summit in mid-July 2018, it would be advisable for all the Allies to come up with concrete plans for how they intend to reach the 2 percent benchmark and keep to it in the future. Conversely, it will not be detrimental but actually helpful to European defense spending increases if the new US administration also makes clear that it will uphold its NATO Treaty commitments in absolute terms and without conditionality to this rebalancing of burden-sharing between the United States and Europe. The statements made by the secretaries of state and defense, Rex Tillerson and James Mattis, during their Senate confirmation hearings and their visits to Europe since then regarding the US view of an aggressive Russia and support for NATO suggest that there will be more continuity than change in the US role in the Alliance, even if President Trump continues to use his tweets and stump speeches to keep the Allies on their toes. More important than the words from the other side of the Atlantic are US actions, and those present a more reassuring picture. President Trump has increased the funding for the US forward presence in Poland and the Baltic states by $1.4 billion and has prolonged the commitment of the US rotational brigade combat team until 2020.

In the face of Russian intimidation in the form of major combined arms maneuvers such as the Zapad 17 snap exercises, provocative flight patterns, and the militarization of Crimea and Kaliningrad, NATO has held firm. It has also kept to its "Three Nos" commitment of 1997 to Russia: not to deploy substantial combat forces or massive infrastructure or nuclear weapons in the east in peacetime. The NATO forward presence will be persistent rather than permanent. Yet the original RAP, notwithstanding its rapid implementation, was not totally satisfactory for the eastern Allies, who do not want to rely only on limited local forces; small-scale, flag-waving exercises; and NATO's ability to decide quickly in a crisis and move thousands of troops across hundreds of kilometers from Western to Eastern Europe. There the availability of roads, railways, ports, and airfields would be a challenge even if NATO deploys in a permissive environment with no or limited Russian interdiction actions, now commonly referred to as antiaccess, area-denial tactics (A2/AD).

Responding to these anxieties, the Warsaw Summit decided to supplement the RAP with the deployment of four battalions in Poland and the Baltic states. These are rotational and multinational to emphasize that an attack against one is an attack against all, and are led by framework nations the United States, the United Kingdom, Germany, and Canada. Eighteen Allies agreed to contribute to these four battalions, which were all finally in place in June 2017. The United States has contributed $3.4 billion to a European Reassurance Initiative to preposition the elements of a third armored brigade in Europe. This is the fund that President Trump has now decided to increase by $1.4 billion.

In January 2017, the first elements of this brigade combat team arrived in Poland. It comprises roughly thirty-five hundred troops and eighty-seven tanks, plus hundreds of other vehicles, including more than forty Bradley Fighting Vehicles. The deployment is significant because it puts some of the US armor, earlier withdrawn from Europe in 2008, back into NATO's forward defense. This armored presence on the ground is supplemented with a combat aviation brigade containing ten Chinook helicopters, fifty Blackhawk helicopters, and eighteen hundred personnel. It is based in Germany, with forward-positioned aircraft in Latvia, Romania, and Poland. There will also be an additional task force of twenty-four Apache helicopters. On top of that, the United States will be prepositioning equipment and ammunition necessary to support an armored-division-sized force. This will help to reduce deployment times, enhance deterrence, and provide additional combat power for contingency operations.

To enhance deterrence in the Black Sea region, Romania will host a multinational division southeast and a brigade headquarters to host and exercise incoming NATO forces. It has also proposed a maritime multinational Black Sea task force to keep track of Russia's more assertive military presence in this sea, a proposal endorsed by NATO defense ministers in February 2017. The exact scope of this naval presence, together with the air defense picture in the region, will now be examined by NATO's military authorities. Canada, Germany, the Netherlands, Poland, Turkey, and the United States have all indicated their willingness to contribute to NATO's presence in this region. In sum, whatever the doubts and anxieties that were generated by President Trump's failure to explicitly endorse the Article 5 commitment during his visit to Brussels, these measures are strong evidence of the US commitment to European security and would be difficult to reverse, given the ongoing momentum. Yet there is no reason for complacency. A US public that is today largely unaware of NATO's role will need to be convinced of its utility and relevance. NATO will need to rebrand itself in the United States by means of a much more robust, sustained public diplomacy effort. A recent Pew survey suggests in this respect that support for NATO is much lower among the dominant Republicans than among Democrats.[1]

The NATO command structure is being reviewed to ensure that it is up to the task of coordinating all the elements of this new force posture. Those include the integration of local and multinational forces and the in-flow of follow-on and reserve forces to bolster NATO's four in-place battalions should a crisis lead to actual conflict. This coordination will require a frequent and more demanding schedule of exercises. Articulating these forces in a way that does not leave large time gaps or major geographical imbalances in the forces involved in these various echelons will be one of the key challenges if NATO ever has to use force to repel an aggression. It is all about balancing light forces with heavy, rapid with slower, and in-place troops with reinforcements—all while acting in a way that serves to dampen a conflict rather than automatically escalate it.

Unfinished Business

The Warsaw decisions did not only concern work in progress but also initiated a great deal of follow-on work. Lurking in the background are some serious questions still in need of an answer.

The most urgent concerns air defense, airspace control, and unfettered sea access to the Baltic, given Russia's possession of a large number of modern fighters and bombers and NATO's reliance hitherto on very modest air policing for the Baltic states. The summit launched a Total Aviation System concept to better identify NATO's future requirements. As a down payment, the summit endorsed work on a concept for a successor to the fleet of airborne early-warning and control aircraft around 2035, and in the margins letters of intent were signed for the development of maritime multimission aircraft and airborne electronic-attack capabilities.

In the missile-defense area, NATO's plans and capabilities are more advanced. The summit declared the initial operational capability of NATO's antiballistic missile-defense system, currently being constructed on a site in Romania and a future one in Poland. This system is supported by US Aegis ships in the Mediterranean and a standing defense plan recently rehearsed by the control center at Ramstein in Germany. The missile defense covers Southeastern Europe and Turkey at this stage of its development, and, whatever the accusations from Moscow, its range and height pose no threat to Russia's nuclear deterrent. It is clearly designed to counter missile threats from states or nonstate actors in the south.

Another concern is in the area of follow-on forces and logistics. Up to now, NATO's return to collective defense has focused mainly on small but high-visibility exercises in Eastern Europe to reassure the eastern Allies and the formation of rapid-response units. These steps were the logical ones to take immediately after Russia's incursion into Ukraine, as deterrence is as much about visibility and political will as it is about large numbers of military forces. But, given that Russia has now deployed 440,000 troops in its Western Military District, is carrying out large-scale exercises (such as Kavkaz 2016 and the Zapad exercise in Belarus in summer 2017), has announced the deployment of Iskander and S-400 missiles in Kaliningrad and other missiles in Crimea, and is building new military bases along its border with Ukraine, NATO has to consider its strength in depth and its ability to mobilize follow-on forces and reinforcements in a timely manner. Therefore, the focus of defense planning has to be to establish the right balance between elite forces able to deploy within forty-eight hours and reserves, which must clearly be on a shorter notice to move than the current one month to three months. As many NATO Allies have severely cut their armed forces to focus on special operations forces and other specialized units for long-distance interventions and counterterrorism operations, there is not the strength in depth that the Alliance enjoyed during the Cold War, especially if NATO identifies a need for on-call reservists extending into the hundreds of thousands.

Key challenges in the years ahead will be to generate follow-on forces in sufficient numbers and to store military equipment and supplies in Eastern Europe. A related challenge has been to ensure that there are adequate airfields, ports, roads, railheads, and other reception facilities in Eastern Europe to allow the reserves to be deployed effectively. The good news is that many of the legal and administrative obstacles that NATO identified back in 2014 to moving forces rapidly across borders (what the commander of US Land Forces in Europe, Gen. Ben Hodges, has called the "military Schengen") have now been removed though amending national legislation. Taken together, these measures should enable the supreme Allied commander, Europe (SACEUR) to have full control over his area of responsibility once a state of emergency (known as "counter surprise" in NATO jargon) has been declared.

Other pieces of unfinished business concern the need to generate more maritime forces for the NRF and to fill NATO's four standing maritime groups. The A2/AD challenge, while not insuperable, will require more sustained military focus and a larger spectrum of electronic warfare capabilities, such as jammers, and stealth aircraft. Before the RAP was promulgated in Wales, NATO's strategic commands had identified sixteen major capability priorities for operations, mainly concerning strategic lift, in-flight refueling, jamming, suppression of air defenses, and precision-guided munitions. By the time of Warsaw, the priority requirements list had grown further, which is not a reflection of the lack of progress since Wales but rather of the fact that the Enhanced Forward Presence has thrown up new requirements, such as more intelligence, surveillance, reconnaissance, antisubmarine warfare, and artillery assets.

Control and sea-denial in the constricted Baltic Sea space require the effective integration of surface ships, submarines, maritime situational-awareness satellites and sensors, air defense, and defense against antiship missiles that can be fired from Kaliningrad. They also require close cooperation with Sweden and Finland, NATO's two key partners in the region. The Atlantic Council in the United States has suggested that in order to combine all these in a coherent command-and-control system, NATO should adopt a framework approach in the Baltic Sea region built around German, Polish, and Swedish ships and antisubmarine warfare capabilities. It is certainly an idea worth exploring.[2]

One key area now commanding more attention is cyber defense. It has moved from being a peripheral technical issue to become an integral part of NATO's overall defense and deterrence strategy. While Wales declared that a severe cyberattack could constitute grounds for invoking Article 5 of the Washington Treaty—namely, collective defense—Allies in Warsaw pledged to strengthen and enhance the cyber defenses of their national critical infrastructures and networks. This Cyber Defense Pledge reflected the fact that cyber defense determines functionality not only in the virtual domain but also increasingly in the more conventional air, land, sea, and space domains as well, as command-and-control and weapon systems are linked to the Internet and made up of advanced electronics. In modern warfare, data has become as valuable as firepower and heavy metal vehicles. Controlling data and exploiting it increasingly determines victory or defeat.

Recognizing this evolution, NATO also declared cyberspace as an operational domain. In doing so, it moved from an earlier focus on information assurance to a focus on protecting its military operations, including exercises and crisis-management procedures, against cyber espionage and attacks. Cyber as a domain will also make it easier for NATO to overhaul its organizational framework to better manage resources, enhance military planning, identify needed skills and abilities, and improve training and decision making for cyber operations. This more coherent effort will need to be reflected in more intensive cyber defense exercises based on more realistic scenarios in which a cyberattack is no longer a temporary nuisance but a real potential showstopper able to inflict lasting damage on equipment, communications, and command and control. Allies will also be able to discuss a mechanism for how national cyber capabilities could be made available to the Alliance as a whole to assist an Ally under attack or to support a NATO mission.

This said, cyber like any other capability designed to produce a military effect, would only be used by NATO defensively and in line with the Alliance's defensive mandate. NATO would act in accordance with international law and in a proportionate manner. Yet the more cyber becomes an inevitable and more decisive element of conflict, the more NATO Allies have an interest in preventing cyberspace from becoming an increasingly contentious, competitive, and hostile domain subject to none of the constraints and international arms-control regimes and associated verification procedures that we have come to expect in dealing with nuclear or chemical weapons. So, in parallel to becoming a more cyber-enabled Alliance militarily, NATO will also need to support voluntary international norms of responsible state behavior and confidence-building measures in cyberspace. The NATO Cooperative Cyber Defence Centre of Excellence in Estonia is helping in this respect by facilitating the *Tallinn Manual* process. Version 2.0 of the manual was released in February 2017. Building on the first edition, released in 2013, it expands the scope to cover peacetime international law and how states should behave in cyberspace in peacetime.

NATO's Hybrid Strategy

NATO's focus on cyber defense is also part and parcel of its preoccupation with hybrid warfare. Russia's incursion into Ukraine was a textbook example of how cyberattacks, sabotage, aggressive propaganda, penetration of intelligence networks, and the infiltration of undercover military operatives (commonly referred to as "little green men") into Crimea could paralyze a region and take administrative control before the victim fully understood what was happening and had time to respond. Not surprisingly, and for historical reasons, Ukraine had many vulner-abilities vis-à-vis Russia, which made it particularly susceptible to hybrid warfare tactics. This is not to say that Allied countries would not be more resilient in a similar crisis situation, and the Enhanced Forward Presence of NATO units in Eastern Europe able to exercise and interact with local forces certainly gives NATO a rapid-response option in dealing with the early manifestations of hybrid warfare, such as incidents along borders.

This said, the cyberattacks against the Democratic National Committee in Washington and attempts to interfere in the 2016 US election campaign through a regular stream of leaks of hacked confidential messages show that even a limited hybrid or information operation, magnified by national media, can achieve a dispro-portionate political impact. Other operations, such as the use of the Black Energy virus against the electricity grid in Western Ukraine in 2016, have demonstrated the disruption that can be caused when a number of different cyber operations (one against industrial control systems, another against internal communications, and a third against the public telephone network) are integrated to produce a cumulative impact.

So, NATO also agreed in Warsaw to intensify its efforts to be better able to anticipate and respond to hybrid forms of aggression below the Article 5 thresh-old. To prepare the way, in 2015, a hybrid strategy was approved by NATO's for-eign ministers, which was followed up by a concrete implementation plan to help NATO identify its vulnerabilities, particularly in the realm of critical infrastruc-ture protection and disinformation, and improve its situational awareness. A key requirement is for more intelligence-sharing within the Alliance and in particular to link civilian to military intelligence networks, as well as to identify early warn-ing indicators that can help to compare intelligence to the key indicators of a hybrid operation and therefore establish a pattern of orchestrated disruption and attribution at an early stage. The heads of state and government in Warsaw noted NATO's intention to establish a new Intelligence Division to spearhead this effort, and this was set up in December 2016. One of its first tasks was to establish a hybrid analysis and fusion cell, which became operational in June 2017. Its aim is to give NATO ambassadors not only more timely but also more accurate infor-mation to ensure that key decisions can be grounded in better evidence of what is actually going on.

NATO and Baltic Sea Security

Yet in attempting to construct a viable long-term defense and deterrence strategy in the east, and the Baltic Sea region in particular, military measures can take you only so far. They are the bedrock, because they establish clear and credible red lines against aggressive risk-taking and hostile probing activities, but they need to be supplemented by political stabilization measures if they are to be fully effective.

The starting point is to enhance NATO's overall strategic awareness of developments and trend lines in the region. In May 2016, NATO foreign ministers asked the Alliance's military authorities to continue to deliver a military assessment of the security situation in the Baltic Sea region every six months. This is to be done in consultation with Finland and Sweden, NATO's two core partners in the region, who have also been designated as enhanced opportunity partners, giving them special access to NATO ministerial meetings, consultations, military planning and training, and exercises.

The Baltic Sea assessments provide an analysis of military and nonmilitary developments, looking at Russia's strategic objectives, hybrid warfare activities and tactics, snap exercises, air safety issues, maritime deployments, and A2/AD measures, such as the stationing of Iskanders in Kaliningrad already referred to. A road map is included in the assessments to identify ways in which NATO can respond to Russia's heightened presence and activity in the Baltic Sea region and also work with Finland and Sweden on mitigation measures to reinforce predictability and stability. The military assessment is also complemented by a political-military assessment, which is conducted by the Alliance's deputy ambassadors (also in association with Finland and Sweden) with the same frequency.

The Warsaw Summit underscored in particular this need for NATO to work closely with partners in order to counter hybrid threats. Consequently, Finland and Sweden are closely involved in the work of the Civil Emergency Planning Committee to develop an assessment of vulnerabilities of maritime transport in the Baltic Sea region. Its advice and recommendations were delivered in the spring of 2017. Another key area of cooperation is crisis management, especially based on scenarios focusing on the Baltic Sea area. Finland and Sweden participated as "potential operational partners" in NATO's Crisis Management Exercise (CMX) 2016 and have also been involved in the subsequent identification of lessons learned. The CMX process has undoubtedly given both Finland and Sweden many useful insights into how the Alliance operates and how crisis management can rapidly give way to collective defense actions. On this basis, they can identify the challenges and responsibilities that they would need to meet at the national level in engaging with NATO not in Afghanistan or the Balkans in a stabilization mission but in a European regional crisis based on overt aggression and with Article 5 implications. Thus the exercises are useful not only to test and harmonize procedures but also to give both NATO and partners a better understanding of what they can expect from each other in an actual crisis affecting the security of both.

Exchanges of information and experiences of hybrid warfare incidents are also an evolving part of this dialogue. The Swedish Institute of International Affairs in Stockholm issued in January 2017 a detailed report on "active measures" that Russia has carried out to influence political developments in Sweden and—allegedly—to prevent the country drawing closer to NATO.[3] These actives measures included deliberate spreading of fake news, troll attacks against the Twitter accounts of well-known Swedish personalities and politicians, and manipulation and misuse of their Twitter feeds to infiltrate false stories into social media. Concrete examples cited in the report include a fake telegram stating that former Swedish foreign minister Carl Bildt was a candidate for the position of prime minister of Ukraine and a fake letter from the defense minister giving details of the sale of lethal weapons to Ukraine. Some of the actions have been more serious, however, such as the mysterious destruction of television transmitters and interference with Swedish activities to track foreign submarines in its offshore waters.

At a time when these campaigns of disinformation and political sabotage are affecting almost all of Russia's neighbors in the Baltic Sea region, it is timely that Finland has decided to establish a Hybrid Warfare Center of Excellence. Although focused initially on the EU, this center will also be open to NATO cooperation and exchanges. Similarly, NATO's own three centers of excellence in the Baltic Sea region (Cyber Defence in Tallinn, Strategic Communications in Riga, and Energy Security in Vilnius) are also open to participation by Finland and Sweden. Finland opened its center on hybrid warfare in June 2017 and has quickly reached out to NATO to establish mechanisms for a joint analysis and exchange on hybrid experiences and with a view to building across the Baltic region a cluster of analysis, training, and exercises that over time can produce among the regional partners a shared culture and strategy in anticipating and defeating hybrid warfare intrusions.

The third focus of Baltic Sea cooperation, in addition to assessment and crisis management, is the effort to achieve greater military transparency, confidence-building, communication, and thus stability in the region. This is all the more important at a time when Russia has stopped its participation in established arms-control regimes, such as the Treaty on Conventional Forces in Europe, and is violating if not the letter then at least the spirit of those regimes still in force, such as the Vienna Document of the Organization for Security and Co-operation in Europe (OSCE) and the Open Skies inspection agreement. For instance, in its Kavkaz 2016 exercise, Russia divided up large numbers of troops that, by its own admission, were part of the same exercise, but doing so is contrary to the Vienna Document.

One issue that has especially preoccupied Allies is air safety. Russia has greatly increased its military flights over the Baltic Sea, often using not only assertive but even provocative and dangerous tactics. NATO aircraft and ships have been "buzzed," there have been a number of airspace violations (also involving Finland and Sweden), and the standard understandings regarding good airmanship and safety have been disregarded. One particular concern has been Russian aircraft flying without their identification transponders switched on, which also poses a risk for civilian air traffic. The European Leadership Network in London issued a detailed report early in 2016 listing a number of near misses in recent times and alerting to the urgent need for a better system of civil-military airspace management in Northern Europe.[4] As NATO has suspended its cooperation with Russia in its Cooperative Airspace Initiative since the 2014 illegal annexation of Crimea, another way needs to be found to address this requirement.

Some useful, constructive work has been carried out by the International Civilian Aviation Organization (ICAO) and a group of experts in the Baltic Sea Project Team (BSPT). When the NATO-Russia Council (NRC) was convened in December 2016, the Allies and Russia were briefed by ICAO and the chairman of the BSPT on the initiatives they have discussed thus far to prevent dangerous incidents and enhance aviation safety. In the meantime, the president of Finland has started an initiative to deal with the transponder problem and to have Helsinki host meetings to bring Russia and the other interested parties of the Baltic Sea region around the same table, as well as to revive the BSPT after it had completed its initial work. In March 2017, the Finnish Transport Safety Agency organized a meeting to discuss the proposal to use transponders for certain state aircraft operations, to review the implementation of previous BSPT recommendations, to consider further steps on enhancing civil-military cooperation, and to explore the possibility of developing a code of practice, based on "Guiding Principles for Good Airmanship."

NATO Allies see merit in these ideas, and the current indications are that Russia is ready to participate in this process. At the time of writing, it is difficult to predict the outcome. NATO will not want to give Russia the impression that it can ignore its existing mandatory commitments (for instance, in the OSCE or ICAO frameworks) simply because new or more regionally specific rules are being discussed. But it still represents a way forward after two years of a significant Russian military buildup and higher tension in the Baltic area. The key will be to try to depoliticize this process as much as possible, looking for technical and practical solutions.

Naturally, the search for stability in the region will depend on how willing Russia is to engage constructively and to seek ways to de-escalate tensions. Equally, can NATO's Warsaw decision to resume a dual-track approach in dealing with Russia, based on deterrence and defense coupled with periodic, focused, and meaningful dialogue, steer Russia in a more constructive direction? The three NRC meetings in 2016, which resumed the NATO-Russia dialogue after the annexation of Crimea, did indeed produce a greater sense of mutual engagement. The atmosphere has been more businesslike, with both sides talking to each other as much as at each other. NATO and Russia are now able to hold reciprocal briefings on military exercises, such as Kavkaz 2017 and Trident Juncture 2018, and with more granularity than in the past. The opening of a structured dialogue at the OSCE in Vienna can also help the Allies and Russia to hold a complementary dialogue on threat perceptions and force postures, leading hopefully over time to a new set of transparency and confidence-building measures.

What would be helpful would be for NATO and Russia to exchange these brief-ings in advance of the exercises rather than several months afterward, to improve transparency and predictability. It would also help to improve military-to-military communication. A hotline already exists between SACEUR and the Russian defense chief, and recently the chairman of NATO's Military Committee held his first meeting with the chief of the Russian armed forces in Baku. This channel could be used more routinely, and other military contacts at lower levels could be initiated to gain a better sense of the thinking in military circles and to identify and try to solve misperceptions and misunderstandings. This will be all the more important with NATO's enhanced forward presence in place in the Baltic states and in Poland, which Russia has dramatically overplayed in public as evidence of "NATO hostil-ity," but it shows very little transparency regarding its own, much larger military reinforcements and infrastructure building in its Western Military District.

All this said, profound differences between NATO and Russia will remain, and the Alliance will need to steer carefully to avoid giving the impression to Russia, as well as to its own domestic audiences, that NATO is returning willy-nilly to "busi-ness as usual" with Moscow after the Crimean interlude. Also NATO will have to avoid its own Baltic-related dialogue with Russia from becoming a bubble impervi-ous to Russia's behavior elsewhere in the world, which could give Russia sanctuary from the consequences and penalties of egregious human rights violations in places such as Syria. Yet if the NRC can become a body where NATO and Russia can discuss these differences in a frank manner and begin looking for some solutions at least, it will have served its purpose.

NATO-EU Relations

There is, of course, another player in Baltic security for which NATO's challenge of engagement will be even more urgent and important in the long run as engagement with Russia. This is the EU, an organization that has many of the political and economic instruments that the Alliance, with its inevitable military focus, lacks and where Finland and Sweden are full members, unlike in NATO. The NATO-EU Joint Declaration signed in Warsaw was a good start and said all the right things, but it will only be as good as its implementation.

Here the good news is that NATO and the EU made rapid progress in devising ideas to give life to this joint declaration and came up with an implementation plan listing seven main cooperation areas and forty-two specific objectives. It was endorsed by NATO foreign ministers and the European Council in December 2016. The plan calls for holding more joint exercises to test the respective hybrid warfare procedures of both organizations and exchanging information between NATO's Computer Incident Response Capability located at Supreme Headquarters Allied Powers Europe and the EU Computer Emerging Response Team. Other ideas are to increase transparency in the area of capability developments and military research and to adopt a more coherent approach to the defense capacity-building efforts not only in the Middle East and North Africa but also in Ukraine, Georgia, and Moldova.

To be successful, the EU will need to embrace the Allies that are not EU members (and the United Kingdom will join this list in due course after Brexit) in the same way that NATO has embraced non-NATO EU countries such as Austria, Finland, and Sweden. Yet if we consider that a few years ago a US ambassador to NATO described NATO and the EU as two institutions in the same city but living on different planets, the implementation of the joint declaration shows that real progress has been made and testifies also to a new willingness on the EU side to publicly recognize the importance of NATO and to commit to working more closely with it. This new spirit has been greatly facilitated by the new EU Global Security Strategy, which identifies many of the same threats and challenges as NATO and also recognizes that the actions of one institution, for instance in Ukraine or the western Balkans, can have a real impact on the other. Hence the need for more coherence and coordination.

As we move forward, the NATO-EU relationship will throw up an additional challenge. The EU has reacted to Brexit and the coolness shown toward it by President Trump, with his call for more burden-sharing, by reviving long-dormant plans to strengthen EU defense cooperation. The EU summit in December 2016 endorsed a number of proposals—for instance, to make better use of the EU battle groups, to pool medical units, to establish a solidarity fund for EU deployments, and to use more civilian research-and-development money for defense research. Even the budget of the European Defence Agency enjoyed its first, albeit modest, increase in a decade. As 2017 unfolded and following the revival of the Franco-German joint leadership in EU matters, these initiatives have been followed up by the creation of a European Defence Fund, with up to €5.5 billion to finance EU multilateral research and capability development programs in the years ahead, and a Military Planning and Conduct Capability, which prefigures the emergence of a stand-alone EU operational headquarters.

Some of the language that these initiatives had generated emphasizes the need for European strategic autonomy vis-à-vis the United States and the need to have a European default option for defense should America turn its back on Europe. To my mind, it would be more useful in the current context if these very welcome and long-overdue efforts at European defense integration could also be presented as a way of strengthening NATO, avoiding unnecessary duplication and also giving the EU more of a stake in the collective defense of the eastern Allies (who are also EU members) and not only to do interventions, training, and capacity-building on Europe's southern periphery. At the very least, NATO and the EU will need to have a dialogue on what collective defense means in the new context, as the EU has an obligation to assist Finland and Sweden under Articles 42.7 and 222 of the

Lisbon Treaty without having the planning or military structures to achieve this, these being naturally the preserve of NATO.

So how would the EU and NATO coordinate in an Article 5–type mission? At the current juncture in transatlantic relations, all our efforts need to be focused on maintaining and strengthening the transatlantic relationship in a much more dangerous world and not on prognosticating a future in which Europe and North America are growing apart and need to act separately. Hence the language, narrative, and strategic communications of European defense as an enhancement and extension of NATO roles are, in my view, as important as the actual budgetary and material effort. This has to be a debate about responsibilities and capabilities and only secondarily and minimally about structures or independent ambitions. This is all the more important when we consider that following Brexit over 80 percent of NATO defense spending would be provided by non-EU Allies, who would also contribute three out of four battalions in the Enhanced Forward Presence in Eastern Europe.

In conclusion, the Warsaw Summit was the moment when NATO moved from immediate crisis management following the shock of Russia's annexation of Crimea and the deterioration of the overall security environment in 2014 toward a more measured and longer-term approach. The policies that it has now devised, and which have been described in this chapter, will have to be applied with patience and tenacity. They may not produce their maximum political benefits for some years to come, but at least they recognize that the Alliance has reached a pivotal moment in world history when the old approaches to security no longer work and a new strategy with a different set of priorities is called for. Warsaw was the moment when NATO brought its core tasks of collective defense, crisis management, and cooperative security out of their separate silos and much closer together. The new NATO strategy, still to be enshrined in a future new Strategic Concept that might be adopted at the seventieth-anniversary NATO summit in 2019, may not be perfect, but it is the best option for keeping Europe safe during this time of troubles and for bringing the day closer when it will once again be permissible to speak of a Europe whole and free.

Notes

The views expressed in this chapter are those of the author alone. They do not represent an official position of NATO.

1. Bruce Stokes, "NATO's Image Improves on Both Sides of Atlantic," Pew Research Center, May 23, 2017, http://www.pewglobal.org/2017/05/23/natos-image-improves-on -both-sides-of-atlantic/.

2. Franklin D. Kramer and Magnus Nordenman, "A Maritime Framework for the Baltic Sea Region," Atlantic Council, March 2016.

3. Martin Kragh and Sebastian Åsberg, "Russia's Strategy for Influence through Public Diplomacy and Active Measures: The Case of Sweden," *Journal of Strategic Studies* (January 2017).

4. Ian Kearns and Denitsa Raynova, "Managing Dangerous Incidents: The Need for a NATO-Russia Memorandum of Understanding," European Leadership Network, http://www.europeanleadershipnetwork.org/managing-dangerous-incidents-the-need-for-a-nato-russia-memorandum-of-understanding_3578.html.

4

The West and Russia

Another Front in the New Cold War?

CHRISTOPHER COKER

Institutions, like species, evolve, or they perish. We used to talk about the "survival of the fittest," a social Darwinist metaphor that has rightly fallen out of fashion. Today scientists speak instead of the survival of the best-informed. Species that know what is going on in the neighborhood tend to survive. The neighborhood we are talking about is the Baltic Sea region, where NATO is challenged to evolve or perish, or at the very best wither away. One of the problems the Alliance faces is that some of its members are far more concerned with other neighborhoods than they are with the Baltic. One is the Mediterranean and the problem of human migration; another is the Greater Middle East and the perennial challenge of Islamic fundamentalism. Its most important member no doubt considers that the real challenge stems not from nonstate forces or even actors such as the Islamic State (IS) but from China, whose actions in the South China Sea are deemed by some to constitute a threat to freedom of navigation and the rules and conventions that underpin the international system.

In the end we should remember that the United States owns a large block of shares in NATO Inc., whose directors are therefore obliged to take into account what it thinks. The American commitment to NATO has been based, in large part, on the conviction that it possesses the capacity to shape Europe's future, usually for the best. Were it ever to conclude that the Europeans are not willing to shape their own future, then it may draw its own conclusions. Whether the European members are geographically grounded in the Mediterranean (the old southern flank) or points further north is unimportant. The Europeans will hang together or hang alone. Europe has a profound interest in fostering a neo-Westphalian order: a society of nation-states willing to share their sovereignty while abiding by certain basic norms. That such an order can advance the well-being of countries that do not yet belong to it (such as Ukraine and Georgia) is a proposition that European statesmen continue to promote. Do they still believe in it, however? The obstacles to creating such an order are many. Preeminent among them, at least at present, is the existence of a country and/or regime bent on challenging or revising the rules-based order that we have all come to take for granted.

Let us begin with the preamble to the European Security Doctrine of 2003: "Europe has never been so prosperous, so secure nor so free. The violence of the first half of the 20th Century has given way to a period of peace and stability unprecedented in European history. Large scale aggression against any member state is now improbable."[1] Such was the comforting belief of the Europeans who drafted their first-ever security doctrine back in 2003. And the preamble is important if we are to take into account the historical significance of the challenge that Europe and the United States now face. It is a challenge, to begin with, to all the post–Cold War platitudes that underpin security thinking. One was globalization. At the time of the Kosovo War, the NATO supreme Allied commander, Wesley Clark, described the Alliance as "a facilitator of globalization."[2] The doctrine of the European Union (EU) was even more explicit. The EU saw itself as a "facilitator of global civil society." All of which was fine, except for the fact that not all the world was globalizing as fast as Europe. Indeed, the Russian foreign minister, Sergei Lavrov, calls his own country a "minority stakeholder" in globalization.

The problem with such Western narratives was that they overlooked the reality of geography. *The Revenge of Geography* is the title of a book by Robert Kaplan.[3] Geography still matters—it matters to Russia (but then it always has); it matters to China in the South China Sea, where there have been sixty-one incidents in the past ten years over territorial control. Another, even more attractive story was that of "soft power." "Weapons of Mass Attraction" was Robert Cooper's definition of the importance of trade and investment, the instruments that the EU thought it could apply with immunity in its eastern neighborhood. The problem is that countries without soft power, or much of it, tend to play up what they have—hard power instead. Russia remains a nuclear power, committed to the modernization of its nuclear program. The impressive display of military power at the Red Square celebration of the sixtieth anniversary of VE Day was meant to overawe an Alliance that has seen a massive reduction in defense expenditure. By comparison, Russia has increased its defense budget by 230 percent in the last ten years. The West was able to tell itself that numbers and size did not matter. "Smart defense" was the answer, except for the fact that it really isn't.

And insofar as Russia deploys soft power, it does so in terms of its social and human capital: the Russian people, including the significant minorities in the Baltic states, as well as the Orthodox faith and the concept of a Russian destiny at a time when the West is distinctly posthistorical, certainly postheroic. What matters most is that soft and hard power in this case have been conjoined: The Russian army has a new task—to "correct historical mistakes" (which probably includes the loss of the Baltic states). This was the reason why the EU had to revise its security doctrine. It now talks of "principled pragmatism" in its relations with neighboring states, including Russia.

But certain things haven't changed. If Russia lost the sense of the "revolutionary" long before the end of the Cold War, the West lost even earlier a role for the heroic in its thinking. Its terms of engagement with history are far more modest. Even with the end of the Cold War, the West knew it had reached the end of an era, but it had no idea what the future era signified. History had become simply too unpredictable to be shaped by any narrative. Or perhaps its range of vision was simply too narrow and confined to allow it to grasp history's essential rhythms. Writing in 1977, Michael Howard posed what he called "the liberal dilemma": Could a peaceful and prosperous community of liberal democracies preserve its interests and extend its influence in pursuit of its highest ideals if it abjured the use of armed force? Today that question is beginning to be answered in a way that many find disturbing.

This is why it is so important to grasp the historical significance of President Vladimir Putin's challenge. I think the French philosopher Jean-Luc Nancy sums it up best: "One could say that everything is historical but also that nothing is 'historic.'"[4] What does "historic" mean? It means significant or memorable. For a long time we have not been able to initiate events that we know will be remembered because of their significance for a future generation. We have for many years now no longer known how to make the present significant for ourselves on the understanding that we can no longer determine what the future will find of note or not. In short, we have lost faith or interest in history itself. In an agnostic age, the "will to power" has been devalued by the suspicion that there is nothing to will for. If that remains the case, then the West, and the Alliance through which it is embodied, will simply shrivel away. If the Western powers are still interested in a better future, is this only on condition that it comes from somewhere else (from East Asia)—on condition, in other words, that they need not bother to conceive of it themselves?

Baltic Security

Until the annexation of Crimea in 2014 (though we should have known this a long time before), we tended to think that Europe was indeed at peace, as its first security doctrine proclaimed with such confidence. The problem is that peace means different things to different people. What does the world understand by peace? asked Susan Sontag in her 2001 Jerusalem Prize acceptance speech.[5] Do we mean the absence of strife or forgetting or forgiveness, or do we mean the great weariness of exhaustion that often follows a war, which can be accompanied, but not always, by an emptying out of rancor? What most people mean by peace, of course, is victory: the victory of their side. Calls for peace for the defeated often appear for that reason fraudulent. There are so many different ways in which peace for oneself can mean oppression or marginalization for others. For Sontag there was very little disagreement about the desirability of peace, but there was about its meaning, and that is because many disagreements are entirely reasonable, even if different parties may think each other profoundly mistaken.

Security, the West proclaims, must be based on a genuine peace, and a genuine peace must in turn promote real security. But that is the problem, for security, like peace itself, is what the philosopher Walter Bryce Gallie called "a contested concept." The example Gallie gives is an interesting one. The statement "this picture is painted in oils" is either true or false and can be exposed as false if we find it to be painted actually in tempera. "This picture is a work of art" is a very different proposition, since anything can be a work of art, from Marcel Duchamp's famous urinal to Yves Tanguy's habit of setting fire to his own monumental works immediately after completing them. The only ways, Gallie suggests, to gain universal agreement would be to coin a new meaning of the term "work of art" to which all parties to a dispute could agree or to force them to accept one meaning or to declare "a work of art" to be a number of different concepts merely employing the same name.

If we take the term "security," we are faced with quite similar problems of definition. Setting aside Gallie's first suggestion, the second—forcing all parties to agree to one meaning—has been historically Russia's policy since it moved into the Baltic Sea region in the early eighteenth century and challenged the dominance of the then great power Sweden. Indeed, the Russian understanding has been broken for only a short period in history in 1920–40 when the Baltic states won their independence. After 1945, Russia effectively managed a Pax Sovietica, which included the Finlandization of its immediate neighbor and a Sweden that was awed (if not shocked) into neutrality. When NATO discussed Baltic security, it did so on the very limited understanding that all it could aspire to achieve was denial of access to the southern part of the sea.

As for the third suggestion, an agreement to disagree, this has never been, nor will ever be, a Russian position. This is clear today from the bullying of Sweden (including unspecified threats if it even aspires to join NATO), regular incursions into the airspace of independent Baltic states, and regular Zapad military exercises every two years, which nearly always end either with the occupation of one of the Baltic states or a nuclear strike against a NATO city (most often Warsaw) or, in some cases, both.

And so if we come to the first of Gallie's ideas, we have to assume that what the West had hoped for—a collective understanding of security—now seems a pipe dream. As Robert Hunter, the former US ambassador to NATO, once remarked, the only hope of permanent security would have been to persuade the Russians to see security in Western terms. If there was ever any possibility of that, this vision quickly faded in the early years of the Putin regime. As Edward Lucas writes in *The New Cold War*, "we are facing a people who want to harm us, frustrate us, and weaken us."[6] Perhaps we should replace the word "people" with the word "regime," but, if when he wrote this back in 2008 the situation seemed as yet unclear, it is surely all too clear today.

All attempts to socialize Russia have effectively failed and perhaps always were going to. Russia is, after all, Russia. It now is run by a neoczarist regime in which the social contract between the people and the state (the legitimating principle for Putin's rule) is the restoration of a sense of national destiny, a historic role. The importance of history should not be underestimated, not least since Russian military doctrine allows the military to be used to "consolidate" historical gains. The annexation of Crimea is itself represented as an attempt to "correct a historical mistake" (even if it was Nikita Khrushchev's gift to Ukraine in 1954). In other words, as we contemplate the present insecurity in the Baltic region, the West has to fall back on NATO's Article 5 guarantee. We rely, once again, not on collective security but collective defense.

Baltic Insecurity

The problem is that the Article 5 guarantee has only been as compelling as Article 3—the ability of every member to actually defend itself. Unfortunately, the Europeans have chosen to cut defense spending drastically in the last twenty years. They have become profoundly preoccupied with socioeconomic programs and activities. Added to the sense that history had come to an "end" in 1989, and that therefore a military dimension was supernumerary, was the growth of positive liberal bias in social science, which obscured the role that conflict is still likely to play in political life.

The liberal societies of the West spent most of the twentieth century engaging illiberal regimes in battle. Those conflicts were fought—on both sides—by citizen armies. By the mid-twentieth century, the process had reached the stage where military historians had begun to write no longer about armies in battle but about entire societies at war. By the end of the twentieth century, however, it had become increasingly difficult to motivate the West's citizens to fight. What we have seen is what social scientists call a process of "civilianization."

Does it matter if liberal societies redefine freedom in negative terms—not as the power to refashion the world on its terms but as the right to be left alone, the right to suffer from one's own mistakes rather than from the malice of others? Well, it may matter a great deal if history returns when least expected. The problem with history is that it can flare up at any time in the most peripheral areas. The West has only recently discovered that it does not live in one time zone—its own, the post-modern era—but that it also lives in several overlapping zones at the same time. It lives in the imagination of a labor-surplus world (if capital will not go to the societies that have an excess of labor, labor will visit societies that are capital-intensive); at least one country on its border has rediscovered its own sense of national destiny and with it the need to revise a post–Cold War order from which it feels deliberately excluded. In the Baltic region, history is fast becoming an interaction between two historical time zones rather than a dialectical relationship within one.

And this is just at the time that the Baltic states discover that they cannot defend themselves. Of the three, Latvia is ripe for the plucking. Sharing a seven-hundred-kilometer border with Russia, it finds itself at a distinct disadvantage. It is the country with the largest regional differences in economic development, the deepest social inequalities, the highest level of political corruption, and a significant percentage of the population that watches Russian television.

Twenty years ago, Robert Cooper, then a special adviser to the EU's higher representative, Javier Solana, warned that it would be ill-advised to allow any country with significant Russian minorities into NATO, for fear that they would constitute an effective Trojan horse. Perhaps he was right. The situation today reminds one of the early 1930s, when the Eastern European states that had signed up to the minority guarantees in the postwar settlements after 1920 felt that they could no longer respect them, given a change of regime in Germany itself.

NATO cannot defend Latvia in the as yet unlikely event that Russia chooses to invade; only Latvia can. And yet, here too Latvia labors under several disadvantages of its own making: It has allowed defense spending to decline, it has not pursued security-sector reforms, and it has no sizable or well-disciplined national territorial force capable of even putting up the resistance that the Finnish or Estonian armies might or that Lithuania hopes to now that it has decided to reintroduce conscription. Were Latvia to be better placed, it would still face some severe challenges. To defend the Baltic states, NATO needs safe sea communications of the kind that made it possible for Germany to hold on longer than imagined to the last two Baltic redoubts in the last year of World War II. In the Cold War, we should remember, NATO did not seek to secure access to the Baltic states—only to deny sea routes in the southern part of the Baltic Sea so that it would be secure from any attempt by the Russians to outflank the central front. Now, of course, it faces a new challenge. In the Cold War at least, it only had to confront a conventional threat. Today war has gone "hybrid." Imagine what would happen if the Russians tried to mine areas of the Baltic Sea (falling back, of course, on [im]plausible deniability).

Add to this the fact that the Baltic states cannot be defended without NATO access to Swedish airspace. Unfortunately, Sweden is not a member of NATO and is not likely to become so any time in the near future. In the Cold War, NATO was able (we now know) to rely on tacit support from the Swedish government. The Swedes operated a turnkey concept; in a crisis, or in war, Swedish equipment would have been interoperable with NATO's, and Swedish air bases would have been made available to NATO air forces. To protect sea access to the Baltic in a crisis today, NATO would need to operate convoys to and from the Baltic ports, for its ships would require access to Gotland and air cover from Swedish bases. At least Sweden has chosen to fortify Gotland to preempt any Russian attempt to seize it.

Finally, none of the Baltic states have been able to create a credible forward defense of their territory. Because of this, Zbigniew Brzezinski has suggested deploying a "tripwire" force of US troops.[7] But the trip wire philosophy of the Cold War was very different. It did not offer a hostage to fortune. It depended on follow-on forces that would have been capable at short notice of reinforcing forward-deployed forces. In those days, of course, NATO did not rely on "smart" defense (a meaningless buzzword if there ever was one); it relied instead on *real* defense, which translated in turn into real deterrence.

Hybrid Warfare

NATO now faces what the former chairman of the Joint Chiefs of Staff Martin Dempsey calls an "inflection point" in modern war. US senator Joe Biden, speaking a few years earlier, also referred to an "inflection point," in this case in reference to deteriorating US-China relations. It is a mathematical term that could be looked up in Wikipedia, but it has no real or military meaning. But it is clear what Dempsey (if not Biden) means by the term. Hybrid warfare is coming to a theater of war near you, the most likely theater being Moldova or the Baltic region.

The Russians themselves don't call it hybrid, of course; they prefer other terms such as "new generation" or "nonlinearity." Nonlinearity is the disproportion between an outcome and the resources spent on achieving it. New generation first appeared in a short story written by one of President Putin's closest political advisers, Vladislav Surkov. It was published under a pseudonym just a few days before the annexation of the Crimea. Surkov is also the man credited with inventing the term "managed democracy." He set his story in a world that was experiencing the "Fifth World War." It is a future in which states can get away with aggression precisely because war has become less political and more fluid. "A few provinces would join one side," Surkov writes, "a few others a different one. One town or generation or gender would join yet another. Then they could switch sides, sometimes mid-battle."[8]

In March 2014, the Russian Federation Council authorized President Putin to use Russian armed forces in the Ukraine. In asking Parliament to revoke this decision in June, he created a facade of legality. Officially Russia was not a party to the conflict, except, of course, that it engaged in intimidating large-scale military exercises that left no doubt in the minds of the politicians in Kiev of its readiness to invade "if necessary." In June, Russia conducted a "snap inspection" in the Central Military District involving more than sixty-five thousand troops, fifty-five hundred vehicles, and over 150 aircraft. Military units in full formation were ready for deployment within seventy-two hours. The Russians also deployed the "little green men" (or "polite people," as Putin spookily liked to call them—Russian special forces in their familiar green apparel acting as "local security forces" without national or other identification tags). In Crimea the presence of these special forces constituted a form of psychological warfare. Would they act peacefully or start shooting? And in all cases Russia denied its involvement in the fighting in Eastern Ukraine, even in the face of growing evidence to the contrary.

When it became impossible to conceal Russian casualties, the official narrative changed. Its servicemen were now "volunteers" fighting for their ethnic cousins. Such thinking seemed to be dominant in the Kremlin during the Ukraine struggle; indeed, the important actors were not armies but local power brokers such as the Donetsk billionaire Rinat Akhmetov (Ukraine's richest man) and Mikhail Dobkin, the former head of the Kharkiv Regional Administration.[9] Cyberattacks were only one weapon in Russia's arsenal but nonetheless an important one. Lengthy analysis showed sustained hacking into sensitive NATO sites as the stand-off continued with the use of "snake" malware against dozens of sensitive computer systems in the Ukrainian government.[10]

What is especially distinctive about nonlinear warfare is that it is intended to avoid direct military confrontations in which lives might be lost and passions ignited. It is designed to avoid what Carl von Clausewitz called war's propensity to escalate. So, how best to avoid escalation? Don't declare war. Don't mount a conventional invasion, but make sure that security is hollowed out from *within* by using local gangs and power brokers. War, in a word, can now be relatively contactless, played out not on a battlefield but in the minds of an enemy and fought at a level of consciousness that erodes self-belief and in turn self-confidence.

It is also asymmetrical in nature, though unusually the asymmetry favors the aggressor, not the defender. It is the aggressor who uses irregular forces, avoids battles, and exploits propaganda. A study by the Russian Academy of Sciences makes clear that "the rules of war have changed significantly. Non-military operations have come to play a greater role in achieving political and strategic goals, and in some situations, are greatly superior to the power of weapons" (this from an article by the chief of the Russian armed forces). Or, to quote a Russian general, "It has always been held that any confrontation without resort to arms is struggle and pursuit of policies by physical force and armed violence is war. Some of our . . .

philosophers, though, maintain that all non-military practices are a contemporary development and suggest, on this assumption, that following those practices, is nothing short of war."[11]

Virtual Violence

War doesn't change. What changes is the way we see it: Perception is everything. Violence is always communicative: It communicates both intent and purpose. And like physical coercion, virtual violence is both instrumental and expressive at the same time. It is an expedient, to be sure, but it is also a bluff. It is a form of status building (because it gets an enemy's attention); what makes it virtual is that one does not necessarily cross the boundaries between life and death. This is the importance of the communicative nature of political violence. In future conflicts, political actors may increasingly circumvent tactical military confrontations or battles and choose instead to deploy other means, from terrorism to cyber warfare, all to maximize political outcomes.

Ultimately the key to virtual violence is self-harm. Children who intentionally harm themselves do so often after being bullied at school or online. Women claim they face "virtual rapes" from network trolls whenever compromising pictures of them are posted on the Web by former friends. This is controversial territory, of course, and we must be careful not to lose ourselves in hollow semantics, for virtual rapes are not "real," however distressing they may be emotionally and psychologically. The greatest power our enemies have over us is to get into our minds, tap into our anxieties, and get us to invest time and effort in dealing with what is not so much virtual as "unreal," such as the prospect that Russia might mine the waters off the Åland Islands to prevent commercial traffic from sailing into Finnish waters, crippling in the process its trade with the rest of the world.

And that is one reason why although NATO now hosts conferences on hybrid warfare, the term itself is not especially in favor in the Baltic states themselves, and that for two reasons. First, many see it as a useful way to locate a major dispute with Russia under the umbrella of war. It is a way in which NATO can talk about maintaining its defense commitments and honoring Article 5, while at the same time ignoring the fact that the Baltic states already feel at war. The first stage of hybrid war, if you read what the Russians write about it themselves, is "information preparation." Take the nuclear threats to Denmark if it joins an American antiballistic missile program, the nuclear blackmail openly discussed by retired Russian generals at the Elbe Group meeting (albeit at an unofficial level), or the regular calls for a "preemptive" occupation of the Baltic states by several prominent Russian political analysts, including those close to Putin.

But there is a more urgent reason why many political scientists and military leaders in the Baltic states themselves dislike the term hybrid warfare, and it is one that goes to the heart of NATO's security dilemma. The Alliance is not *doctrinally* prepared for what may happen next. It is, after all, a defensive alliance, ill-placed to respond to challenges in ambiguous areas of security. Remember, Article 5 requires the agreement of its members that an armed attack has actually occurred. How easy do we think it would be to achieve such agreement if the Russians were to engage in a series of "salami tactics" in which over months, even years, the sovereignty and independence of the Baltic States is sliced away by Russian actions? Perhaps it is time to even admit the heretical thought that Article 5, as presently constituted, may be NATO's greatest weakness. Some years ago, and only reluctantly, Article 5 was revised in effect to take into account the prospects of cyber warfare (the very first of which may have been directed against a Baltic state—Estonia in 2007—in what its defense minister at the time called "the first act of World War III"). If introducing cyber warfare into the equation was difficult enough, what hope is there of reaching a consensus on putting hybrid warfare into the commitment?

Notes

1. *European Security Strategy* (Brussels: December 12, 2003), Council of the European Union, https://www.consilium.europa.eu/uedocs/cmsUpload/78367.pdf.

2. *Times* (London), September 8, 1999.

3. Robert Kaplan, *The Revenge of Geography* (New York: Random House, 2012).

4. Jean-Luc Nancy, *The Birth to Presence* (Palo Alto, CA: Stanford University Press, 1993).

5. Susan Sontag, *At the Same Time* (London: Penguin, 2007).

6. Edward Lucas, *The New Cold War* (London: Bloomsbury, 2012).

7. Zbigniew Brzezinski, interview, Agence France-Presse, January 21, 2015.

8. John Robb, "Putin and Open Source Warfare," Global Guerrillas, May 7, 2014, http://globalguerrillas.typepad.com/globalguerrillas/2014/05/putin-and-open-source-warfare.html.

9. Peter Pomerantsev, "How Putin Is Reinventing Warfare," *Foreign Policy*, May 5, 2014, http://foreignpolicy.com/2014/05/05/how-putin-is-reinventing-warfare/.

10. *Financial Times*, October 29, 2013.

11. S. J. Checkinov, "The Nature and Context of a New Generation War," *Military Thought*, no. 4 (2013).

PART II

NATO Allies *and* Baltic Sea Security

5

Are the Baltic States Next?

Estonia, Latvia, and Lithuania

ANDRES KASEKAMP

Since the Russian annexation of Crimea, the question of whether the Baltic states are next has been on everybody's minds. The international media has descended on Narva, an Estonian border town with a 95 percent Russian-speaking population eighty miles from St. Petersburg, to ask whether "little green men" could suddenly appear there.[1] Narva is a symbol for the larger Baltic question, though it could also just as easily be the Latvian city of Daugavpils. A chorus of prominent analysts and public figures, starting with the former NATO secretary-general Anders Fogh Rasmussen, have warned of the "high probability" of future Russian action against the Baltic states.[2] Since March 2014, the Baltic issue has become a question of the future of NATO itself. The BBC actually produced a television program in February 2016 titled "World War Three: Inside the War Room," which begins with the scenario of imaginary Latgalian separatists in eastern Latvia.[3]

The evidence of increasing military activity in the Baltic Sea region as a spillover from the Ukrainian conflict is indeed abundant. Russian air force planes have been flying recklessly with transponders switched off, and Russian warships have made their presence felt. In response, NATO has beefed up its air-policing mission and increased troop deployment for exercises to reassure the Baltic states and deter Russia.[4] The "information war" has reached unprecedented levels.

Parallels with Ukraine

Though at first glance there might be some superficial similarities with what transpired in Ukraine, the differences are clearly more significant in the Baltic case. First of all, the Baltic states are members of NATO and the European Union (EU), and thus Russian action against them would have immeasurably graver consequences. Therefore, a clear-sighted analysis of the situation is all the more important.

The success of the Crimean operation depended on an element of surprise: Few expected or planned for Ukraine to be militarily attacked by Russia. Russian preparations were not detected (or at least not correctly understood). Russia was able to use its military bases already existing on Ukrainian territory. Top Ukrainian commanders in Crimea defected to the Russian side. Russian actions exploited a unique postrevolutionary situation with confusion about the legitimacy of the interim authorities in Kiev. The border with Russia in Eastern Ukraine was lengthy, porous, and weakly guarded.

In contrast to Ukraine, the Baltic states have the capacity to respond immediately. They are well-governed countries with greater transparency and lower levels of corruption than most postcommunist states. The Ukrainian administration, military command, and intelligence services were riddled with pro-Moscow senior officials appointed by the government of Viktor Yanukovych. Additionally, Europe and the United States counseled Kiev not to respond militarily to Russia's aggression in Crimea. The fact that Ukrainian forces did not open fire in Crimea encouraged Putin to believe that the same could be easily achieved in the Donbas region. However, when Ukrainian forces resisted the separatists, they succeeded in winning back territory before Russian forces intervened directly. The Baltic states had capitulated meekly to the USSR in 1940 in the vain hope of not provoking Moscow. The lesson drawn for the contemporary Baltic national security doctrine is to always offer military resistance. The commander of the Estonian Defense Forces has stated that the first "little green man" to appear on Estonian soil will be shot immediately.[5]

Hybrid war is not new to the Baltic states. They have already experienced some of its elements: cyberattacks, economic pressure, energy supply disruptions, and disinformation campaigns. Even the Soviet-sponsored failed communist insurrection of 1924 in Estonia had many features in common with events in 2014, as did the simultaneous incorporation of the Baltic countries into the Soviet Union in 1940. Balts instinctively and immediately recognized the familiar choreography of the staged voluntary annexation of Crimea. A key part of the Russian operations in Ukraine has been the deniability of direct military involvement. Thus, the separatists claimed to have obtained their Russian arms and equipment from captured Ukrainian bases—which would be impossible in the Baltic states since Baltic forces use only NATO standard equipment.

Russian president Vladimir Putin does not consider Ukraine to be a genuine nation but part of the larger Russian nation (and many Russians agree with him). However, even Putin understands that the Baltic states are completely distinct. During the Soviet era, Russians perceived the Baltic republics as the Soviet West, a clearly different and more advanced region. There is no historical territorial dispute; Lenin recognized the three Baltic states and their territories, and Stalin subsequently shifted the Estonian-Russian and Latvian-Russian borders in Russia's favor. Narva has always indisputably belonged to Estonia. This acknowledgment of difference is important because undoubtedly one of the prime motivations for Putin's aggression was to ensure that a successful democratic Ukraine did not emerge out of the Maidan demonstrations. Witnessing a fraternal Slavic nation replace a corrupt authoritarian-leaning regime with a successful democratic government would pose an unacceptable example for the Russian people, with consequences that could undermine the Putin regime. What happens in Ukraine matters for Russia, whereas the Baltic states' political development is considered unique and without any domestic ramifications for Russia.

The Russian Minority and Societal Security

Perhaps the West's greatest concern has not been the military aspect but rather the ethnic factor. Putin justified aggression against Ukraine with the need to "protect" Russian speakers. This is a dangerous fallback to the pre-1945 world, where dictators claimed the right to change borders by force to bring coethnics into their fold. Putin's reasoning is a dramatic escalation from the spurious excuse used six years earlier in South Ossetia, of protecting Russian *citizens*. There, Russian passports were distributed to Ossetians, which later provided a convenient excuse for intervention. In southeastern Ukraine, there was a wider claim of "protection" of all ethnic Russians. This allowed Moscow to establish a narrative that the conflict was a "civil war between East and West." However, this simplistic, yet effective, propagandistic claim is easily debunked by the fact that a large proportion of those fighting on the Ukrainian side are actually ethnic Russians.

The ethnic Russians in Ukraine were initially swayed by the demonstration of might and a rational calculation to side with the victor in a confused situation where government authority had dissipated. Material considerations also played a role; for instance, pensions are higher in Russia than in Ukraine. Such incentives do not apply in the Baltic case since the standard of living is considerably higher there than in Russia. This is especially evident in the border areas; the Pskov oblast, bordering Estonia and Latvia, is one of the poorest in the entire Russian Federation. People in Narva regularly cross the bridge to Ivangorod and know very well for themselves that life is more miserable on the Russian side of the border. For a while, Narva's supermarkets became a popular destination for consumers

from St. Petersburg after Putin slapped countersanctions on EU agricultural produce. Wages are lower and unemployment higher in Narva than in Tallinn, and
the same applies for Daugavpils vis-à-vis Riga. These economic indicators are,
however, characteristic of general regional disparities in economic development
between the center and periphery, not a function of ethnicity.

While most Estonian and Latvian Russians believe that Crimea should belong
to Russia, it would be wrong to jump to the conclusion that they would desire a
similar Russian intervention at home. Indeed, the images of carnage in Donbas are
a powerful argument in favor of maintaining peace. Rather than asking Russian-
speaking residents of Narva or Daugavpils their opinion about Crimea or Putin, it
would be more insightful to ask whether they would prefer rubles to euros or the
Russian health-care system to the Estonian or Latvian one. Even those Estonian
and Latvian Russians who are stateless enjoy the right to freely travel and work
within the EU, a privilege that would be sorely missed. Although there is a sharp
contrast between the titular national groups and ethnic Russians on the support
for NATO and the perception of a threat from Moscow, it is more important that
there is little difference regarding the will to defend their country.[6] Some analysts
have warned, though, that it is not important what people in Narva or Daugavpils
actually think because Russia could ignite trouble simply by inserting a few outsiders. In such a scenario, Putin wouldn't need the support of a majority of locals for
success. Their indifference would suffice.

Russia's Capabilities

Russia's military activity in the Baltic Sea region has increased sharply after Crimea.
In 2015, NATO fighters from the Baltic air-policing mission intercepted Russian
air force planes on 160 occasions, a fourfold increase from 2013.[7] Russian warships
have obtrusively skirted the territorial waters of the Baltic states and have even
interfered with the laying of the underwater electricity cable between Lithuania
and Sweden. Russia has deployed its most advanced weapon systems—Iskander-M
ballistic missiles and the S-400 long-range air-defense system—to the region.[8] It
has been modernizing and expanding its armed forces while the West has been
continuously cutting its defense spending. In the beginning of 2016, it was
announced that Russia intends to establish three new army divisions in the western
region adjacent to the Baltic states.

Nevertheless, this aggressive military posturing is not new—it is a continuation
of the trend characterized by massive military exercises in the region with offensive
scenarios, such as Zapad 2009, Zapad 2013, and Zapad 2017. A worrisome new
development is the recent penchant for "snap" exercises with very little forewarn-
ing. The Crimea operation actually began as a snap exercise. These increasingly
frequent exercises might serve to lessen NATO's sensitivity and alertness to signs of
imminent danger.[9] Currently there is a focus on the fashionable little green men

and "hybrid warfare," but there is a risk that everyone expects the next war to be like the previous one.[10] However, it could be something much more conventional. After the initial use of *maskirovka* (deception) in Donbas, the decisive factor in the subsequent combat was old-fashioned Russian artillery.

The Kaliningrad oblast, the Russian exclave between Poland and Lithuania—in essence a huge military base—gives Russia the ability to master the strategic environment in the southeastern Baltic Sea region. With their formidable antiaccess/area-denial capabilities, the Russian forces stationed in Kaliningrad could impede the transportation of Allied reinforcements by air or sea to the Baltic states. A related further vulnerability for NATO is the Suwalki gap. Potential Russian control over this narrow strip of Polish and Lithuanian territory between Kaliningrad and Belarus could prevent NATO forces from coming to the assistance of the Baltic states via Poland, the only land route.[11] A RAND Corporation study published in February 2016 based on war-gaming scenarios concluded that Russian armed forces would have control over Tallinn and Riga within sixty hours and NATO would face certain defeat.[12]

In terms of military logic, the answer to the question whether the Baltic states are next is clearly "no" while the Russian operation in Donbas remains incomplete. A land corridor connecting Donbas to Crimea would be the logical next step if territorial expansion were the Kremlin's goal. Territorial expansion, however, appears to have been shelved in favor of a protracted frozen conflict that would be a constant drain and pressure point on Ukraine. However, if any other post-Soviet country would be next, then the obvious candidate would be Moldova with its separatist enclave of Transnistria.

Putin has shifted the focus of international attention from Ukraine to the Russian military intervention in Syria. The EU's political attention has been diverted by Islamic terrorism and the flood of refugees entering European territory. Sanctions, plummeting oil prices, and the accompanying decline of the Russian currency have led to domestic retrenchment and increasing repression of the opposition. In such a situation, it would be entirely natural for the regime to deflect attention from domestic difficulties to external enemies. The big question all along has been to discern Russia's intentions, but reading Putin's mind is impossible. One thing that can be said for certain is that Putin purposely has sought to create an atmosphere of uncertainty and anxiety about Russia's potential next moves. Catching the West off balance and by surprise has been his forte, as witnessed by Russia's intervention in Syria. At least one strategic objective is clear and consistent: dividing Europe from America and dividing Europe itself.

A military operation limited to Narva, for example, could serve to achieve that objective by placing the NATO Allies in an unpalatable situation where they must answer the question whether or not to send their citizens to "die for Narva."[13] The logic of this hypothetical argument is that Putin's ultimate aim is not territorial expansion but undermining NATO. Such an operation limited to a small area could leave NATO in a dilemma of how to respond, especially since Russian military policy includes the "de-escalation" of conflicts by nuclear means—that is, threatening to carry out a limited tactical nuclear strike in order to convince NATO to refrain from coming to the assistance of an Ally under attack. Failure to invoke Article 5 and respond would be fatal for the credibility of the Alliance. Andrei Piontkovsky has turned the question around and asked whether Putin is willing to die for Narva.[14] Such a gamble obviously wouldn't be worth the risk for Putin, but he has consistently demonstrated that he is much less risk-averse than Western leaders.

The Response of the Baltic States

The Baltic states were among the first to call for immediate EU sanctions against Russia after the annexation of Crimea and have staunchly supported maintaining the sanctions for as long as necessary. Preserving international law is especially important for small states that rely on it to persuade the great powers to respect their sovereignty. The sanctions have not achieved their stated aim of inducing the Putin regime to reverse its policies, but they have been successful in preventing Russia from attempting further military advances in Ukraine. The cost of inaction will certainly be higher next time, as the West's tepid response to Russia's invasion of Georgia in 2008 showed. From the Baltic perspective, Russian behavior is part of a larger pattern, and if the West does not demonstrate resolve then the Baltic states could indeed be next. A fundamental insight from their historical experience of living with the Bear is that weakness invites aggression. Putin's Russia is constantly testing the limits of what the West will tolerate and thus forcing others to accept the "new normal."

EU sanctions against Russia have hurt the Baltic economies more than most European countries, but upholding the principle at stake is more important for Estonians, Latvians, and Lithuanians than the commercial advantages. To be precise, it is not the EU sanctions but the Russian countersanctions against agricultural produce from the EU that have had the greatest negative impact on Baltic trade. The hardest-hit sectors have been transportation and the export of dairy products and canned fish.[15] In addition, the sharp decline in the market price for oil and the subsequent fall in the value of the Russian ruble have diminished the inflow of Russian tourists and investors to the Baltic states. However, the increasing repressiveness of the Putin regime has led individual Russians, who have lost hope that things will get better before they get worse, to move to the Baltic states.

The Baltic states reacted quickly to the perceived threat from Russia. Latvia and Lithuania, which had cut their defense budgets during the financial crisis to around only 1 percent of gross domestic product, announced a sharp boost in defense spending, pledging to reach 2 percent by 2018. Estonia, which was one of the few NATO countries to actually spend 2 percent, also directed additional resources into defense. Even more remarkably, Lithuania, which had followed NATO recommendations to fully professionalize its military, decided to reintroduce conscription. Estonia was the only Baltic country that had ignored NATO's recommendation to eliminate conscription, influenced by the territorial defense model of neighboring Finland and drawing conclusions from the Russian-Georgian war of 2008. In the Estonian case, obligatory military service has also been one of the most effective methods of integration of the Russian minority.

Though their regular armies are numerically small, all three countries rely on extensive volunteer reserves. Russian aggression resulted in renewed enthusiasm for self-defense among the population, as evidenced by a sharp increase in enrollment in the home guard. In 2015, Estonia carried out its largest and most comprehensive military exercise ever (Hedgehog), thus testing the volunteer reserves' readiness for territorial defense.

As a result of Russian aggression in Ukraine, the external security environment has deteriorated dramatically, but paradoxically the security of the Baltic states is stronger than ever. In little more than one year, Baltic defense planners have achieved goals that were set for the longer-term future. In January 2014, Estonian defense minister Urmas Reinsalu faced a barrage of criticism at home for voicing unrealistic views after he commented at a think tank conference in Washington that Estonia would ideally prefer American boots on the ground. By the time of the NATO summit in Wales in September 2014, the situation had undergone an enormous change. NATO Allies had begun to deploy troops on a constant rotating basis for exercises, but the Baltic media now expressed some disappointment that the establishment of permanent bases on Baltic soil was ruled out.

NATO pledged in the 1997 NATO-Russia Founding Act that in "the current and foreseeable security environment" it would refrain from "additional permanent stationing of substantial combat forces" in Central and Eastern Europe.[16] Former Estonian president Toomas Hendrik Ilves has argued that these provisions are no longer valid because Russian actions have significantly altered the security environment. Furthermore, the proposed amount of forces that the Allies might station in the Baltic states could not be categorized as "substantial" in objective military terms. Nevertheless, leaders of NATO countries, most prominently German chancellor Angela Merkel, have reiterated NATO's intention to honor the restrictions imposed by the founding act.

The method of Russia's incursion in Ukraine, particularly its justification of protection of compatriots, has raised the issue of the integration of the Russian minority in the Baltic states to the fore once again.[17] There is a sense of déjà vu: a return to the concerns of the 1990s and the reemergence of an issue that seemed to be largely overcome with EU enlargement in 2004. Russian actions have not created new divisions in Estonian and Latvian society but simply exacerbated existing cleavages. Roughly one-quarter of the Estonian population and one-third of the Latvian population are Russians who mostly settled in the Baltic region during the

Soviet period. In contrast, Lithuania does not have a significant number of ethnic Russians; its largest minority is Polish.

Previously, it was generally believed that the integration of the Russian minority would be resolved by time—that Soviet nostalgia would fade with the passing of the older generation. The first warning that this assumption was false came with the conflict over the relocation of the Soviet war monument in Tallinn ("the Bronze Soldier") in 2007.[18] The use of memory politics, especially the sacralization of the Soviet victory in the "Great Patriotic War," has been the cornerstone of constructing a *Russkii mir* ("Russian world"). Russia has instrumentalized its "compatriots" in order to undermine societal integration and to maintain a sense of grievance and sow mistrust. Ensuring that a significant part of the Russian minority remains alienated serves Russia's interests, as does making Estonians and Latvians view their local Russians as a potential fifth column. The conflict in Ukraine has been accompanied by an unprecedented level and sophistication of hostile information warfare. Most Estonians and Latvians live in separate information spaces from ethnic Russians, with Russian television channels the prime source for the latter.[19]

The Baltic states were among those that proposed that the EU take countermeasures to combat Russian-inspired media falsifications. In 2015, the small East StratCom Task Force within the European External Action Service was set up (also employing officials seconded from the Baltic states) and began a disinformation review debunking the most blatant lies that surfaced in the media. In 2014, the NATO Cooperative Center of Excellence for Strategic Communication was launched in Riga. It had already been in the works for a few years (Estonia had already established the NATO Center for Cyber Defense and Lithuania the NATO Center for Energy Security), but it was finally launched at a highly opportune moment. Previously many had wondered about the pressing need and purpose for establishing a new center, but its relevance became clearly apparent after Crimea.

In addressing the information challenge to societal integration, the Estonian government decided to establish a new Russian-language television channel in 2015. This may not actually have much of an impact in shaping the attitudes of Estonian Russians, but it was still an important step to show that the government is attempting to address the issue. The initiative also had strong diplomatic backing from Allies such as Germany, which was keen to help with soft power (such as the international public broadcaster Deutsche Welle) rather than hard power. The idea had been discussed already in 2007 after the Bronze Soldier riots but was not implemented because the Estonian government already had enough financial challenges with maintaining quality public broadcasting in the state language, and there was little faith that an Estonian channel could successfully compete with the blockbuster entertainment produced by Moscow television channels. Thus, the strategy pursued by the new channel is not to provide counterpropaganda but to focus on stories of local interest to the Estonian Russian community.[20] On the other side, the Russian media outlet Sputnik has been seeking to get registered in each of the Baltic countries; Estonian, Latvian, and Lithuanian authorities have struggled to respond to the broadcasting of hostile propaganda without restricting free speech.

A test of Baltic responses and Allied solidarity came in September 2014 when an Estonian security police officer, Eston Kohver, was abducted by the Russian Federal Security Service from the Estonian side of the Estonian-Russia border. He was only returned to Estonia one year later through a "spy swap." This action prompted Estonia to put more resources into securing its border zone and building a border fence. Nevertheless, the picture of Baltic-Russian relations is not only one of confrontation; Estonia is still prepared to ratify its border treaty with Russia. It was signed by both countries' foreign ministers in Moscow on February 18, 2014, just days before President Viktor Yanukovych fled Kiev. One could argue that it represented a high point in a positive trend in bilateral relations.[21] Despite Russia's violation of Ukraine's borders, the first reading of the ratification bill passed the Estonian Parliament in November 2015. The onus is now on the Russian Duma to initiate its ratification procedures.

NATO's Reassurance and Deterrence

The most tangible sign of NATO's presence in the Baltic states prior to the Ukraine conflict was the air-policing mission stationed in Šiauliai, Lithuania. The ad hoc mission with four fighter planes from individual NATO nations rotating on a four-month schedule was confirmed as an official component of NATO's "smart defense" at the 2012 NATO summit after intensive Baltic lobbying. Before Crimea, Estonia and Lithuania had been involved in a behind-the-scenes tug-of-war over the NATO air-policing mission. Estonia had invested heavily into making its brand-new Ämari airbase operational and did not want to see it unused, while Lithuania was afraid that sharing capacities would diminish its own. Crimea resolved that problem; suddenly there were enough NATO fighter planes to go around for both countries. This was the most immediate response by the NATO Allies, especially the United States, in reassuring the Baltic states after Crimea. By the end of 2014, there was a record number of sixteen NATO planes in the Baltic states, but in the fall of 2015 the number was halved—four in Estonia and four in Lithuania, which was a sufficient number for carrying out the mission in peacetime.

In response to the Baltic states' concerns, NATO announced the creation of a Very High Readiness Joint Task Force (VJTF), as an enhancement of the existing NATO Response Force, at its Wales Summit in 2014. The VJTF comprises a multinational brigade that is fully deployable within seven days and a small spearhead force deployable in forty-eight hours.[22] An integral element of this reassurance are the NATO Force Integration Units—small command-and-control centers that were established in each of three Baltic states during 2015. Of the NATO Allies, the United States has beefed up its presence in the Baltic region most noticeably. It has placed 150 US troops in each of the three countries on a rotating basis for exercises. The Barack Obama administration included a fourfold increase in funding for the US military presence in Europe in its 2017 budget request.[23] Thus far the deployments have been limited to a "constant rotation," which is now being called a "persistent presence." This falls short of a "permanent basing," which would make it the genuine "trip wire" force that the Baltic states desire. Nevertheless, in a sense the Baltic states today are the equivalent of West Berlin during the Cold War.

NATO has moved relatively quickly to provide "reassurance" to the Baltic states, but what is really necessary is to put in place "deterrence" for Russia.[24] In the run-up to the NATO summit in Warsaw in July 2016, the Baltic states were expecting the full implementation of the decisions made at the Wales Summit and, ideally, permanent basing of NATO personnel and the prepositioning of military hardware for the VJTF in the Baltic states. The decisions announced at Warsaw went a considerable way toward allaying Baltic anxieties and demonstrating Alliance solidarity and seriousness of purpose toward Russia. Most significantly, it was decided that one multinational battalion will be stationed in each of the Baltic states on a "toe to heel" rotational basis. Canada, Germany, and the United Kingdom pledged to serve as the framework nations for Latvia, Lithuania, and Estonia, respectively.[25] The troops and equipment of the NATO Enhanced Forward Presence in the Baltic states were deployed during the spring of 2017.

Russia's aggression in Ukraine has also had the consequence of stimulating debate about security policy in other Baltic Sea region states. The Nordic countries have enhanced cooperation among themselves, with an unprecedented joint declaration by the Nordic defense ministers explicitly mentioning Russia as the gravest threat to European security.[26] Important small steps toward closer cooperation with NATO are the memorandums of understanding with Sweden and Finland that will enable hosting facilities and were signed at the Wales Summit. This has a significant positive impact on the defensibility of the Baltic states. In the summer of 2016, US forces for the first time participated in military exercises on Finnish soil. From a Baltic point of view, the best thing that could possibly happen to alleviate their security dilemma would be Finland and Sweden joining NATO and the creation of a genuine security community in the Baltic Sea region.

The most high-profile reassurance came when President Obama visited Tallinn immediately prior to the NATO Wales Summit in September 2014. He stated that the "the defense of Tallinn and Riga and Vilnius is just as important as the defense of Berlin and Paris and London."[27] In order for the validity of his statement not to be tested, deterrence must be credible. President Donald Trump's early statements have raised some doubts about his commitment to NATO's Article 5 in the eyes of European allies. However, his actions—a dramatic increase in defense spending in the proposed fiscal year 2018 budget, including the European Reassurance Initiative—speak a different language than his words.[28]

Notes

1. Daniel Berman, "Will Narva Be Russia's Next Crimea?," *Diplomat*, April 8, 2014, http://thediplomat.com/2014/04/will-narva-be-russias-next-crimea; Gordon F. Sander, "Could Estonia Be the Next Target of Russian Annexation?," *Christian Science Monitor*, April 3, 2014, http://www.csmonitor.com/World/Europe/2014/0403/Could-Estonia-be-the-next-target -of-Russian-annexation; Ben Nimmo, "Are the Baltics Next on Putin's List?," Central European Policy Institute, March 6, 2015, http://www.cepolicy.org/publications/are-baltics-next-putins -list; and David J. Trimbach and Shannon O'Lear, "Russians in Estonia: Is Narva the Next Crimea?," *Eurasian Geography and Economics* 56 (2015): 493–504.

2. Ambrose Evans-Pritchard, "Putin Could Attack Baltic States Warns Former Nato Chief," *Telegraph*, February 5, 2015.

3. "World War Three: Inside the War Room," February 3, 2016, http://www.bbc.co.uk /mediacentre/proginfo/2016/05/inside-the-war-room.

4. Michael Birnbaum, "Fearing Russian Expansion, Baltic Nations Step Up Military Exercises," *Washington Post*, May 16, 2015; and Eric Schmitt and Steven Lee Meyers, "U.S. Is Poised to Put Heavy Weaponry in Eastern Europe," *New York Times*, June 13, 2015.

5. Sam Jones, "Estonia Ready to Deal with Russia's 'Little Green Men,'" *Financial Times*, May 13, 2015.

6. Juhan Kivirähk, *Integrating Estonia's Russian-Speaking Population: Findings of National Defense Opinion Surveys* (Tallinn: International Centre for Defence and Security, December 2014), http://www.icds.ee/publications/article/integrating-estonias-russian-speaking -population-findings-of-national-defense-opinion-surveys/.

7. Łukasz Kulesa, *Towards a New Equilibrium: Minimising the Risks of NATO and Russia's New Military Postures*, European Leadership Network Policy Brief, February 2016, 8, http://www.europeanleadershipnetwork.org/medialibrary/2016/02/07/180d69f6 /Towards%20a%20New%20Equilibrium%202016.pdf.

8. Henrik Praks, "Hybrid or Not: Deterring and Defeating Russia's Ways of Warfare in the Baltics; The Case of Estonia," Research Paper No. 124, NATO Defense College, Rome, December 2015.

9. Riina Kaljurand, "The Annexation of Crimea and Its Implications for the Baltic States' Security," in *Fortress Russia: Political, Economic, and Security Development in Russia following the Annexation of Crimea and Its Consequences for the Baltic States*, edited by Andis Kudors (Riga: Centre for East European Policy Studies, 2016), 178.

10. Andres Vosman, "Learning the Right Lessons from Ukraine," in *European Defence Planning and the Ukraine Crisis: Two Contrasting Views*, Focus Stratégique no. 58 (Paris: IFRI Security Studies, 2015).

11. Agnia Grigas, "NATO's Vulnerable Link in Europe: Poland's Suwalki Gap," http:// www.atlanticcouncil.org/blogs/natosource/nato-s-vulnerable-link-in-europe-poland-s -suwalki-gap.

12. David A. Shalpak and Michael Johnson, *Reinforcing Deterrence on NATO's Eastern Flank: Wargaming the Defense of the Baltics*, RAND Corp., 2016, http://www.rand.org/pubs /research_reports/RR1253.html.

13. Ahto Lobjakas, "Letter from Tallinn," Judy Dempsey's Strategic Europe, Carnegie Europe, May 15, 2015, http://carnegieeurope.eu/strategiceurope/?fa=60096.

14. Paul Goble, "Refusing to 'Die for Narva' Would Be End of NATO and the West, Piontkovsky Says" *Interpreter*, April 29, 2015, http://www.interpretermag.com/refusing-to-die-for-narva-would-be-end-of-nato-and-the-west-piontkovsky-says/.

15. Liudas Zdanavičius, "Economic Development in Russia after 2014 and Its Consequences for the Baltic States" in Kudors, *Fortress Russia*, 136–37.

16. Founding Act on Mutual Relations, Cooperation and Security between NATO and the Russian Federation, http://www.nato.int/cps/en/natohq/official_texts_25468.htm.

17. Mike Winnerstig, ed., *Tools of Destabilization: Russian Soft-Power and Non-military Influence in the Baltic States* (Stockholm: Swedish Defence Research Agency, December 2014).

18. Karsten Brüggemann and Andres Kasekamp, "The Politics of History and the 'War of Monuments' in Estonia," *Nationalities Papers* 36 (2007): 425–48.

19. Jill Dougherty and Riina Kaljurand, "Estonia's 'Virtual Russian World': The Influence of Russian Media on Estonia's Russian Speakers," International Centre for Defence Studies, Tallinn, October 2015, http://www.icds.ee/publications/article/estonias-virtual-russian-world-the-influence-of-russian-media-on-estonias-russian-speakers-1/.

20. Ibid.

21. Latvia and Lithuania already have border treaties with Russia.

22. Supreme Headquarters Allied Powers Europe, *NATO Response Force Fact Sheet*, https://jfcbs.nato.int/page5725819/nato-response-force-nrf-fact-sheet.

23. US Department of Defense, "Carter Previews FY2017 Defense Budget Request," http://www.defense.gov/News-Article-View/Article/648373/carter-previews-fy2017-defense-budget-request.

25. Justyna Gotkowska, "NATO's Presence in the Baltic States: Reassurance for Its Allies or Deterrence for Russia?," *OSW Commentary*, no. 169 (April 29, 2015), Centre for Eastern Studies, Warsaw.

25. "Warsaw Summit Communiqué: Issued by the Heads of State and Government Participating in the Meeting of the North Atlantic Council in Warsaw July 8–9, 2016," http://www.nato.int/cps/en/natohq/official_texts_133169.htm.

26. "Russian Aggression: Nordic States Extend Their Military Cooperation," *Aftenposten*, April 9, 2015, http://www.aftenposten.no/nyheter/uriks/Russian-aggression-Nordic-states-extend-their-military-cooperation-7975109.html. See also note 4.

27. White House, "Remarks by President Obama to the People of Estonia," Tallinn, Estonia, September 3, 2014, https://www.whitehouse.gov/the-press-office/2014/09/03/remarks-president-obama-people-estonia.

28. Anna Wieslander, "Beyond the Article Five Backlash: What Really Happened with Trump and NATO," *EurActiv*, June 2, 2017, http://www.euractiv.com/section/global-europe/opinion/beyond-the-article-5-backlash-what-really-happened-with-trump-and-nato/.

6

Deterring Russia

An A2/AD Strategy in the Baltic Sea

MIKKEL VEDBY RASMUSSEN

Christian's Island sits in the Baltic Sea as the easternmost point of Denmark. The island remains the property of the Ministry of Defence, with a commandant appointed by the minister, as a reminder of the war that Denmark fought against Britain from 1807 to 1814. The conflict was mainly a naval confrontation that occasionally spilled onto land, as when Royal Marines occupied the island of Anholt in 1809, fortifying the light tower and renaming it Fort York. Having been deprived of its main ships of the line after the British bombardment of Copenhagen in 1807, the Danish navy had to rely on smaller ships such as the *Kalundborg* class, which was twenty meters long with a crew of seventy sailors who manned the oars and the two guns. The *Kalundborg* class was part of a fleet of 250 vessels, which might seem feeble compared to the previous standards of the Danish navy, but nonetheless the Danes were able to offer so much resistance that the British had to commit ninety-six British naval vessels, including sixteen ships of the line, and thirty thousand sailors and marines as the British tried to keep the Baltic trade open. The Danish skirmishers forced British ships into convoys, but in spite of Royal Navy protection the Danes were able to seize British shipping valued at half the Danish Crown's annual prewar revenue.

Today one finds the remains of one of the privateer bases on Christian's Island. The main fortifications, however, were around Copenhagen and at Kronborg (Elsinore), which were the strongpoints of a system of ninety-six fortifications with nine hundred guns in Denmark and supplemented by a thousand guns on Norwegian fortifications.[1] Using these fortifications and the small vessels, the Danes were able to deny the British command of the sea and increase the cost of maintaining control of sea to a point where Britain paid a considerable military and commercial price for operating in the Baltic and the Kattegat. This was a nineteenth-century version of what current American strategists term antiaccess/area-denial (A2/AD).[2]

A2/AD is the key concept to understand how to deter Russia in the Baltic Sea region. It has become a commonplace assumption that Russian incursions into the Baltic states would follow the script from Ukraine, with Russia using "hybrid warfare" tactics.[3] Consensus has it that such Russian infiltration would be extremely hard for the Baltic states and the NATO Allies to handle.[4] On the contrary, I would argue that it is the conventional scenario that is much more difficult for the Allies because it rebels against the theory and practice of Western armed forces since the end of the Cold War. A "counter-little-green-men" campaign—the little green men being the masked soldiers in green uniforms carrying Russian military weapons who first appeared in the Ukrainian crisis in 2014—would be a type of campaign for which Western military forces have an extensive, if sometimes painful, experience from ten to twenty years of counterinsurgency campaigns in such places as Iraq and Afghanistan.[5]

Russia would probably not have much success in deploying its troops to the Baltic countries as it did in Ukraine, and one should therefore expect that such a campaign would quickly evolve into something more akin to domestic terrorism (in this case sponsored by and perhaps even perpetrated by an outside power) than the staged rebellion we witnessed in Eastern Ukraine. American and other NATO militaries have extensive experience in dealing with such contingencies and would fairly quickly be able to contain the efforts of "little green men." At this point, the Kremlin would have to decide whether to intervene with conventional forces, as was the case in Ukraine.[6] The Alliance's ability to mount a conventional deterrent would then become most important. By focusing on hybrid warfare, NATO has thus conveniently sidestepped the real challenge: how to provide a credible conventional deterrence.

In order to provide a credible deterrence, the Allies must have the capabilities to limit the Kremlin's options and increase the costs of an intervention in Baltic countries. NATO can do this by turning the tables on Russia and developing the Alliance's A2/AD capabilities in the Baltic. Two lines of operation underpin such a deterrence posture: (1) the ability to make the Baltic Sea a "poisoned lake," thereby preventing Russian shipping and naval assets from operating, and (2) the ability to send forces to support the Baltic countries—in other words, assuring the Balts and the Russians that the cavalry would come to the rescue. First, the A2/AD capabilities will be addressed.

Russian A2/AD Capabilities

The US Marine Corps explains the challenge of A2/AD this way:

> Over the past two decades, the development and proliferation of advanced weapons, targeting perceived U.S. vulnerabilities, have the potential to create an A2/AD environment that increasingly challenges U.S. military access to and freedom of action within potentially contested areas. . . . If these advances continue and are not addressed effectively, U.S. forces could soon face increasing risk in deploying to and operating within previously secure forward areas—and over time in rear areas and sanctuaries—ultimately affecting our ability to respond effectively to coercion and crises that directly threaten the strategic interests of the U.S., our allies, and partners.[7]

A2/AD is the US perspective on the Chinese investment in missiles, submarines, command-and-control assets, and other military systems that dramatically increase the cost of US power projection west of Japan. A2/AD strategies present the United States with the prospect of losing planes and even carriers in a military confrontation for which the US is largely unprepared after fifteen years' focus on counterinsurgency operations and the following period of austerity. This means that the US force structure depends on very low levels of attrition. By increasing the costs of intervention this way, the Chinese are attempting to deter the US and ultimately challenge its status as a Western Pacific power.[8]

A2/AD is changing the premise for the use of force by Western powers, which since the end of the Cold War have relied on the ability to project power virtually unopposed. Russia's intervention in Syria in November 2015 demonstrated its ability to deny Western forces the easy dominance of the airspace on which Western interventions have depended since the end of the Cold War. "As we see the very capable air defense [systems] beginning to show up in Syria," supreme Allied commander (SACEUR) Gen. Philip Breedlove noted, "we're a little worried about another A2/AD bubble being created in the Eastern Mediterranean." According to General Breedlove, the "A2/AD bubble" in Syria was the third such Russian manifestation of power in the general's European Command's area: "One was established in the Black Sea and the other in the Baltic Sea."

General Breedlove was referring to the fact that, in the words of the Danish Defence Intelligence Service (DDIS), "Russia already has the military capability to threaten the access of substantial NATO reinforcements to the Baltic countries in the form of air defence missile systems in Western Russia that cover most of the air space of the Baltic countries." The DDIS further notes that Russia is "highly likely to improve its access denial capability with the deployment of new surface-to-surface missiles and coastal defence missiles to the Kaliningrad region."[9] This

Russian A2/AD capability means, according to Richard Fontaine and Julianne Smith, that the Kremlin can "deny access to the countries on NATO's Eastern flank long enough to establish facts on the ground that would be hard, and perhaps impossible, to reverse."[10] Britain's House of Commons Defence Committee followed the same line of argument when it concluded in a 2014 report that NATO "was poorly prepared for a Russian attack on the Baltic, and that poor state of preparation might itself increase the likelihood of a Russian attack."[11]

NATO can come to the aid of the Baltic countries via three routes: by land via the narrow corridor between Kaliningrad and Belarus where the Polish and Lithuanian borders meet, by sea via the Danish Straits, and by air over the Baltic Sea or through Polish airspace. In all three instances the lines of communication of NATO forces would be vulnerable to a Russian counterattack. A2/AD reduces the value of deterrence because it increases the costs of helping Allies to the point where the commitment to do so might be called into question. In 2001, General Breedlove's predecessor as SACEUR, Gen. Wesley Clark, was asked during a Senate hearing whether the Baltic countries were too vulnerable to be defended. General Clark answered, "I can't imagine a crisis involving the Baltic states that wouldn't affect the security of Europe."[12] Therefore, Clark argued in favor of NATO membership for the Baltic countries because he wanted NATO, and thus the United States, to have the ability to manage a crisis involving the Baltic states rather than being dragged into one because Baltic membership in the European Union would mean that NATO members had a commitment to defend the Baltic states.

A2/AD capabilities could turn General Clark's argument on its head. Today Europe's security is formally linked to the Baltic countries, but the consequence is that an escalation of a conflict with Russia in the Baltics would have direct consequences for the rest of Europe—and for the United States. Russian A2/AD capabilities mean that an attempt to expel Russian forces from one or more of the Baltic countries would involve Western forces so large that their deployment would in itself constitute a war with Russia. This point is underscored by the fact that these forces should expect to suffer such casualties that, once undertaken, the operation would mean a commitment to serious warfighting. The size and risk of an operation to defend the Baltic countries makes living up to the Article 5 commitment a risk in and of itself. The logic of a risk argument is such that from a NATO perspective the Baltic states might seem to be responsible for the risk they constitute, even if it is Russian military capabilities and possible intentions that constitute this risk.[13]

The Kremlin might speculate that the answer to "Who will die for Vilnius?" is "Not that many." Therefore, the Kremlin needs to keep high the casualty figure European governments would have to consider when committing to assist the Baltic states. The fact that Russia can force NATO to field a substantial force with a high risk of losing a substantial part of it constitutes a deterrence in itself. The current force levels in NATO are such that it would be difficult for the Alliance to assemble an appropriate force at the appropriate time. Having assembled the force, NATO governments would not be pleased with the prospect of losing assets that would be very difficult to replace in the current budgetary environment—especially if General Clark's notion that a conflict in the Baltic region would be a subset of a larger European confrontation. In that case, the Europeans might want to save their limited assets for another theater.

Deterrence is a political commitment made credible by military capabilities and military contingency planning. A2/AD capabilities erode the effect of military capabilities and thus makes contingency planning much more difficult. In order to make the A2/AD capabilities themselves credible, either capability has to be demonstrated. It is in this context that one should regard Russian exercises in the region, such as the one in October 2015 when Russian Su-24s trained for the "bombing of targets and the positions of mock command centers, engineering facilities, personnel and the military hardware of a simulated enemy" in the region.[14] Another example is the stationing in Kaliningrad of Iskander missiles, with their range of five hundred kilometers.[15] This reflects a new Russian exercise regime in the region.[16] After the Russian intervention in Ukraine, the Baltic region became a focal point for Russian challenges to the West, even though Russian military capabilities there are nowhere near the military assets that the USSR used to be able to deploy.[17] Still, Russia's Western Military District is home to one tank division and a tank brigade as well as a mechanized division and four mechanized brigades supported by two artillery brigades, missile brigades, and so forth. The Russian air force has a strong presence, and the Baltic Fleet includes three submarines and fifty-six surface combatants.[18] In order to pursue an A2/AD strategy, the full spectrum of Cold War capabilities is, however, hardly necessary.

Russia has thus increased its military activity in the Baltic Sea region. The European Leadership Network counted forty air incidents and three naval incidents in the region from March 2014 to March 2015.[19] The air incidents are more than a third of the total number of NATO's incidents with Russia in that period. (Note that Sweden and Finland are not members of the Alliance.) The majority of these incidents were the habitual harassment of NATO aircraft that took part in the NATO air-policing operation in the Baltic countries. A number of more dramatic incidents did occur, however. In November 2014, there were sightings of what was deemed to be a Russian submarine in the Stockholm archipelago. In March and December 2014, a Russian military aircraft flying without using its transponders nearly collided with a commercial airliner. According to the DDIS, the increased Russian air activity in the region took place as part of the largest Russian air exercise in the region since 1991. In its Risk Assessment 2014, DDIS concludes that "even though most flight patterns were familiar, some of the activities were of a more offensive character than observed in recent years and likely also involved simulated missile attacks by tactical aircraft against Danish territory."[20]

Russia has thus demonstrated its A2/AD capability and its willingness to use this asset. By focusing on the Russian demonstration of its military capabilities and political willingness to use them, the West risks playing the Kremlin's game, when Russia actually might very well be more vulnerable to A2/AD strategies in the Baltic Sea. A2/AD capabilities can, in fact, become an effective countermeasure to Russian incursions and thus demonstrate solidarity, Alliance commitments, and military capabilities of countries in the region.

Turning the Tables: Deterring Russia

Just like the Danes were able to deny the Royal Navy easy access to the Baltic Sea and dramatically increased the costs for operating there during the Napoleonic Wars, A2/AD capabilities can underscore and enhance the deterrence capabilities of the Alliance and its partners in the region. The Danish experience two hundred years ago demonstrates that in the brown-water maritime environment of the region, A2/AD makes a lot of sense. This was also the experience during the Cold War when NATO planning and that of Sweden and Finland were focusing on closing the Baltic Sea to Warsaw Pact forces in the event of an attack and preventing Warsaw Pact forces access to the territory of Denmark, Sweden, and Finland.

Since the end of the Cold War, military technology and the geopolitical realities around the Baltic Sea have changed, but this only increases A2/AD capabilities; a coherent effort between NATO and partner countries in the region would deny Russia the possibility of operating in ways that challenge the deterrence posture. One cannot prevent reckless flying by Russian military planes, but the significance of these actions can be greatly diminished by a coherent response that demonstrates a capability to counter the access of Russian military platforms to the region and close the Baltic Sea as an area of operation for Russian forces in the event of hostilities.

The strategic aim for an A2/AD approach in the Baltic Sea region should be to (1) demonstrate the ability to make the Baltics a "poisoned lake" and (2) demonstrate the ability to rapidly support the Baltic countries in the event of a crisis—in other words, show that "the cavalry will come to the rescue."

Poisoned Lake

The West might feel vulnerable in view of Russian Baltic capabilities, but these capabilities reflect the fact that the Baltic Sea is a vital area for Russia. In 2016, 2,015,000 twenty-foot-equivalent units of cargo sailed on the Baltic Sea to Russian ports.[21] This is more than half the container throughput in Russian ports, and, if one includes the substantial traffic on Baltic and Finnish ports with Russia as its ultimate destination, this constitutes Russia's main sea-trade route. Pipelines in the Baltic Sea also transport Russian gas to Western Europe. In military terms, Russia feels the need to control the Baltic Sea because otherwise there would be direct access to one of its main population areas. Apart from Finland and the Baltic countries, none of the other states around the Baltic Sea depends on Baltic lines of communication in a similar way. Russia depends on open Baltic lines of communications but is unable to control them. This constitutes a major vulnerability for the Kremlin, even if Russia in the long term were able to transfer its container trade to its Asian and Arctic ports, which would increase costs and leave Russian ships vulnerable to Allied blockade, especially in the latter, which are easily within NATO's area of operation. In response to Russian incursions into the Baltic countries, NATO's stated policy would be to close off the Baltic for trade in Russian ports and prevent Russian naval and air assets from operating in the Baltic Sea.

NATO would be able to close off the Baltic Sea with little consequence for NATO members but with great costs to the Russians. A blockade would have potentially serious results for the Russian economy. This would enable what T. X. Hammes has termed "off-shore control."[22] Obviously, this would not seriously influence the all-important Russian oil and gas sector, nor would it prevent Russia from redirecting trade to its Arctic or Pacific ports, but it would increase the costs for the Kremlin dramatically. Western sanctions in the wake of Russia's intervention in Ukraine did not affect the Kremlin's policies—at least not in the short term—and one should not expect a blockade to do that either. However, the costs of a blockade would be much larger and more immediately felt, which would have to figure in any calculation made in the Kremlin about whether to invade the Baltic countries.

The key part of a plan for a blockade would thus be NATO's demonstrated ability to carry out such an operation. Denmark's role would be crucial because, as the Danes demonstrated during the Napoleonic Wars, the Danish Straits are where any traffic to and from the Baltic Sea can be effectively stopped. A blockade would require a substantial number of ships and a large command-and-control setup to direct it. In order for the blockade to be a credible deterrence, NATO would thus have to pool its Baltic assets in a naval force with a headquarters able to carry out a blockade and the ships to do the job. Such a "Standing Naval Command Baltic" should be headquartered in Denmark in order to use that country's superior picture on naval movements in and out of the Baltic Sea. In order to secure commitment from the larger NATO nations, command should alternate between a British and a German admiral. A Baltic naval command would be able to pool national assets but also point to deficiencies in current forces. Such a command would also be able to include Finnish and Swedish naval forces in close cooperation.

NATO planners should of course not expect Russia to simply accept a blockade, and Russia would do its best to challenge NATO's ability to carry it out. This would include aggressive rhetoric and provocations in relation to exercises. Actually, making a naval force the main vehicle for NATO-Russia shows of force in the region would be beneficial compared to disputes on the borders between the Baltic states and Russia. A great naval game would be much easier to contain and move focus from the Baltic countries to the Allies. From a planning perspective, the naval blockade would form the lynchpin of a review of NATO capabilities in the region, and to that extent they would need to be reinforced by the participating states by new procurement or, in the event of a crisis, by naval powers such as the United States and Britain. Because of geography, a blockade would not be an exclusively naval operation. In the narrow waters of the Baltic Sea, air cover would be provided from land. By establishing the military infrastructure to support a blockade, NATO could thus increase the credibility of its deterrence, but a naval response would not be sufficient to deter an attack on the Baltic countries.

Cavalry to the Rescue

If a blockade is to deter Russia by increasing the costs of an invasion of one or more of the Baltic countries, then rapid military support is needed to stop such a military adventure in its tracks. NATO has clearly identified this as an area in need of improvement, and the establishment of the Very High Readiness Joint Task Force at the Newport Summit in 2014 is an example of how the Alliance is trying to make sure it can get troops to Vilnius faster than the Russians.[23] The US decision to preposition heavy military equipment such as tanks, Bradley Fighting Vehicles, and artillery in Eastern Europe, including in the Baltic countries,[24] and other parts of the Barack Obama administration's $985 million European Reassurance Initiative, which was continued and significantly increased by President Donald Trump,[25] will further add to the Alliance's ability to actually make good on the security commitment to the Baltic countries. So will the British decision in the Strategic Security and Defence Review to organize two rapid-deployment brigades.[26]

Thus, Britain and the United States are reprising the role they played in NATO defense planning during the Cold War. The crucial difference between the 1980s and the 2010s is that the smaller NATO Allies are no longer on the front line waiting for the Americans and the British to come to their aid. Apart from Poland, NATO Allies that want to come to the aid of the Baltic countries have some traveling to do. This takes careful preparation and repeated training to get it right, on the part of those who travel to the front as well as those who are to receive the forces.

The smaller NATO Allies, therefore, need to make their own preparations if conventional deterrence of Russia in the case of the Baltic countries is going to work. There are a number of ways to this. First, forces can take part in NATO or national exercises in the Baltic countries, thus providing the continued presence that works as a trip wire for a Russian incursion. Second, countries can team up with Poland or with the Baltic states themselves in joint brigades or similar formations. Third, Allies could train to use existing deployable capabilities in a Baltic context. Denmark has, for example, combined all three approaches in response to the new security situation. In 2014, the Danish army deployed a task force of nine hundred armored infantry with tanks to Lithuania to take part in a national exercise (Saber Strike). The Danish army did this on short notice by using the logistical arrangements in place from its deployments to Afghanistan with a chartered roll-on/roll-off ship.[27] This was one of a number of Danish initiatives to demonstrate and train the ability to deploy to the Baltic states and was supplemented by the seconding of Danish officers to NATO's Multinational Corps Headquarters Northeast in Poland—a Danish-German-Polish headquarters that was to organize NATO training and operations in the Baltic area.[28]

Heavy investment in the infrastructure to receive forces and the increased ability of forces to arrive in theater in a timely fashion would make it harder for Russia to utilize its superior lines of communication and the large forces stationed in its Western Military District. By virtue of geography, Russia has the mass and the lines of communication to prevail in a conventional military confrontation. In exercises, Russia has demonstrated the ability to mobilize a hundred thousand troops and move tanks to Ukraine from hundreds of kilometers away.[29] War games run by the RAND Corporation for the Pentagon in 2014 ended with Russia prevailing over NATO forces in an all-out confrontation in the Baltic countries.[30] The war games should be treated with some caution, however: Whatever you can learn from them on NATO's ability to support the Baltic states, you can also learn about the US military's desire to get more funding for new contingencies in Europe. That need for funding was grounded in the fact that the war games apparently demonstrated the very different costs associated with planning for battle with a peer adversary as opposed to conducting counterinsurgency operations in, for example, Afghanistan.

Even if investment in conventional capabilities increases in NATO, it would still take time for such capabilities to make a difference in deterring Russia. The Kremlin might even speculate on making a move before an increase of Western capabilities becomes operational. Therefore, Western military planning must focus on how to offset Russian conventional superiority. It is hardly the first time NATO was faced with such a challenge. An oft-repeated phrase at a meeting of NATO army chiefs in October 2015 was "It's like what we were doing as lieutenants."[31]

During the Cold War, nuclear weapons were to offset Soviet superiority in numbers, but in the late 1970s British and American forces in Germany began to experiment with what would become AirLand Battle, which was essentially a way to attack Soviet forces in depth, thus making it possible for Allied forces to outmaneuver the Red Army.[32] If one is to draw some lessons from that experience, then Allied forces must be willing and able to increase the area of operation beyond the Baltic states. NATO should be able to attack Russian forces in Kaliningrad and other places in the Baltic Sea region and Europe where NATO has the advantage. It is in Russia's interest to keep the conflict a limited one, and therefore NATO should not accept that limitation. Furthermore, NATO air forces should be prepared to strike deep into Russia to attack the Russian army's lines of communication, and NATO should be able to conduct offensive cyber operations against Russian forces, intelligence services, and the like. In order to avoid provoking NATO into conducting deep strikes for which the Alliance are much better equipped than Russia, the Kremlin would probably seek to keep the conflict, at least initially, under the military horizon by using hybrid warfare rather than combined-arms operations. And in assessing options, the Kremlin would probably not only look to the situation on land but also be influenced by NATO's ability to make the Baltic Sea a "poisoned lake."

Conclusions

In the nineteenth century, the Danish fight against the British demonstrated the ability to use asymmetrical strategies to great advantage in the Baltic Sea. Proving that point did not win the war for the Danes, however. The current security environment is very much different and presents more opportunities for an A2/AD strategy, with the most crucial difference being that Denmark is allied (in various ways) with all the countries surrounding the Baltic Sea—except Russia. This should make an A2/AD strategy a credible deterrent. It is also a type of deterrent that is inherently defensive and thus will suit the strategic culture of the cautious Danes, Germans, Norwegians, and Swedes. This is important because what Russia is really challenging with aggressive exercises and other actions is the credibility of deterrence in the region. The complicated Alliance structure in the region, which includes NATO members and nonaligned partner countries with separate and sometimes complicated bilateral relations with Russia, gives the Kremlin scope for probing the cohesion of the countries in the region. This scope is dangerous and should be overcome by a precise catalog of measures to demonstrate to the Russians that the cost of intervention in the Baltic states is too high.

If the Baltic Sea is turned into a poisoned lake, the costs of incursions into it would increase dramatically. Since the issue is deterrence, increasing the potential costs of operations should serve to direct Russian ambitions elsewhere. This would be an obvious benefit to the nations in the region but also to NATO, since Russia's ambitions are more manageable elsewhere. If a blockade is to deter Russia by increasing the costs of an invasion of one or more of the Baltic states, then rapid military support should stop such a military adventure in its tracks.

One more lesson is worth remembering, however. After the English Wars, Anglo-Danish relations fairly quickly returned to normal and in time developed to the close ties we see today. If history teaches us anything, it is to be good at deterrence but equally good at furthering a peaceful dialogue.

Notes

1. Ole Frantzen et al., *Danmarks krigshistorie, 700–2010* (Copenhagen: Gyldendal, Gads Forlag, 2010).

2. Andrew Krepinevich, Barry Watts, and Robert Work, *Meeting the Anti-Access and Area-Denial Challenge* (Washington, DC: CBSA, 2003).

3. "Nato to Counter 'Hybrid Warfare' from Russia," May 15, 2015, BBC, http://www .bbc.com/news/world-europe-32741688. On hybrid war, see Frank G. Hoffman, *Conflict in the 21st Century: The Rise of Hybrid Wars* (Arlington, VA: Potomac Institute, December 2007), http://www.potomacinstitute.org/images/stories/publications/potomac_hybridwar_0108 .pdf.

4. International Institute for Strategic Studies, *Hybrid Warfare: Challenge and Response* (London: Routledge, 2015), 17–20.

5. Joint and Coalition Operational Analysis, *Decade of War: Volume I; Enduring Lessons from the Past Decade of Operations* (Suffolk, VA: Joint Staff, 2012).

6. Igor Sutyagin, *Russian Forces in Ukraine*, Royal United Services Institute (hereafter RUSI) Briefing Paper, March 2015, https://rusi.org/sites/default/files/201503_bp_russian _forces_in_ukraine.pdf.

7. Air Sea Battle Office, "The Air Sea Battle Concept," Navy.mil, November 9, 2011, http://www.navy.mil/submit/display.asp?story_id=63730.

8. Mikkel Vedby Rasmussen, *The Military's Business: Designing Military Power for the Future* (Cambridge: Cambridge University Press, 2015), 116–25.

9. Danish Defence Intelligence Service (hereafter DDIS), *Intelligence Risk Assessment 2015: An Assessment of Developments Abroad Impacting on Danish Security* (Copenhagen: DDIS, November 2015), https://fe-ddis.dk/SiteCollectionDocuments/FE/Efterretningsmaes sigeRisikovurderinger/Risikovurdering2015_EnglishVersion.pdf, 19.

10. Richard Fontaine and Julianne Smith, "Anti-Access/Area Denial Isn't Just for Asia Any-more," *DefenseOne*, April 2, 2015, http://www.defenseone.com/ideas/2015/04/anti-accessarea -denial-isnt-just-asia-anymore/109108/.

11. House of Commons Defence Committee, *Towards the Next Defence and Security Review: Part Two; NATO*, July 22, 2014, §41, http://www.publications.parliament.uk/pa /cm201415/cmselect/cmdfence/358/35807.htm.

12. Wesley Clark, "NATO: Facing the Challenges Ahead; Testimony, Senate Foreign Rela-tions Committee," Washington, DC, February 27, 2001, http://www.gpo.gov/fdsys/pkg /CHRG-107shrg71538/html/CHRG-107shrg71538.htm.

13. Mikkel Vedby Rasmussen, *The Risk Society at War* (Cambridge: Cambridge University Press, 2006).

14. "Russian Baltic Fleet Naval Aviation Holds Air Combat Drills," Sputnik, October 30, 2015, http://sputniknews.com/military/20151030/1029330020/russian-baltic-fleet-aviation -drills.html#ixzz3sIxURAUF.

15. Vladimir Isachenkov, "Russia Placing State-of-the-Art Missiles in Kaliningrad," *Business Insider* (Associated Press), March 18, 2015, http://uk.businessinsider.com/russia -placing-state-of-the-art-missiles-in-kaliningrad-2015-3?r=US&IR=T.

16. DDIS, *Intelligence Risk Assessment 2015*, 19.

17. DDIS, *Intelligence Risk Assessment 2014: An Assessment of Developments Abroad Impacting on Danish Security*, Copenhagen 2014, https://fe-ddis.dk/sitecollectiondocuments/fe /efterretningsmaessigerisikovurderinger/risikovurdering_2014_englishversionrv.pdf, 14–15.

18. International Institute for Strategic Studies, *The Military Balance* (London: Routledge, 2015), 191–92.

19. *Avoiding War in Europe: How to Reduce the Risk of a Military Encounter between Russia and NATO*, European Leadership Network, August 28, 2015, http://www.europeanleadership network.org/medialibrary/2015/08/18/2f868dfd/Task%20Force%20Position%20Paper%20 III%20July%202015%20-%20English.pdf.

20. DDIS, *Intelligence Risk Assessment*, 15.

21. "Key Russian Gateways," Global Ports, accessed July 13, 2017, http://www.globalports .com/globalports/about-us/our-industry-overview/container-market/key-russian-gateways.

22. T. X. Hammes, "Off-Shore Control: A Proposed Strategy for an Unlikely Conflict," *Strategic Forum*, National Defence University, June 2012, http://www.dtic.mil/dtic/tr/fulltext /u2/a577602.pdf.

23. *NATO Response Force / Very High Readiness Joint Task Force*, NATO official website, November 2015, https://www.shape.nato.int/nato-response-force—very-high-readiness-joint -task-force.

24. Phil Stewart and David Mardiste, "U.S. to Pre-Position Tanks, Artillery in Baltics, Eastern Europe," Reuters, June 23, 2015, http://www.reuters.com/article/2015/06/23/us-usa -europe-defense-idUSKBN0P315620150623#TMUx8zC85OqG2eFl.99.

25. European Reassurance Initiative, US Department of Defense, http://comptroller .defense.gov/Portals/45/Documents/defbudget/fy2016/FY2016_ERI_J-Book.pdf.

26. "Cameron to Announce New Strike Brigades in Strategic Defence Review," *Guardian*, November 22, 2015, http://www.theguardian.com/politics/2015/nov/23/cameron-to-announce -new-strike-brigades-in-strategic-defence-review.

27. Forsvaret, Kunsten at deployere 900 mand [Danish defense, the art of deploying 900 troops] http://forsvaret.dk/FST/Nyt%20og%20Presse/Pages/Kunstenatdeployere900mandog tonsvisafgods.aspx.

28. "Dansk NATO-bidrag skal opveje det lave forsvarsbudget" [Danish NATO-contribution to make up for low defense budget], Berlingske, September 4, 2014, http:// www.b.dk/nationalt/dansk-nato-bidrag-skal-opveje-det-lave-forsvarsbudget.

29. Ben Nimmon, *Reinventing European Deterrence*, RUSI News Brief, November 20, 2015, https://rusi.org/publication/newsbrief/reinventing-european-deterrence.

30. Julia Ioffe, "Exclusive: The Pentagon Is Preparing New War Plans for a Baltic Battle against Russia," *Foreign Policy*, September 18, 2015, http://foreignpolicy.com/2015/09/18 /exclusive-the-pentagon-is-preparing-new-war-plans-for-a-baltic-battle-against-russia/.

31. Ibid.

32. Frederick W. Kagan, *Finding the Target: The Transformation of American Military Policy* (New York: Encounter Books, 2006), 3–74.

7

Russia as a Challenge in the Baltic Sea Region

A View from Warsaw

JUSTYNA GOTKOWSKA

From Russia's perspective, the Baltic Sea region may be a convenient test case for trying to achieve its geopolitical objectives: to divide the West, to undermine the trust in NATO's collective defense principle and credibility, and to demonstrate that US security guarantees are nonbinding. The politico-military geography of the Baltic Sea region allows that. The three Baltic states with a small military potential constitute NATO's exposed peninsula, at least metaphorically. They are surrounded to the southwest by Russia's highly militarized Kaliningrad Oblast, to the southeast by Belarus, whose military system is integrated with Russia, to the east by Russia, and to the north by the non-NATO countries Sweden and Finland. As a result of diminished defense capabilities, the two nonaligned countries are vulnerable to Russian military pressure or even a preemptive occupation of parts of their territory (e.g., Gotland or the Åland Islands) in order to close the access for NATO forces to the region. But also Poland, the biggest country on NATO's eastern flank, with middle-sized armed forces that are undergoing a modernization process, may be exposed to potential aggressive Russian actions directed against its territory.

Until 2014, there had been no significant NATO military infrastructure or military forces placed in the Baltic states or in Poland, apart from four rotational fighter jets from NATO countries conducting air policing in the Baltic states' airspace from the base in Šiauliai, Lithuania. Simultaneously with diminishing

European military budgets and capabilities and a gradual withdrawal of US forces from Europe, Russia has been increasing its military expenditures and developing conventional and nuclear capabilities, along with abilities for rapid deployment of troops in its Western Military District. This imbalance of forces along NATO's eastern flank, and especially in the Baltic Sea region, has steadily been increasing. Since 2008, Russian military activities in the region have been growing, with a significant increase after the annexation of Crimea. NATO as well as Sweden and Finland have confirmed the new patterns of Russian provocative behavior.

Russia's more confrontational actions have included violations of national airspace and territorial waters, intimidation of planes and vessels in international airspace and waters, and an increasing number of military exercises based on aggressive scenarios, including a nuclear attack on Warsaw (Zapad 2009) and simulated bombing raids against Sweden and Denmark. By these military shows of force, Russia wants to demonstrate political will and military capabilities in the region—capabilities needed for an attack on NATO member states and nonaligned countries and for denying access to NATO reinforcement forces. In the Baltic states, Russia has been trying to undermine the local trust in NATO's collective defense, to destabilize internal politics, and ultimately to cause the countries to accommodate Russian interests. In Sweden and Finland, Russia has been attempting to politically and militarily "neutralize" the two nonaligned countries—that is, to stop them from joining or deepening their cooperation with NATO. Russia's goal with regard to the West is to intimidate both elites and societies in order to convince them that it is better to compromise with Russia than to risk a state of permanent instability or even an open military conflict. Moscow is seeking to make the West feel threatened, as was very well illustrated by the title of the Valdai International Discussion Club meeting in October 2014, "The World Order: New Rules or a Game without Rules?"[1]

The near future may be an uncertain and unstable period of time for the Baltic Sea region. First, the risk of unintended clashes has increased with the rise of provocative behavior of the Russian air force and navy units. Second, since the Russian military show of force in the region has brought limited or even contradictory results so far, there is a risk that the Russian provocations may increase. Russia may be willing to militarily confront NATO by infringing on the sovereignty or territorial integrity of the states in the Baltic Sea region, which would be a relatively easy endeavor considering the regional military balance of power and Russian military capabilities. In such a scenario, NATO would need to militarily counter Russian actions in order to fulfill the Article 5 obligations of the North Atlantic Treaty, which could lead to full-scale military confrontation. If Russia perceives that there is a good chance to achieve its strategic goals by the use of military force—that is, to undermine NATO's credibility and to show that US security guarantees are nonbinding—it would attempt to do that.

Such a move would be based on the Kremlin's assumption that NATO would hesitate about how to respond—with the United States preoccupied with its domestic affairs while shouldering the responsibility of protecting the Europeans, which Moscow considers as divided. The Kremlin may bet on the assumption that NATO would be more willing to compromise than be ready for an open war with Russia. NATO's priority is therefore to avoid such a scenario in which the US and NATO have to contemplate how to regain occupied Allied territory. The West thus needs to convince the Kremlin that there are no political or military doubts about NATO's reaction to Russia's hostile actions against its eastern member states.

NATO's deterrence posture in the Baltic Sea region should therefore be strengthened in order not to allow for misperceptions and miscalculations in Moscow that could lead to aggressive Russian actions. Only a substantial NATO and US military presence in the Baltic states and Poland will convince Russia that all Allies are politically and militarily committed to the principle of collective defense. The Kremlin is a rational actor that calculates the chances and risks of its actions; it is aware of its own military predominance in the region but also of Western and US military superiority in general.[2] Since Russia's posture will not change in the foreseeable future, NATO and the United States must be prepared to deal with this situation in the coming five to ten years.[3]

How Should We Meet the Challenge?

NATO and its member states need to send the right signals to Russia: that they are serious about their own security and defense and that they treat the challenge posed by Russia as a strategic one. The worsening regional security environment in the recent years has motivated Poland to develop a three-dimensional security and defense policy focused on strengthening national defense, increasing its political-military ties with relevant Allies and partners, and advocating a greater focus on collective defense within NATO.

First, Poland has been trying to maintain a relatively high level of defense spending in recent years—an increase from the obligatory 1.95 percent of gross domestic product (GDP), with some variations depending on the implementation of the budget, to 2 percent of GDP in 2016—and plans to raise the military expenditure to 2.3 percent in 2025 and 2.5 percent in 2030. Poland has also announced an ambitious program of modernization and reforms for its armed forces, with a focus on acquisition of systems to, on the one hand, deny entry to enemy forces (e.g., planned purchase of short- and medium-range air and missile-defense systems) and punish them on the other (e.g., purchase of JASSM air-to-surface long-range cruise missiles for the Polish F-16 and planned purchase of new submarines with long-range sea-to-surface cruise missiles). A priority is also to strengthen the antitank potential of the land forces by acquiring new tanks and antitank guided munitions. The introduction of territorial defense forces similar to the Scandinavian model of home guards is ongoing.[4]

Second, Poland has started to invest in the relationship with its Allies and partners along NATO's eastern flank as well as with its crucial Allies, the United States and Germany. Poland has been trying to reinvigorate the military potential of its main regional cooperation partners from the Visegrad Group (V4)—the Czech Republic, Slovakia, and Hungary. One example of these efforts is the jointly established V4 Battle Group, on standby in the European Union (EU) in the first half of 2016, which will be developed as a permanent format of cooperation designed for EU, NATO, and United Nations operations. It will be on standby in 2019 again within the EU. Poland has also been deepening its political (and military) ties with the Baltic states and Romania, which share the Polish perspective on Russia and the Polish view on the future transformation of the Alliance. In addition, Poland has been looking forward to deepening its bilateral military ties with the two NATO partners, Sweden and Finland. In particular, the first country is seen as of great importance from the point of view of conducting NATO's operations in the Baltic Sea region. The US and Germany are also seen as key Allies that are crucial for the national defense of Poland; American and German troops would constitute the bulk of NATO's reinforcement for Poland, if the need for Allied help arises. Therefore, Polish governments have been trying to deepen the military contacts and cooperation and increase interoperability, exercises, and training as well as the presence of US and German units on Polish territory.

Until 2016, cooperation with the United States has been developed mainly between the air forces as a result of Poland's purchase of F-16 combat aircraft, in the form of pilot training, joint exercises, and modernization. Since 2012, it has been complemented by the rotational presence of US combat and transport aircraft in Poland (the US Aviation Detachment). Another important element of the US-Polish cooperation is Poland's participation in the US ballistic-missile-defense development program in Europe (European Phased Adaptive Approach), which as of 2011 is found under the umbrella of NATO's missile-defense architecture. A US SM-3 missile-interceptor site in northwestern Poland will be fully operational by 2018. The ongoing modernization programs of the Polish armed forces offer a wide scope for further deepening the US-Polish military-technical collaboration. So far, the cooperation with Germany has primarily been between the heavy armored units of the land forces, as a consequence of the Polish army's purchase of the Leopard battle tanks used by the Bundeswehr. It also has been initiated between the air forces (e.g., joint training activities of combat aircraft) and navies (e.g., joint exercises of German frigates and the Polish navy's helicopters).

Third, already after the 2008 Russo-Georgian War, Poland argued in favor of a greater focus on collective defense within NATO and for bolstering the Alliance's deterrence posture. These arguments found resonance after the annexation of

Crimea and the Russian intervention in Eastern Ukraine in 2014. Since Russian actions in Ukraine imposed a profound change on Europe's security order, Poland also advocated renouncing the NATO-Russia Founding Act, which would allow substantial NATO combat forces to be placed on a permanent basis on the eastern flank. This, however, did not find approval by all Allies. A compromise reached at the 2014 NATO summit in Newport stipulated the need to unilaterally abide by the NATO-Russia Founding Act but at the same time articulated the necessity to step up NATO's presence on the eastern flank and to adapt its structures to new challenges in collective defense. The adopted Readiness Action Plan (RAP) was based on two pillars—reassurance and adaptation measures.[5]

Up to the 2016 NATO summit in Warsaw, Poland argued for the full implementation of the RAP and for the need for further changes in the Alliance. Poland was arguing for NATO to take the next step, from reassuring Allies to deterring Russia. Poland also advocated in favor of further enhancing the Allied presence in the Baltic Sea region by placing more rotational companies (including not only US troops but also German, UK, and other European units), by increasing the Allied participation in exercises, and by prepositioning US military equipment in the region. The 2014–15 rotational presence, with one rotational US company in each country and a rotational presence by European Allies, was deemed insufficient for serving as a credible deterrent vis-à-vis Russia.

With regard to the adaptation measures within the RAP, three elements have been highlighted by Warsaw. First, emphasis should be put on the full implementation of the reforms of the NATO Response Force (NRF). This includes making its new high-readiness component, the Very High Readiness Joint Task Force (VJTF), fully operational in the form of a multinational brigade, as well as implementing the new concept and raising the readiness of the two multinational brigades in the Initial Follow-on Forces Group. Second, NATO's command structures should be effectively adapted to the new realities on the eastern flank. This should be done by making fully operational the new elements of the command structure that is being established in the countries on NATO's eastern flank, the NATO Force Integration Units (NFIUs).

The NFIUs should provide support to VJTF operations in these countries as well as enable support planning and exercises based on Article 5 scenarios. Moreover, the Polish-German-Danish Headquarters Multinational Corps Northeast (HQ MNC NE) in Szczecin, Poland, should continue to adjust to the new role and tasks that it will be fulfilling in the future. The HQ MNC NE would become the operational headquarters for the NRF forces in the event of their deployment in the region. It is important to further increase the international (US and regional, including Swedish and Finnish) participation in the HQ MNC NE and turn it into a regional hub for enhancing military cooperation. Third, NATO's advanced planning for collective-defense operations on the eastern flank should be improved since it is key for conducting Article 5 operations in the region. Without detailed defense planning, there is no real improvement of NATO's ability to react to threats on NATO's eastern flank.

Moreover, from a Polish perspective, NATO needs a strategic and long-term adaptation—that is, a strengthening of collective-defense capabilities and force structure. Prior to NATO's Warsaw Summit in 2016, Poland, as the host country, put forward a number of proposals.[6] They included (1) changing the profile of NATO's force structure to allow NATO to respond not only with a brigade but also with a division and more, (2) improving the heavy capabilities to increase the credibility of conventional deterrence, and (3) increasing NATO's common funding for the development of the military infrastructure that enables NATO to receive reinforcement forces on the eastern flank. Furthermore, NATO has to acknowledge the Russian nuclear doctrine (first use of tactical nuclear weapons on a conventional battlefield to "de-escalate" a conflict). The Alliance has to be prepared to deal with such scenarios and has to develop a clear strategy and show political will with regard to such threats.

From a Polish perspective, the decisions reached at the Warsaw Summit in July 2016 marked a significant shift in the nature of NATO's presence on its eastern flank.[7] NATO's members have deemed it necessary to ensure that a larger presence of NATO forces is suited for combat, not just exercises. Four battalion-sized battle groups (each totaling approximately a thousand troops and composed of US and Western European forces), fully armed and provided with military equipment, were deployed on a rotational basis in Poland, Lithuania, Latvia, and Estonia in the first quarter of 2017. These four battle groups, which would engage in combat in the event of Russian aggression, would trigger the chain of NATO military response and engage the Alliance in a conflict with Russia. A multinational division headquarters in Elbląg was established in Poland and will be responsible for commanding all battalion-sized battle groups.

This NATO presence aims to deter the Kremlin from undertaking aggressive actions; Moscow can no longer count on NATO to avoid responding and must calculate with the implications of an engagement by US, German, or British troops in a potential conflict. At the Warsaw Summit, Poland secured a large US military presence on its territory and has been transforming to a hub of US military activity on the eastern flank. Within the NATO framework, the United States became the leading nation for establishing the battalion-sized battle group in Poland, with up to a thousand US soldiers rotationally stationed in the northeastern region of the country. Under the Pentagon's European Reassurance Initiative (ERI), main components of the US heavy armored brigade combat team, together with US division tactical headquarters, have been deployed in Poland since 2017. Parts of this brigade started to exercise in the Baltic states, Poland, Romania, and Bulgaria in 2017. Under the Donald Trump administration, the US presence on the eastern flank has been sustained and even reinforced, with an increase from $3.4 billion to $4.8 billion for fiscal year 2018 in funding for the ERI in the Pentagon's budget.

The Warsaw Summit sent a strong signal that NATO is adapting its deterrence posture. However, in order to create a cohesive and reliable deterrence strategy, a lot of postsummit work needs to be done with regard to adjusting military structures and political processes. As NATO's former deputy secretary-general, Alexander Vershbow, put it, "the goal of deterrence hasn't changed: it's about convincing potential adversaries that the costs of any form of attack would be disproportionately high, and that such action would be a serious mistake."[8]

Notes

1. "Meeting of the Valdai International Discussion Club," President of Russia website, October 24, 2014, http://en.kremlin.ru/events/president/news/46860.

2. Justyna Gotkowska, "Russia's Game in the Baltic Sea Region: A Polish Perspective," European Council on Foreign Relations, December 16, 2014, http://www.ecfr.eu/article /commentary_russias_game_in_the_baltic_sea_region_a_polish_perspective381.

3. Jeffrey Rathke, "Can NATO Deter Russia in View of the Conventional Military Imbalance in the East?," Center for Strategic and International Studies (hereafter CSIS), November 30, 2015, https://www.csis.org/analysis/can-nato-deter-russia-view-conventional -military-imbalance-east.

4. Polish Ministry of National Defence, "Koncepcja Obronna Rzeczypospolitej Polskiej" [The concept of defense of the Republic of Poland], May 23, 2017, http://www.mon.gov.pl /aktualnosci/artykul/najnowsze/prezentacja-koncepcji-obronnej-rp-w2017-05-21/.

5. NATO, Wales Summit Declaration, September 5, 2014, http://www.nato.int/cps/en /natohq/official_texts_112964.htm#rap.

6. CSIS, "Statesmen's Forum: H. E. Tomasz Siemoniak, Polish Deputy Prime Minister and Minister of Defense Polish Defense: Priorities in a Changed European Security Environment," May 19, 2015, https://www.csis.org/events/statesmens-forum-he-tomasz-siemoniak -polish-deputy-prime-minister-and-minister-defense.

7. NATO, Warsaw Summit Communiqué, July 9, 2016, http://www.nato.int/cps/en /natohq/official_texts_133169.htm.

8. NATO, "21st Century Deterrence: Remarks by NATO Deputy Secretary General Alexander Vershbow at the Snow Meeting in Trakai, Lithuania," January 15, 2016, http:// www.nato.int/cps/en/natohq/opinions_127099.htm.

8

Germany: The Silent Baltic State

CLAUDIA MAJOR AND ALICIA VON VOSS

The countries around the Baltic Sea are among Europe's frontline states affected by the conflict between Russia and Western Europe. The Baltics and Nordics share a common concern about a revisionist, aggressive, and rearming Russia: Since the onset of the crisis in and around Ukraine in 2014, these countries have felt increasingly exposed to Russian military and nonmilitary intimidation. Currently, they can neither defend nor maintain regional security by themselves. Their capacities are limited, and their memberships in different security institutions (the European Union [EU] and NATO) complicate a common assessment and response, as do their diverging security policies. Also their geography is unfavorable in the sense that they share long borders with Russia (Estonia, Lithuania, Finland), which are often difficult to access and are sparsely populated (such as in Norway) or have exposed outposts (such as the Swedish island of Gotland). They depend on the deterrence and defense efforts of their partners and NATO.

This has turned the regional Nordic-Baltic security challenge into a European and transatlantic one. NATO's credibility depends on whether it can guarantee the security of these countries and in particular the three states most vulnerable to a Russian attack: Estonia, Latvia, and Lithuania. Germany, as one of the largest and most capable countries bordering the Baltic Sea, increasingly aims to contribute toward improving regional security by supporting regional cooperation and by sharpening the Nordic-Baltic dimension of its security policy.

Germany remains a puzzling element of Nordic-Baltic security. While it is one of the biggest states bordering the Baltic Sea, a member of the Council of the Baltic Sea States, and a key player in NATO's military adaption since the crisis in Ukraine, it does not have a clear Baltic or Nordic focus in its security and defense policy. To Germany, the region has until recently (2014 and the Ukraine crisis) been of friendly disinterest in terms of security policy, also because it was not a trouble area. It did not feature high on Berlin's security political agenda, as its security policy was rather built on an east-west axis, with the northern and southern dimensions receiving less attention. This did not exclude institutional cooperation and regular consultations with the Nordic and Baltic states, but there was less of a strategic approach with clear objectives.

The crisis with Russia brought the region to the forefront of security and defense considerations and back on Germany's security political agenda. While Germany responded with substantial commitments in NATO, the EU, the Organization for Security and Co-operation in Europe (OSCE), and multilateral and bilateral formats, a conceptual answer, such as a northern or northeastern axis of German security and defense policy, is emerging rather slowly. Berlin is still in the process of defining the conceptual underpinning of a northern or northeastern axis in its security policy.

As a result, the German answer to the security conundrum in the Baltic Sea region, which is considerable, particularly within NATO, might not be perceived in its entire scope and raises some questions.[1] On the one hand, Berlin committed itself faster and more substantially to the Alliance's adaptation measures decided on at the 2014 Wales Summit than its previous behavior in NATO and its reputation as a status quo ally would have suggested.[2] It confirmed its political and military commitment at the 2016 Warsaw Summit. On the other hand, Berlin has been criticized for its assessment of the security situation. It is precisely the role as a broker between East and West that leads the German government to insist on both: *deterrence* and *détente* vis-à-vis Russia, while at the same time advocating a military posture for NATO that focuses on responsiveness and readiness rather than on strong forward defense. Deterrence and détente, in reference to the 1967 Harmel Report, has indeed become the German leitmotif.[3] Thus, while Germany, quite surprisingly in view of some of its previous positions, turned into a backbone for NATO's strategic adaptation, it takes the blame for supposedly not responding adequately to the worries and needs articulated particularly by the Eastern European Allies.

The Backbone of NATO's Adaptation

Germany has played a considerable part in shaping the strategic adaptation agreed on in Wales in 2014 but has also committed itself to providing a substantial contribution to the implementation of both pillars of the Readiness Action Plan (RAP), reassurance and adaptation. Germany confirmed its commitment at the 2016 Warsaw Summit, which brought back the concept of deterrence.

With regard to reassurance measures, Berlin has, for instance, increased its naval participation in the Baltic Sea and is sending significantly more soldiers to the exercises in the region. In 2015, Germany sent about forty-five hundred soldiers. After the United States, Germany was until 2017 the second-biggest troop contributor to the reassurance measures in the east—that is, the biggest European one. As for the adaptation measures, Berlin is taking part in all NATO Force Integration Units (NFIUs). It has doubled its personnel (from 60 to 120) at the Multinational Corps Headquarters Northeast (MNC NE) in Szczecin, Poland.

Germany was also the first Ally to take on the command of the new spearhead force in 2015, the Very High Readiness Joint Task Force (VJTF). Germany, the Netherlands, and Norway provided the majority of the troops in the 2015 setup phase and carried the associated costs. With approximately twenty-seven hundred of the total of approximately five thousand soldiers, Germany provided the majority of troops. Besides, Berlin volunteered to take again the lead of the VJTF in 2019. After the 2016 Warsaw Summit, Berlin took over the lead of one of the four Enhanced Forward Presence (EFP) battalions that NATO decided to station in the three Baltic states and Poland.

At a quick glance, the German contributions may appear rather compartmentalized: the VJTF, the MNC NE, contributions to reassurance measures, and additional personnel for NATO exercises. However, when taking a closer look, it appears that Germany is in fact providing the backbone for the successful implementation of NATO's strategic adaptation. In addition, Berlin's commitment to the north and the Baltic region is considerable in terms of leading one of the four EFP battalions, sending personnel to NFIUs and the MNC NE (which it jointly runs with Poland and Denmark), participating in exercises, and maintaining its general standing contribution to NATO forces (that is, the German forces assigned to NATO).

The current focus on collective defense as the primus inter pares among the three NATO core tasks—the other tasks being crisis management and cooperative security—suits German political preferences well. Berlin never really warmed to the idea of out-of-area operations, such as in Afghanistan or Libya.[4] Besides, the German public—still skeptical of the use of military force—seems to prefer the deployment of the Bundeswehr in a scenario of collective defense rather than in crisis-management operations in faraway countries, such as on NATO's southern flank and against the so-called Islamic State (IS).

Quite ironically, the return to collective defense nevertheless poses a challenge to the German armed forces, since it was first and foremost crisis management (particularly the operation in Afghanistan) that informed strategic thinking over the last decade and guided decisions on how to structure, train, and equip the armed forces. In order to again ensure collective defense, the planning, equipment, training and exercises, and force structure of the armed forces need to be adapted.

Germany's Political, Military, and Financial Challenge

However, this realization raises some daunting political, military, and financial questions for Berlin. Politically, Germany needs to be able to decide about its military contributions. Therefore, it has to create the preconditions for rapid decision making on any deployment and Germany's share therein, including in multinational structures where applicable. This implies that the Bundestag needs to be enabled to make quick decisions. Therefore, the Bundestag needs to be informed comprehensively about German contributions as well as about its potential role in case of an Article 5 situation and about NATO's decision-making procedures. The so-called Rühe Commission, which assessed whether the parliamentary approval procedures should be reformed to accommodate the rights of the Bundestag on the one hand and assure Allies of Germany's commitment on the other, was a first step in that direction.

Militarily, German obligations signify a long-term increased requirement for personnel, equipment, and exercises as well as reform of existing plans and processes. Many reports and articles have questioned the readiness and deployability of the German armed forces. Certain equipment is not fully operational (for instance, the Tornados), while other capabilities are available only to a limited extent (such as air transport). Moreover, logistical issues need to be sorted out: If troops are to be relocated faster, then the corresponding transportation capacities need to be made available, as well as legal requirements established for heavy military equipment to be moved in Germany and Europe. And not least, more military exercises are needed to reconnect with the collective defense task and to make sure the interoperability with Allies and partners can be guaranteed. These challenges require long-term and sustainable solutions. The Framework Nation Concept (FNC), introduced in 2013, addresses some of these issues. As a tool to systematically organize defense cooperation, the FNC offers an opportunity for smaller states to contribute some specialized capabilities to larger framework nations, which provide the organizational backbone of the multilateral force structure.[5] Together, they form a cluster that would become more effective and sustainable— that is, capable of carrying out longer operations.

Financially, the substantial contributions and the associated changes cannot be born from the current level of funding. The budget increase decided on in 2015 will be spent to a large extent on personnel. The announcement in January 2016 to spend an additional €130 billion on equipment until 2030 is an important first step yet might not be sufficient either. In fact, Germany is unlikely to reach the spending goal of 2 percent of gross domestic product agreed on at the 2014 Wales Summit.

Détente

While contributing substantially to the deterrence and defense efforts in Europe, Berlin—in reference to the 1967 Harmel Report—maintains that in order to reach security, the complementary component next to deterrence is détente.[6] Thus, Berlin has suggested initiatives to keep the channels of dialogue with Moscow open. This explains, on the one hand, its commitment to the OSCE (where Berlin assumed the chairmanship in 2016), the EU, and formats such as the Normandy contact group and the Minsk group. On the other hand, this German approach is also visible in initiatives such as calls for meetings of the NATO-Russia Council, the objections to an abrogation of the 1997 NATO-Russia Founding Act, the setup of a Russia-NATO crisis mechanism as suggested by Berlin in December 2014, and the commitment within NATO to initiate rules of behavior with Russia for the safety of air and maritime encounters. This resulted in criticism of Berlin as being too Russia-friendly and not taking the fears of other Allies seriously enough.

A debate unfolded that questioned whether NATO should not do more to ensure credible deterrence and reassurance, including the permanent stationing of troops and equipment in Eastern Europe (which was later agreed on in Warsaw at the 2016 NATO summit). In the past, this has been an issue that has caused considerable tension within the Alliance. While the Baltic states and Poland in particular have pushed for the permanent stationing of equipment and NATO troops on their territories, other countries, and Germany in particular, have treated this subject with caution. Berlin—supported by Paris, Oslo, and Washington—did not want to alienate Moscow further and was not convinced it was the adequate solution in terms of defense. Berlin and others feared that the permanent stationing of troops in the eastern NATO members would not improve the security situation but could contribute to an escalation. Therefore, Berlin has sought to strike a balance between deterrence and dialogue by reassuring Allies and building a credible deterrence and defense on which then to engage in dialogue with Russia.[7]

Among other initiatives, Germany has thus sought to strengthen bilateral military support as a means to reassure eastern partners. Germany has launched, together with the United States, the Transatlantic Capability Enhancement and Training Initiative (TACET). TACET is about ensuring better coordination between the US and Germany in their training and exercises in Eastern Europe.[8] Following the decisions at the summit in Warsaw to establish an EFP in the three Baltic states and Poland, Germany now also leads the multinational battalion in Lithuania.

In addition to the commitment to the RAP, Germany sought to develop answers within NATO, the EU, and the OSCE and on a bilateral basis on how to deal with hybrid aggressions. The distinguishing feature of hybrid tactics is the use of civilian and military tools—which the EU is better suited to use.[9] The goal of hybrid approaches is to exploit the weaknesses of the opponent, such as the vulnerabilities of societies. Military responses by NATO forces are therefore not the first or most appropriate tool to address them. For Berlin, countering hybrid threats thus requires an appropriate mix of civilian and military instruments to systematically deal with Europe's vulnerabilities. To this end, concerted efforts are needed to improve prevention, resilience, communication, deterrence, and defense. This also means that EU-NATO relations need to be improved in order to achieve the appropriate mix, as undertaken with the Joint EU-NATO Declaration signed at the Warsaw Summit in July 2016.

When the German foreign and defense ministers visited the Baltic countries in April 2015, a series of cooperation agreements in areas such as energy, culture, education, and civil society were signed to improve the ability to counter hybrid threats. A particular focus was on media and communication, with the overarching goal to foster and promote independent, objective, and professional media to counter Russian propaganda.[10] This includes exchange programs and grants for journalists and students, cooperation in the training of journalists, an extended program of Deutsche Welle (Germany's international news channel) in Russian, and programs to foster competences in dealing with media at school. While Germany's Allies have welcomed this commitment, some also criticized it as a way of avoiding a stronger military commitment. But it is an equally important measure to strengthen the Baltic societies.

The interconnectedness of Western societies is a great strength, but at the same time it is also one of the greatest weaknesses of the West. Therefore, the resilience of European societies needs to be bolstered. In this context, prevention measures become essential, including early warning mechanisms. Since those weaknesses that could be exploited range from economic dependence to discontent minorities, the measures need to cover a range of issues, from infrastructure to the freedom of the press. The resilience pledge adopted at the 2016 Warsaw Summit and the focus on resilience in the EU show the rising importance of the topic.

A Test Case for a New German Policy or Leading by Default?

Germany's reaction to the Ukrainian crisis is part of the broader debate launched in 2013 and 2014 about whether Berlin should assume a greater share in international security—that is, one that corresponds to its political and economic weight. Following the arrival of the new government in December 2013, the president, the defense, and the foreign ministers delivered strong speeches at the Munich Security Conference in January 2014.[11] The key messages conveyed that Germany must be ready for earlier, more decisive, and more substantive engagement and that while Germany's traditional culture of military restraint remains valid, it must not become an excuse for staying on the sidelines. Germany, in many ways the central European power and a country deeply connected to global networks, must also be ready to do more to guarantee the security that others have provided for decades and to protect the international order from which it benefits. These speeches marked the official beginning of (at least) a rhetorical change in German foreign and security policy.

The German reaction to the Ukraine crisis in various formats (EU, NATO, OSCE, Minsk, Normandy, bilateral) can indeed be interpreted as the expression of a greater willingness to live up to international responsibilities. There are further examples that show a greater German commitment in political-diplomatic but also military terms beyond the crisis in and around Ukraine, such as the delivery of arms to the Kurdish Peshmerga in 2014; the increased commitment in Mali in support of France, the EU, and the United Nations; and, since the 2015 November attacks in Paris, the military contribution to the fight against IS. However, this does not entail that Germany will always make the decisions that other Allies expect or that it will act consistently.

Overall, in view of its various contributions, Germany has gained a certain political weight. Yet this commitment remains to a great extent crisis-driven and pushed by external developments. Generally speaking, Germany has become most active when partners or events created the necessary pressure, such as in the Ukraine crisis, that forced Berlin to take over diplomatic and military leadership. In other cases, such as the fight against IS, Germany became active only when the crisis turned into a domestic issue (for instance, as refugee flows to Europe grew) or when it was critical for an important partner (for example, following the Paris attacks). Yet the biggest commitment remains the one to collective defense in the east. It also shaped the new White Book on Defense published in July 2016 and the new conception of the Bundeswehr, which was expected for the summer of 2017 but to date has not been passed.

It is therefore not surprising that the countries in the Baltic Sea region look to Germany as a key security and defense player and call for Berlin to get more involved in their regional security. However, Germany and the countries of the region need to clarify their expectations and the scope of what they are realistically willing and able to commit. Overall, regional security would benefit from a clearer perspective on what role Germany should play, what other countries in the region can contribute to regional security, and how the transatlantic relations factor in.

Notes

The authors would like to thank Amélie Lohmann for her kind support in finalizing this chapter.

1. Claudia Major, "NATO's Strategic Adaptation: Germany Is the Backbone for the Alliance's Military Reorganisation," German Institute for International and Security Affairs (hereafter SWP), *SWP Comments* 16 (March 2015). See also Claudia Major and Alicia von Voss, "Nordic-Baltic Security, Germany and NATO: The Baltic Sea Region Is a Test Case for European Security," SWP, *SWP Comments* 13 (March 2016).

2. Patrick Keller, "Germany in NATO: The Status Quo Ally," *Survival* 54 (2012): 95–110.

3. NATO, "The Harmel Report," Nato.com, January 30, 2017, http://www.nato.int/cps
/en/natohq/topics_67927.htm. See also Helga Haftendorn, "Entstehung und Bedeutung des
Harmel-Berichts der NATO von 1967" [Evolution and significance of the 1968 NATO Harmel Report], *Vierteljahrshefte für Zeitgeschichte* 40 (1992): 169–220. See also Claudia Major
and Jeffrey Rathke, "NATO Needs Deterrence and Dialogue," SWP, *SWP Comments* 18
(April 2016).

4. Keller, "Germany in NATO," 95–110.

5. Major, "NATO's Strategic Adaptation." See also Claudia Major and Christian Mölling,
"The Framework Nations Concept: Germany's Contribution to a Capable European Defence,"
SWP, *SWP Comments* 52 (December 2014).

6. Claudia Major and Christian Mölling, "Entspannung braucht Abschreckung—
Abschreckung braucht Entspannung" [Détente needs deterrence—deterrence needs détente],
S&F Sicherheit und Frieden 35 (2017): 13–18.

7. Major and Rathke, "NATO Needs Deterrence and Dialogue."

8. Federal Foreign Office, "United States of America," Auswaertiges-amt.de, April 2017,
accessed June 5, 2017, http://www.auswaertiges-amt.de/EN/Aussenpolitik/Laender/Laender
infos/01-Nodes/UsaVereinigteStaaten_node.html.

9. Claudia Major and Christian Mölling, "A Hybrid Security Policy for Europe," SWP,
SWP Comments 22 (April 2015).

10. Anton Troianovski, "Germany Seeks to Counter Russian 'Propaganda' in Baltics,"
Wall Street Journal, April 17, 2015, https://www.wsj.com/articles/germany-seeks-to-counter
-russian-propaganda-in-baltics-1429294362. See also Federal Foreign Office, "Enge Koopera-
tion und Solidarität mit baltischen Partnern" [Close cooperation and solidarity with Baltic
partners], Auswaertiges-amt.de, April 17, 2015.

11. Claudia Major and Christian Mölling, "Zwischen Krisen und Verantwortung: eine
erste Bilanz der neuen deutschen Verteidigungspolitik" [Between crises and responsibility: A
first assessment of the new German defense policy], Institut français des relations internatio-
nales, Paris, *Note du Cerfa* 127 (2015).

9

Norwegian Perspectives on Baltic Sea Security

HÅKON LUNDE SAXI

Norway has access to rich natural resources in vast ocean areas, and borders on a great power in the north. These two factors largely define [Norway's] regional dimension.

Norwegian Ministry of Defence

Since the end of the Cold War, the official Norwegian policy has been that the Baltic Sea region is of high importance to Norway.[1] In reality, this has been only partially true. While Norway has not been uninterested in the Baltic Sea region, it has tended to be overshadowed by more pressing Norwegian priorities. The main priority in Norwegian foreign and security policy has been twofold. Geographically, Norway's priorities have been its High North and Arctic regions, including Norway's maritime economic zones in the Norwegian Sea, the Barents Sea, and around Svalbard. The Baltic "near abroad" has by comparison been delegated to the back burner. As for partnerships, Norwegian security policy has favored building close relations with the larger Allies to the west over the Nordic-Baltic neighbors to the east.

Thus, the Baltic Sea region has until very recently not figured prominently in Norwegian security policy. To its east, Norway has been linked by shared bonds of common values, histories, and identities to the other Nordic countries and to a lesser extent to the Baltic ones. However, hardnosed calculations of Norwegian interests have continued to favor focusing on developing good and close relations with the maritime Anglo-Saxon powers to the west. As has been the case since Norwegian independence in 1905 and since Norway joined NATO in 1949, they remain the ultimate guarantors of Norwegian security.[2]

This main pattern, which still endures, has been somewhat modified by NATO's enlargements in 1999 and 2004 as well as by the 2014 Ukrainian crisis. Norway has only recently discovered that it now has vital security interests in the Baltic Sea region. Nevertheless, for Norway the main security priority remains its maritime High North and Arctic regions. It is presently seeking to bolster the awareness, presence, and involvement of the transatlantic Alliance in this area.

The Pre-2014 Period: The Baltic Near Abroad as a Peripheral Region

While Norway joined the Council of the Baltic Sea States in 1992, this was almost as an afterthought. Economically and in terms of security, Norway's stakes in the Baltic Sea region were far lower than for the states that shared a Baltic Sea coastline. Meanwhile, its political, economic, and security stakes in the developments in the High North region were far higher. Norwegian leaders and officials therefore devoted far more attention and energy toward developing a successful regional cooperation in the Barents region through, for example, the Barents Regional Council established in 1993. For Norwegian foreign ministers such as Thorvald Stoltenberg (1990–93) and Bjørn Tore Godal (1994–97), it seemed vital to build trust, familiarity, and economic integration between Norway and the northwestern regions of Russia. Ideally, Russia should become a "partner" and be integrated into the Euro-Atlantic security community.[3]

However, that Russia would develop favorably and become a stable, liberal, and democratic partner could not be taken for granted. After the end of the Cold War, Russia was perceived as an unstable and unpredictable great power, with which Norway shared a 196-kilometer border. The political, economic, and military relationship between Norway and Russia was characterized by asymmetry. Following the recommendations of the 1992 defense commission, post–Cold War Norwegian defense policy remained focused on invasion defense in northern Norway. The main reason for this continuity was concern about the "lingering threat" emanating from Russia. From 1998 to 2002, defense policy became somewhat less focused on territorial defense and Russia.[4] Since 2002, invasion defense has given way to the dual tasks of participating in international military operations abroad and carrying out robust short-notice military crisis management at home. Nevertheless, the main scenario for which the armed forces were designed was a security policy crisis between Norway and Russia in the High North region.[5] Such a limited political-military crisis was expected to be short in duration, take place in international waters and airspace, and involve mainly air and maritime forces.[6]

All the Nordic states began to extend considerable amounts of military and security assistance to the Baltic states after 1990, especially following the withdrawal of Russian forces in 1994. Norway's engagement was, however, of a lesser order than that of Denmark, Sweden, and Finland.[7] Norway was also at the time perceived, with some justification, as one of the countries that was more skeptical about NATO enlargement eastward. Instead, Norwegian officials tended to advocate integrating "our Baltic friends" as far as possible into the Euro-Atlantic institutions but without full membership in the European Union (EU) and—especially—in NATO in the near term. Norwegian officials were on the one hand concerned with not "diluting" NATO's Article 5 security guarantees, stressing that the ability to carry out collective defense of member states also had to be preserved in the "new" post–Cold War alliance.

Conversely, while carefully stressing that a Russian veto on enlargement was not acceptable, they were also worried about the consequences for Western-Russian relations. If enlargement caused a backlash to Russia's integration as a "normal" member of the European security community, this would not be in Norway's interests.[8] In this careful and "gradualist" policy toward enlargement, Norway differed from Denmark.[9] Being geographically more distant from Russia and standing to benefit more directly from enlargement, Copenhagen much more quickly came to champion full NATO membership for Poland and the Baltic states.[10]

By the time NATO enlarged to more countries around the Baltic Sea—Poland in 1999 and Estonia, Latvia, and Lithuania in 2004—these Norwegian concerns had largely been laid to rest. Norway at the time had come to support enlargement. Both before and after enlargement, the Norwegian armed forces worked closely with their Nordic and Baltic counterparts in NATO operations in the Balkans and in Afghanistan. The enlargements also meant that the Baltic Sea became a virtual "NATO and EU lake." However, this did not immediately increase Norway's preoccupation with the Baltic Sea region.

The foreign policy priorities of long-serving minister of foreign affairs Jonas Gahr Støre (2005–12) were not directed eastward but northward: toward the High North and the Arctic, with their crucial oil, gas, and fishery resources.[11] The minister repeatedly emphasized that "the High North is the Government's number one foreign policy priority." Støre was fond of quoting at length from a poem by the Norwegian poet Rolf Jacobsen that suggests its listeners "look north more often" (*se oftere mot nord*).[12] On the one hand, the government's policy reflected long-standing economic realities. The Norwegian economy remains heavily dependent on natural resources extracted from its huge exclusive economic zone. Since oil was discovered in 1969, the petroleum sector alone has grown to account for about 20 percent of gross domestic product and 50 percent of the country's exports.[13] Fisheries and shipping were also key sectors. Unsurprisingly, this maritime dependence heavily influenced Norwegian foreign policy. On the other hand, since at least 2007, Norwegian defense policy experienced a "retro-tendency" to meet growing Russian capabilities and assertiveness.[14] In 2008, Norway introduced a Core Area Initiative within NATO, which aimed at strengthening the focus in the Alliance on more traditional "in-area" security.[15]

To accompany his story about the importance of the north, Støre was fond of showing his audiences a map that was centered on the North Pole and showed Norway's vast northern maritime areas. On this map the Baltic Sea appeared only as a small lake in the lower right-hand corner. Its appearance on the map reflects its position in Norwegian foreign and security policy: at the periphery and off to the side, an afterthought.[16]

Nordic-Baltic Cooperation in the 2000s

In the second half of the 2000s, there was a surge toward greater Nordic and Nordic-Baltic cooperation on security and defense. In 2009, many of these defense initiatives among the Nordic countries were brought together under the Nordic Defence Cooperation (NORDEFCO) framework. Simultaneously, the by then elder statesman Thorvald Stoltenberg was asked to present proposals for more Nordic foreign and security policy cooperation. These in February 2009 became the so-called Stoltenberg Report.[17]

The Norwegian military identified a strong need to cooperate internationally to meet the dual challenge of rising costs and shrinking force size and found the Nordic neighbors to be agreeable and willing partners. The Baltic states were, however, seen as less interesting. They were small, had fewer relevant capabilities and less equipment commonality, were culturally more dissimilar, and were geographically not adjacent to Norway. Nonaligned Sweden and Finland, and especially NATO member Denmark, appeared as more appropriate partners to meet the Norwegian military's cooperative needs.

However, for the wider Norwegian security policy establishment, even the Nordic framework was seen as problematic. The preference was rather for building close cooperation with the Allies to the west and south that would ultimately guarantee Norway's security in a crisis. This applied particularly to the major maritime powers to Norway's west, the United States and the United Kingdom, but also to the southern continental powers, Germany and France. The Nordic and Baltic states were too small to offer much in the way of support in a crisis, even if Sweden and Finland would abandon nonalignment and become members of NATO. For this reason, the Norwegian security policy community warmly welcomed the British initiative to establish the so-called Northern Group in 2010. The Northern Group was more of a security policy talking shop than NORDEFCO, which aimed toward more concrete military cooperation on training, education, acquisition, and maintenance. However, it had a strong security-policy appeal in the inclusion of several key NATO countries: It consisted of the Nordic-Baltic states but, more important, also the United Kingdom, Germany, Poland, and the Netherlands.[18]

The 2009 Stoltenberg Report contained a number of suggestions for joint action favored by Norway, since they focused on northern maritime issues. These included surveillance of Icelandic airspace, satellite-based maritime monitoring in the Baltic Sea, joint sea patrols, and more political cooperation on Arctic issues.[19] In Sweden and Finland, officials stressed that this emphasis on the High North and the Arctic needed to be balanced by a greater focus on the Baltic Sea area.[20] Norway, however, demonstrated a limited willingness to invest political and economic capital in Baltic Sea security. Typically, when a wise-men group convened in 2010 to identify how to advance the cooperation between the Nordic and Baltic countries (NB8), it was a result of a joint initiative by Denmark and Latvia.[21]

The Sea Surveillance Cooperation in the Baltic Sea (SUCBAS) provides an interesting case of Norwegian noninvolvement in Baltic Sea security. Originally launched in 2006 as a Swedish-Finnish undertaking, SUCBAS has since enlarged to also include all the NATO member states around the Baltic Sea (Denmark, Estonia, Latvia, Lithuania, Poland, and Germany). In 2015, the United Kingdom also joined. Norway remained skeptical about its usefulness, though, and did not wish to pay the entry costs. Oslo was, however, eager to encourage the other Nordic states to join a very similar Norwegian project, Barents Watch, which focused on maritime situational awareness in the High North, the Barents Sea, and the Arctic.[22]

NATO air-policing in the Baltic states and Iceland also provides tangible clues to national priorities. Norway, with its long Atlantic coastline, contributed to both missions but concentrated more on patrolling Icelandic airspace. Denmark, with both an Atlantic and a Baltic Sea coastline, split its efforts more equally between the two.[23]

The 2014 Ukraine Crisis: Norway Discovers the Baltic Sea

With the 2014 Ukrainian crisis, Norway—a neighbor of Russia—now viewed the security situation as significantly changed. In an interview conducted a year after the start of the crisis, Norwegian minister of defense Ine Eriksen Søreide told CNN in an unusually clear, but not alarmist, way that "I want to warn against the fact that some people see this as something that is going to pass. The situation has changed. And it has changed profoundly." She argued that there was now "no going back to some sort of normality."[24]

Considering its relatively small size, Norway now took an unusually prominent and active role in NATO's Immediate Assurance Measures toward the Baltic states in the wake of the crisis. In April 2014, following an Alliance request, Norway assumed out-of-rotation command of NATO Mine Countermeasure Group 1, contributing the flagship KNM *Valkyrien* and the minesweeper KNM *Otra*. The naval force was active in the Baltic Sea as part of NATO's reassurance measures. In June and October, Norwegian infantry companies also trained in Latvia for several months in exercises with a similar purpose.[25] Following the September Wales Summit, Germany, the Netherlands, and Norway also agreed to contribute to NATO's interim Very High Readiness Joint Task Force (VJTF) in 2015. This brigade-sized force (approximately five thousand troops) should be able to rapidly reinforce frontline Allies, thereby acting as a deterrent to potential aggressors. The VJTF was to form a more responsive core of the existing NATO Response Force (NRF), which the three countries had already been slated to provide. The Norwegian army committed its high-readiness force, the Telemark Battalion battle group, to the interim VJTF.

Some of these land exercises, as well as the Norwegian commitment to the NRF, had been planned already before the Russian annexation of Crimea but were now framed in the completely new context of deterrence and reassurance. To explain the increased Norwegian military presence in the Baltic states, the Norwegian chief of defense stressed that Norway's actions were intended to communicate "clearly" to Russia that the Baltic states were behind "NATO's red line."[26] Søreide told reporters, "When one is a member of NATO, one has to respond when Allies request support, just as we would expect support if we needed it."[27]

Norway had come to discover two vital interests in Baltic Sea security: preserving the inviolability of international law in general and upholding NATO's Article 5 security guarantees in particular. These were long-standing priorities in Norwegian security policy, sometimes described as the UN track versus the NATO track.[28] As a small state with limited military resources but with huge maritime areas rich in resources, Norway considered the upholding of international law to be its "first line of defense."[29] Furthermore, within NATO, Norway was often grouped together with the "new" Central and Eastern European member states as "Article 5ers": countries that first and foremost see the Alliance as a provider of (primarily American) security guarantees. These countries all bordered or were located close to Russia.[30] For the Article 5ers, the credibility of Alliance collective defense was the bedrock on which their security rested. The seeming vulnerability of the Baltic states now threatened to undermine this vital foundation. Additionally, with key Norwegian Allies such as the United States, the United Kingdom, and Germany leading the efforts to reassure the Baltic states and Poland, Norway viewed it as important to work closely with these major powers.[31]

All Quiet on the Northern Front

One reason why Norway could commit itself to such an extent to the reassurance of its Allies on the "eastern front" was that things were comparatively quiet on the "northern front."[32] The situation in the High North and the Arctic regions was not considered to have changed in the same alarming way after February and March 2014. As Søreide told the press in February 2015, the Russians "have not breached our territory and that is different from what is happening in the Baltic Sea area. They are breaching territory there all the time."[33] By October 2014, the number of intercepts of Russian aircraft by NATO in the Baltic area had tripled compared to 2013. In what was described as "dangerous brinkmanship," Russian pilots were also reported to be acting aggressively and unpredictably.[34] This new pattern of activity was very different from that in the Norwegian High North.

The Norwegian Intelligence Service had for years closely watched the increase in Russia's air and naval activity in the Arctic. Since 2007, this had included the resumption of strategic bomber patrols over the Barents Sea and Norwegian Sea. The Northern Fleet had also increased its activities in the Arctic. This Russian resurgence include a revitalized "bastion defense concept" intended to protect its strategic submarines in the European Arctic Ocean, with ambitions of sea-denial extending west and south to the Greenland-Iceland-UK gap. However, the increases in Russian capabilities in the High North and Arctic regions were seen as a "normal" part of Russia's long-term military modernization, and developments had taken place gradually over many years.[35]

In the Norwegian High North, there was also, unlike in the Baltic Sea area, no sudden change in the patterns of Russian military behavior following the outbreak of the Ukrainian crisis. The two Norwegian F-16 fighter aircraft assigned to act as NATO's Quick Reaction Alert in Norway had intercepted and identified more or less the same number of Russian aircraft in 2014 as in 2013.[36] The relative continuity in Russian behavior in the High North gave Norway the necessary freedom of action to increase its efforts to strengthen Baltic Sea security in 2014 and 2015.

In light of the tense situation in Norway's near abroad, the country nevertheless did increase its national military preparedness and situational awareness efforts at home. This, together with the already mentioned in-NATO-area efforts on the eastern front, was given priority over out-of-NATO-area missions on the Mediterranean, North African, and Middle Eastern "southern front." In 2011, during NATO's UN-sanctioned air war over Libya, Norway and Denmark provided almost identical contributions to the Alliance effort: six F-16 combat aircraft.[37] In October 2014, Norway differed markedly from Denmark. Unlike Copenhagen, Oslo now declined a request to provide combat aircraft to support the US-led coalition in Iraq fighting against the Islamic State group.

At the time, Norway's F-16AM/BM aircraft were showing signs of aging. Cracks had been discovered in their 1980s-era fuselage, which meant that many aircraft were at least temporarily unavailable. This forced the government to prioritize. Prime Minister Erna Solberg (Conservative Party) argued that, "due to our border with Russia, Norway is in a different situation than countries such as Denmark, Holland and Belgium." The government's decision and reasoning enjoyed bipartisan support. Jonas Gahr Støre (Labor Party), now the leader of the largest opposition party, stated that "we not only have a long coast to patrol, but we also have assumed responsibility for large sea areas which has strategic importance for NATO."[38] The minister of defense echoed this sentiment: "Right now and today, we have to make sure we can keep our situational awareness and . . . keep up our presence in the High North, both with frigates and planes."[39] Norwegian leaders effectively argued that the Alliance expected Norway to keep its house in order at home, maintaining good situational awareness, presence, and readiness on NATO's northern front.

The 2016 Warsaw Summit: Making NATO "Look North More Often"

Moving into 2015 and 2016, Norway continued to maintain its strong support for NATO's reassurance and deterrence measures on the "eastern front" of the Alliance. From May until September 2015, Norway assumed lead-nation responsibility for NATO's air-policing mission in the Baltic states, providing four F-16s and seventy personnel.[40] At the 2016 Warsaw Summit, Norway pledged to provide a company-sized unit as part of NATO's Enhanced Forward Presence in the Baltic states.[41] The security of the Baltic states also enjoyed a newfound prominence in Norwegian security thinking. In October 2015, a government-appointed expert commission on defense delivered its advice for the next long-term plan for the armed forces. The commission allotted high priority to the defense of the Baltic states.

The expert commission outlined three scenarios to illustrate some of the situations the armed forces now had to prepare for. Scenario one was an (initially) bilateral crisis involving Norway and Russia in the High North. Scenario two was a NATO collective-defense operation in the Baltic Sea area in defense of the Baltic states. The third was a nonstate terrorist attack on Norway. Considering that Norway was itself a "frontline" state bordering Russia and vulnerable to Russian "horizontal escalation" in case of a NATO-Russian conflict, the commission recommended a high level of ambition for Norway's participation in the collective defense of the Baltic states: "The Norwegian Armed Forces must be able to rapidly provide and transfer units to the Baltic area, to demonstrate political will and an actual ability to exercise collective defense. . . . The Norwegian forces must be prepared for both military combat and to remain in the area for a protracted period of time."[42]

However, in spite of the immediate relative calm in the High North compared with the Baltic Sea region, Norwegian politicians and government officials nevertheless soon came to champion an increased NATO focus on the maritime High North. In the run-up to the 2016 NATO summit in Warsaw, Søreide stressed that the "new security environment" required "maritime power and presence" and the need to "raise NATO's profile in the maritime domain." Russia's new high-end military capabilities and infrastructure in the Arctic, such as its submarines, aircraft, and long-range missiles, were identified as the challenge.[43] At the summit, Norway joined forces with the United Kingdom, France, and Iceland to successfully champion new proposals to strengthen NATO's activities and force posture in the North Atlantic.[44] The summit communiqué reflected this effort. It added the North Atlantic to the list of strategically important areas where the Alliance faced "evolving challenges" and committed NATO to strengthen it maritime posture and situational awareness. The Alliance would deter and defend against threats to "sea lines of communication and maritime approaches of NATO territory."[45]

The high priority given to the defense of the Baltic states and the wider eastern front in Norwegian defense policy has to be understood as part of Norway's priorities as an Article 5er. If NATO's security guarantees were tested and proved ineffective, it would have devastating repercussions for Norwegian security. For this reason, making NATO's deterrence efforts credible and effective was of key importance for Norway. On the one hand from this point of view, strengthening Norwegian security and strengthening the security of Norway's Baltic Sea Allies and partners were two sides of the same coin. There were mutual interests both in Norway and among the Baltic Sea states in strengthening the security of the latter.

On the other hand, Norwegian leaders simultaneously worried that the deterrence, defense, and reassurance measures so far enacted after 2014 were too reactive and one-sidedly focused toward the eastern front. NATO's military efforts—such as the VJTF—were also perceived as too land-centric. Norway's desire to see NATO revitalize collective defense in the Northern Atlantic maritime area, while strengthening its maritime capabilities, should be read as a reaction to this perceived one-sidedness.[46] *If* one regards the attention, focus, and military capabilities of the Alliance as zero-sum—which is debatable—then such a shift toward an increased northern maritime presence would necessarily have to come at the expense of the eastern or southern fronts. From this point of view, there were also some competing interests at work.

Conclusions

In 1939, the Swedish embassy in Oslo wrote home to Stockholm complaining about the "complete lack of interest from the Norwegian side for all Baltic Sea problems."[47] If we had had access to the same kind of correspondence written sixty or seventy years later, it would probably have revealed a similar disinterest in Oslo for Baltic Sea security issues. As Thorvald Stoltenberg once lamented, "It was not always easy to get the Icelanders and Norwegians to realize that what was happening in the Baltic also affected their safety."[48] Until the 2014 Ukrainian crisis, the Baltic Sea area in general and the security of the Baltic states in particular were issues of relatively minor importance in Norwegian security and defense policy.

From a Norwegian point of view, the Baltic states were Allies, friends, and partners, but their importance was limited. Sweden and Finland, with which Norway has a 2,366-kilometer border (92 percent of its total land border), and which are far more populous, economically significant, and arguably also more similar to Norway culturally, figured much more prominently in Norwegian thinking. However, this interest did not carry as far as the Baltic Sea or to the Baltic states. Among the Nordic capitals, with the possible exception of Reykjavík, Oslo paid the least attention to the Baltic Sea region. Instead, Norwegian attention was directed northward and westward. In the north, Norway sought to develop and protect is huge exclusive economic zones, with their rich natural resources. In the west, Norway sought to maintain and strengthen its ties with those Western powers that ultimately guaranteed its security.

The 2014 Ukrainian crisis generated an upsurge in Norwegian interest in the Baltic Sea and, in particular, in the security of the Baltic states. Russian revisionism now appeared to threaten the law-based international order and Western security guarantees on which Norwegian prosperity and security relied. In response, Oslo committed political and military resources to ensure a more credible deterrence posture for the Baltic states. However, Norwegian attention soon turned toward bringing NATO to engage more strongly in the North Atlantic. While it did not abandon the newfound awareness of the Baltic Sea, Norwegian security policy returned in a sense to its classical pursuit: to tie the Western (maritime) powers more closely to the defense and security of Norway and the wider northern flank of the Alliance.

Notes

I am grateful to all those who have offered their valuable insights and advice in writing this chapter, especially Rolf Tamnes, Paal Sigurd Hilde, and Magnus Petersson. Any mistakes or omissions are entirely my own.

Epigraph: Norwegian Ministry of Defence, *Styrke og relevans: Strategisk konsept for Forsvaret* [Strength and relevance: Strategic concept for the Norwegian armed forces] (Oslo: Ministry of Defence, 2004), 42.

1. See, for example, the pamphlet published when Norway chaired the Council of the Baltic Sea States in 1999 and 2000: Norwegian Ministry of Foreign Affairs, *Norge of Østersjørådet* [Norway and the Baltic Sea Council] (Oslo: Ministry of Foreign Affairs, 2000).

2. Olav Riste, "Was 1949 a Turning Point? Norway and the Western Powers 1947–1950," in *Western Security: The Formative Years; European and Atlantic Defence, 1947–1953*, ed. Olav Riste (Oslo: Norwegian University Press, 1985).

3. Thorvald Stoltenberg, *Det handler om mennesker* [It's about people] (Oslo: Gyldendal, 2001), 249–58; and Bjørn Tore Godal, *Utsikter* [Views] (Oslo: Aschehoug, 2003), 104–19.

4. Norwegian Defence Commission of 1990, *NOU 1992: 12; Forsvarskommisjonen av 1990* [Norwegian Defence Commission of 1990] (Oslo: Statens forvaltningstjeneste, 1992); Norwegian Ministry of Defence, *Hovedretningslinjer for Forsvarets virksomhet og utvikling i*

tiden 1994–1998 [Main guidelines for the armed forces' activity for the years 1994–98], Report to the Storting, no. 16 (1992–93); and *Hovedretningslinjer for Forsvarets virksomhet og utvikling i tiden 1999–2002* [Main guidelines for the armed forces' activity for the years 1999–2002], Report to the Storting, no. 22 (1997–98).

5. *Omleggingen av Forsvaret i perioden 2002–2005* [The restructuring of the armed forces in the period 2002–2005], Proposition to the Storting, no. 45 (2000–1), chap. 4 and chap. 5; and *Den videre moderniseringen av Forsvaret i perioden 2005–2008* [The further modernization of the Norwegian armed forces 2005–2008], Proposition to the Storting, no. 42 (2003–4), chap. 1.

6. Norwegian Chief of Defence, *Forsvarssjefens Forsvarsstudie 2000: Sluttrapport* [The chief of defense's defense review 2000] (Oslo: Forsvarets overkommando, 2000), 7–9; *Forsvarssjefens militærfaglige utredning 2003* [The chief of defense's defense review 2003] (Oslo: Forsvarets overkommando, 2003), 3–4; *Forsvarssjefens Forsvarsstudie 2007: Sluttrapport* [The chief of defense's defense review 2007] (Oslo: Ministry of Defence, 2007), 5–6; and Gen. Sverre Diesen, "Security and the Northern Region," in *High North: High Stakes: Security, Energy, Transportation, Environment,* ed. Rose Gottemoeller and Rolf Tamnes (Bergen: Fagbokforlaget, 2008).

7. Clive Archer, "Nordic Involvement in the Baltic States Security: Needs, Response and Success," *European Security* 7, no. 3 (1998); "Nordic Swans and Baltic Cygnets," *Cooperation and Conflict* 34, no. 1 (1999); and Rolf Tamnes, *Oljealder, 1965–1995* [Entering the Oil Age, 1965–1995], vol. 6, *Norsk utenrikspolitikks historie* [The history of Norwegian foreign policy] (Oslo: Universitetsforlaget, 1997), 145.

8. See, e.g., the book by the permanent representative to NATO (1992–98), Leif Mevik, *Det nye NATO: En personlig beretning* [The new NATO: A personal account] (Bergen: Eide forlag, 1999), 51–56, 61–62.

9. For a historical comparison of Norwegian and Danish defense policy, see Håkon Lunde Saxi, *Norwegian and Danish Defence Policy: A Comparative Study of the Post–Cold War Era,* Defence and Security Studies no. 1 (Oslo: Norwegian Institute for Defence Studies, 2010).

10. See interview with Danish minister of foreign affairs (1982–93), Uffe Ellemann-Jensen, in Jakob Kvist and Jon Bloch Skipper, *Udenrigsminister: Seks politiske portrætter* [Foreign minister: Six political portraits] (Copenhagen: People's Press, 2007), 227–28. See also the biography by the Danish minister of defense (1993–2000), Hans Hækkerup, *På skansen: Dansk forsvarspolitik fra Murens fald til Kosovo* [On the redoubt: Danish defense policy from the fall of the wall to Kosovo] (Copenhagen: Lindhardt og Ringhof, 2002), 15, 66; and Archer, "Nordic Swans and Baltic Cygnets," 59.

11. These themes, which formed the leitmotif of Jonas Gahr Støre's tenure as minister, are well reflected in his book *Å gjøre en forskjell: Refleksjoner fra en norsk utenriksminister* [Making a difference: Reflections from a Norwegian foreign minister] (Oslo: Cappelen Damm, 2008).

12. Jonas Gahr Støre, "Most Is North: The High North and the Way Ahead—an International Perspective," lecture at the University of Tromsø, April 29, 2010 (Oslo: Ministry of Foreign Affairs, 2010), https://www.regjeringen.no/en/aktuelt/Most-is-north/id602113/.

13. International Monetary Fund, *Norway: Selected Issues,* IMF Country Report no. 13/273 (Washington, DC: IMF, September 2013), 21.

14. Rolf Tamnes, "Et lite land i stormaktspolitikken" [A small country in great power politics], *Internasjonal Politikk* 73, no. 3 (2015): 389; and Svein Efjestad, "Norway and the North Atlantic: Defence of the Northern Flank," in *NATO and the North Atlantic: Revitalising Collective Defence,* ed. John Andreas Olsen (London: RUSI, 2017), 62–66. See also Olav Bogen and

Magnus Håkenstad, *Balansegang: Forsvarets omstilling etter den kalde krigen* [Balancing act: The reforms of the Norwegian armed forces after the Cold War] (Oslo: Dreyers forlag, 2015), chap. 6.

15. Paal Sigurd Hilde and Helene F. Widerberg, "NATOs nye strategiske konsept og Norge" [NATO's new Strategic Concept and Norway], *Norsk Militært Tidsskrift* [Norwegian military journal] no. 4 (2010): 13–19.

16. See maps at very beginning and end of Støre, *Å gjøre en forskjell.*

17. On the "surge" and the founding of NORDEFCO, see Håkon Lunde Saxi, *Nordic Defence Cooperation after the Cold War*, Oslo Files on Defence and Security no. 1 (Oslo: Norwegian Institute for Defence Studies, March 2011); and Thorvald Stoltenberg, *Nordic Cooperation on Foreign and Security Policy* (Oslo: Ministry of Foreign Affairs, February 9, 2009).

18. Paal Sigurd Hilde, "Nordic-Baltic Security and Defence Cooperation: The Norwegian Perspective," in *Northern Security and Global Politics: Nordic-Baltic Strategic Influence in a Post-unipolar World*, ed. Ann-Sofie Dahl and Pauli Järvenpää (London: Routledge, 2014), 93–94, 103.

19. See proposals 2–6 in Stoltenberg, *Nordic Cooperation on Foreign and Security Policy.*

20. Saxi, *Nordic Defence Cooperation*, 37–39, 43–44.

21. Danish and Latvian Ministries of Foreign Affairs, *NB8 Wise Men Report* (Copenhagen and Riga: Danish and Latvian Ministries of Foreign Affairs, 2010).

22. Saxi, *Nordic Defence Cooperation*, 43–44. See also the SUCBAS and BarentsWatch webpages, available at http://sucbas.org/ and https://www.barentswatch.no/en/about/.

23. NATO, *The Secretary General's Annual Report 2013* (Brussels: NATO Public Diplomacy Division, 2014), 21. Note that Baltic air-policing began in 2004. The NATO air-surveillance mission over Iceland began in 2008.

24. Mick Krever, "Norway: 'We Are Faced with a Different Russia,'" CNN, February 26, 2015.

25. Norwegian Armed Forces, *Forsvarets årsrapport 2014* [Annual report 2014] (Oslo: Norwegian Armed Forces, 2015), 62, 94.

26. Quoted in Rune Thomas Ege, "Tydelig beskjed til Russland" [Clear message to Russia], *Verdens Gang*, November 19, 2014.

27. Quoted in Håkon Eikesdal, "Her øver norske soldater i Putins nabolag" [Norwegian soldiers on exercises in Putin's neighbourhood], *Dagbladet*, October 1, 2014.

28. Tamnes, "Et lite land i stormaktspolitikken," 392.

29. Norwegian Ministry of Foreign Affairs, *Interesser, ansvar og muligheter: Hovedlinjer i norsk utenrikspolitikk* [Interests, responsibilities, and opportunities: The main features of Norwegian foreign policy], Report to the Storting, no. 15 (2008–9), 37, 43.

30. See, e.g., Jens Ringsmose, "NATO: A Provider of Public Goods," in *Theorizing NATO*, ed. Mark Webber and Adrian Hyde-Price (London: Routledge, 2016), 214–15. See also Hilde, *Nordic-Baltic Security and Defence Cooperation.*

31. The United States, the United Kingdom, Germany, France, and the Netherlands were subsequently identified by Norway as key Allies with whom it hoped to build especially close military relationships. Norwegian Ministry of Foreign Affairs, *Veivalg i norsk utenriks- og sikkerhetspolitikk* [Setting the course for Norwegian foreign and security policy], Report to the Storting, no. 36 (2016–2017) (Oslo: Norwegian Ministry of Foreign Affairs, 2017), 33. On Norwegian military cooperation with the UK and Germany, see Håkon Lunde Saxi, "British and German Initiatives for Defence Cooperation: The Joint Expeditionary Force and the Framework Nations Concept," *Defence Studies* 17, no. 2 (2017): 171–97.

32. Paal Sigurd Hilde, "Norway, the Ukraine Crisis and Baltic Sea Security," in *Baltic Sea Security: How Can Allies and Partners Meet the New Challenges in the Region?*, ed. Ann-Sofie Dahl (Copenhagen: Centre for Military Studies, 2014).

33. Quoted in Julian Borger, "Norway to Restructure Military in Response to Russian 'Aggression,'" *Guardian*, February 25, 2015.

34. Thomas Frear, Łukasz Kulesa, and Ian Kearns, *Dangerous Brinkmanship: Close Military Encounters between Russia and the West in 2014* (London: European Leadership Network, November 2014).

35. See, e.g., Norwegian Intelligence Service, *FOCUS 2013: Annual Assessment* (Oslo: Norwegian Intelligence Service, 2013), 8–13. On the Russian bastion defense concept today and during the Cold War, see Rolf Tamnes, "The Significance of the North Atlantic and the Norwegian Contribution," in *NATO and the North Atlantic: Revitalising Collective Defence*, ed. John Andreas Olsen (London: RUSI, 2017).

36. Norwegian Armed Forces, *Forsvarets årsrapport 2014*, 68.

37. Håkon Lunde Saxi, "So Similar, yet So Different: Explaining Divergence in Nordic Defence Policies," in *Common or Divided Security? German and Norwegian Perspectives on Euro-Atlantic Security*, ed. Robin Allers, Carlo Masala, and Rolf Tamnes (Bern: Peter Lang, 2014), 257–59.

38. Quoted in Alf Bjarne Johnsen, "Derfor holder hun F-16 hjemme" [That's why she's keeping the F-16 at home], *Verdens Gang*, October 22, 2014; NTB (Norwegian news agency), "Solberg: Naturlig at norske kampfly blir i Norge" [Solberg: Only natural that Norwegian combat aircraft remain in Norway], *Norsk Telegrambyrå*, October 17, 2014.

39. Quoted in Borger, "Norway to Restructure Military in Response to Russian 'Aggression.'"

40. NTB, "Norge vokter baltisk luftrom" [Norway is guarding Baltic airspace], *Norsk Telegrambyrå*, March 21, 2015.

41. Øystein Kløvstad Langberg, "Norske styrker sendes til Øst-Europa: Skal lage 'snubletråd' mot Russland" [Norwegian forces are being sent to Eastern Europe: To constitute trip wire against Russia], *Aftenposten*, July 9, 2016.

42. Expert Commission on Norwegian Security and Defence Policy, *Unified Effort* (Oslo: Ministry of Defence, 2015), 57.

43. Ine Eriksen Søreide, "Strategic Shift in the North: A Call For NATO Maritime Power, Presence," *Defense News International*, December 14, 2015, 15.

44. Efjestad, "Norway and the North Atlantic," 66–68.

45. NATO Heads of State and Government, *Warsaw Summit Communiqué* (Brussels: NATO, 2016), para. 23.

46. See the recent book chapter by the policy director at the Norwegian Ministry of Defence, Efjestad, "Norway and the North Atlantic," 66–74.

47. Envoy Christian Günther, quoted in Wilhelm Carlgren, *Mellan Hitler och Stalin: Förslag och försök till försvars- och utrikespolitisk samverkan mellan Sverige och Finland under krigsåren* [Between Hitler and Stalin: Proposals for military and foreign policy cooperation between Sweden and Finland during the war) (Stockholm: Militärhistoriska förlaget, 1981), 12.

48. Thorvald Stoltenberg, "Introduction," in *One for All, All for One: New Nordic Defence Policy?*, ed. Michael Funch and Jesper Schou-Knuden (Copenhagen: Nordic Council of Ministers, 2009), 14.

PART III

NATO's Nordic Partners

10

The Strategic Role of Gotland

JOHAN RAEDER

In 2016, some 160 years after the Crimean War, conflict was again brewing between Turkey and its allies on the one hand and Russia on the other over differences in the Middle East, and Crimea was again an object of conflict between Russia and the West. In the 1850s, the conflict in Crimea soon led to military operations between the belligerents also in the Baltic Sea theater. Today Russia's military buildup, its disregard of the established international order and international law, and its behavior toward its Baltic neighbors are again sources of concern within the West. The growing military power of Russia has led to an interest of the Western powers to increase their presence in the Baltic Sea region. As was the case 160 years ago, Sweden shares this interest.

The lessons that we draw from earlier conflicts and of history in general may vary, but the Crimean War of the nineteenth century shows that the security of the Baltic Sea region is dependent on relations between the great powers of Europe and their alliances and that smaller countries in the region have to adapt to this reality. It also shows that any discussion of the role of Gotland in a conflict needs to take the wider geographical and political circumstances into consideration. What, then, is the role of Gotland in Baltic Sea security today?

The Political Role of Gotland's Defense

Gotland's significance for hard security in the Baltic Sea region has varied over time, reflecting the specific circumstances of different periods. The value ascribed to Gotland in a military conflict in the Baltic Sea region differs, depending on whom you are and what you want to achieve. It might be merely political, or it might be of a more practical nature. It might also, of course, be both.

For Sweden, its political value is self-evident. Sweden has clearly stated that it intends to defend all of its territory and would not recognize any claims by any other party to any of it. Should Gotland be attacked, Sweden would make a determined effort to defend it by forces deployed on Gotland and by forces deployed elsewhere.[1] For Russia, there might also be a political value in attacking or occupying Gotland, since it could show that the Swedish government and its armed forces are unable to protect its citizens and territory. During the Cold War, a situation where the Warsaw Pact had control of Swedish territory and could use it in support for offensive operations against its main opponent would have been unacceptable to NATO. As a consequence, it was assumed that if Sweden were attacked by the Soviet Union, the Western Alliance would give Sweden its support. The military capabilities of NATO and of the United States, including its strategic nuclear capabilities, were therefore part of the general deterrent against the Soviet Union and the Warsaw Pact. Sweden was, although not a member of the Alliance, under the nuclear umbrella of the United States.[2]

Sweden's aim was thus to convince the Soviet Union that, if it attacked Sweden without crossing the nuclear threshold, it would have to engage in a costly and time-consuming effort to degrade the Swedish air force and navy. This would give the Swedish land forces time to mobilize and to further prevent the Soviet Union from focusing on its main operational goals. In the case of a coastal invasion, the defense of potential entry points of the eastern part of central and southern Sweden, including Gotland, was of priority.

The defense of Gotland was thus conceived as part of an overarching strategy of a defense in depth.[3] Sweden maintained a military force on Gotland that would contribute to inflicting unacceptable losses on the Soviet Union should it try to undertake a coastal invasion of mainland Sweden or take possession of the island itself but not large enough to severely drain resources from other objectives of higher priority. With air- and sea-surveillance radars and coastal artillery based on Gotland, the island served as a barrier, providing early warning and limiting the prospects for a Soviet landing on the Swedish coast. A strong Swedish military presence was part of the effort to deter the Soviet Union from attempting to attack mainland Sweden.[4]

The Post–Cold War Period, 1991–2008

The collapse of the Soviet Union along with its ideological base and military power resulted in a profoundly different security political situation in the Baltic Sea region. The changes in military geography were of immense benefit to Sweden. Soviet bases in the Baltic states were evacuated, and Estonia, Latvia, and Lithuania slowly built their own defense forces.

For Russia, its nuclear deterrent, its bases on the Kola Peninsula, and the air defense of western Russia continued to be of fundamental importance, and it still maintained forces in the Baltic states. Russia's military-strategic objectives in the region did not, however, include the ability to support a large-scale Soviet-style offensive in Central Europe but were more centered on limiting NATO's ability to conduct offensive operations against Russia or the northern part of the Baltic Sea. A Russian attack on Sweden would be more likely to have the objective to deny an opponent the possibility of using Swedish territory in support of an attack on Russia. A coastal invasion of southern Sweden was no longer a realistic threat.

The Swedish government still included a long-term scenario in its defense planning with a Russia that would again be able to pursue its central interests in the region from a position of military strength. The Swedish defense decision in 1992 therefore initiated a modernization of the armed forces; while the size of the armed forces was reduced, their remaining units would become more capable. For Gotland the results were that the forces there would be modernized and include training units for one mechanized brigade, one air-defense battalion, and one amphibious company, as well as the forward deployment of a detachment of multirole fighters to Visby.

A Russian move on the Baltic states would constitute a clear warning signal. It would take time for Russia, with its deteriorating military capability, to be able to conduct offensive operations out of that territory. The integrity of the Baltic states, which was central to the maintaining of the international security order in and of itself, was therefore also a strategic Swedish interest with direct influence on the defense of Sweden.[5]

Sweden took part in the international effort to support the Baltic states in building their defense capabilities, which apart from establishing national defense forces also increased their prospects to become members of NATO, a goal supported by nonaligned Sweden. Sweden became one of the largest donors of defense matériel, donating the equipment for one full brigade and one air-defense company each to Estonia, Latvia, and Lithuania. This was accompanied by support structures such as training facilities, storage, workshops, and a training program for the armed forces, as well as for the respective ministries.[6]

The effect Gotland had had as a barrier to a Soviet invasion during the Cold War for a defense of Sweden in depth was gradually complemented by a similar effect in the Baltic states. The support to the Baltic states thus had the added benefit of serving the same underlying purpose as maintaining a military presence on Gotland. Militarily capable forces in Estonia, Latvia, and Lithuania would contribute to the strategic depth of the defense of Northern and Western Europe.[7]

By the mid-1990s, the political and military prerequisites for a large-scale conflict in Europe no longer existed. Russian offensive military capabilities in the region were very limited. NATO's military capabilities in the region had also been scaled down significantly, but Russia was in a state of weakness and was not for the foreseeable future considered to be able to constitute a threat against Europe as a whole in the way that the Soviet Union had during the Cold War. As a consequence, Sweden reduced its defense forces and its defense spending. Even so, Gotland's strategic location and importance motivated a continued presence of air- and coastal-defense capabilities with accompanying training facilities. A defense in depth was still the guiding principle for the defense of Sweden, and Gotland's role in that remained.

By the end of the century, a military invasion of Sweden was not considered to be possible during the next decade, provided that Sweden maintained a basic military capability. The development of the Swedish military capabilities was instead focused on developing interoperability with other states in order to increase Sweden's ability to contribute to international peace-support operations. This led to a significant development of Sweden's cooperation with NATO within the framework of the Partnership for Peace. Small-scale attacks on Sweden were still not ruled out but were seen as possible results of limited military crises in the region. Such attacks could include the use of long-range weapons such as cruise and ballistic missiles, as well as limited naval and air forces. Russia's objective in such a scenario would be to punish or intimidate Sweden. The basic defense capability Sweden deemed necessary to handle such situations included a continued, although reduced, military presence on Gotland.[8]

In the beginning of the new century, a military invasion of Sweden seemed even more remote. Armed conflict and operational aspects coupled to it were no longer the basis for the development of the Swedish defense forces. All activities directly aimed at that task ceased. Sweden's armed forces would now be organized as a small, deployable, and technically advanced force, ready to conduct operations as part of international peace-support operations. The conceptual basis for the armed forces had a strong emphasis on intelligence and situational awareness. It was believed that this would reduce the necessity for large forces since information superiority and precision engagement would lead to the early detection of an enemy's preparations. This would provide Sweden with the opportunity to quickly counter such moves, threaten to attack, or, if needed and with minimal use of force and minimal risk for casualties, attack enemy targets preemptively, thus preventing attacks on Sweden. This concept went under the name of the Revolution in Military Affairs (RMA).[9]

The RMA fit well into the thinking of proponents for a limited Swedish defense force, with further cuts in defense spending in sight. It also corroborated the popular idea that future military conflicts were to be more clinical, with a minimal number of casualties. In retrospect, the idea that limited strikes or even threats of such strikes on selected enemy targets would stop Russia from preparing for an attack seems to have been an overestimation of the investments Sweden was willing to make in developing such capabilities and of the extent of losses a militarily rearmed and aggressive Russia would be ready to accept. Nor was it accompanied by a political discussion on the extent to which Sweden would be prepared to engage in preemptive military strikes. As the concept was presented, it did not take the potential threat of nuclear weapons against a small, concentrated, although modern force fully into account. It also did not clearly explain how a small, militarily nonaligned, conventionally armed state such as Sweden could back up its warnings with any credibility similar to that of a superpower such as the United States.

In September 2004, the Swedish government assessed that a direct military attack on Sweden was unlikely to happen for at least the next ten years, even though smaller incidents could not be ruled out. Estonia, Latvia, and Lithuania had become members of NATO and of the European Union (EU), with their security guaranteed by the only remaining superpower. Russia's relationship with NATO was considered to be good, and Russia participated in various cooperative arrangements in the Baltic Sea region. The EU had decided on the Treaty of Nice, and Sweden's view was that its EU membership increased security and created solidarity between the member states. Sweden did not expect to be alone in handling a crisis in its region. Sweden's security situation had thus improved significantly.

Sweden decided on very substantial reductions in the number of military units. The armed forces were now tasked with maintaining a capability of conducting two battalion-sized operations simultaneously within the conceptual framework of the RMA. The assumption was that this would give Sweden enough time to rebuild its military capability if a threat reemerged. The military presence on Gotland was reduced to a temporary detachment of fighter aircraft from southern Sweden. Maintaining a basic Swedish defense capability in order to be able to meet a future emerging Russian threat was no longer a basis for Swedish defense planning. The threat of an invasion of Sweden was considered to be gone and more limited attacks to be highly unlikely.[10] The role of Gotland for the security of the Baltic Sea region had become a question of little relevance.

Toward a New Cold War, 2008–16

The Swedish decision on defense in 2009 was taken against the background of the Russian invasion of Georgia the previous year. Russia's preparedness to use military violence to resolve political conflicts had increased, although the membership of the Baltic states and of Poland in the EU and NATO rendered any such development in the Baltic Sea region unlikely. The Russian rhetoric, focusing on its right to defend Russian minorities wherever they were, showed, however, that military crises and incidents in the Baltic Sea region could not be ruled out. Russia's military capabilities were slowly developing, but it still had a limited ability to conduct operations outside of its own territory.

As a consequence, Sweden shifted the focus of its defense efforts back toward the defense of Sweden. The territorial defense of Sweden did, however, not mean going back to a stance of military nonalignment aiming at armed neutrality in potential conflicts in the region. It was also not conceivable that a military conflict in the Baltic Sea region would affect only one country. Article 42.7 of the Lisbon Treaty, signed in December 2007, clearly stated that EU member states have an obligation to support each other, and Sweden presented a solidarity declaration stating that it would not remain passive if an EU member or a Nordic country suffered an attack. Challenges to Swedish security would be met in cooperation with other countries and organizations at an early stage. The war in Georgia had shown that future conflicts could develop rapidly and that the existing Swedish armed forces, based on mobilization, were not flexible enough. Conscription as a basis for recruitment was laid dormant, and instead a new force structure, based on standing units, was set up. Main battle tanks for a tank company were prepositioned on Gotland in order to ensure early access to heavy matériel in the remote case that Gotland would have to be defended, but without any basing of units there.[11]

The drawdown of the Swedish armed forces had in part been based on the conclusion that a future threat in all likelihood would be different than the threat of the late 1980s and that there would be enough time to increase Swedish defense efforts should the Russian military again develop the capability to pose a threat against Sweden. The 2009 defense agreement continued to focus on creating a modern defense force, but there was no increase in the resources allocated to defense. Shortfalls remained, for instance, in precision strike capabilities needed to engage a modern, capable adversary (and the backbone of the earlier guiding RMA concept), as well as in more basic matériel. The numerical strength of the armed forces continued to be very limited.

By 2015, Sweden's ability to defend itself was at the center of the country's defense policy. The security situation in the Baltic Sea region had deteriorated further as a consequence of the illegal Russian aggression in Ukraine, the most severe challenge to the existing world order for the last twenty-five years. Russia had shown its capability to, without warning, rapidly mobilize forces to conduct complex operations in its vicinity. This capability was expected to increase further as new weapon systems would be fielded as a result of the armaments program and increased exercise activities. The capability to conduct operations far from its borders was also expected to increase over time. The military expenditures continued to be prioritized in the Russian economy, and the Russian armed forces were behaving increasingly aggressive in and around the Baltic Sea. The Russian military capability in the Baltic Sea region had increased significantly since 2008, and the expansion of Russian ports had increased the importance of its trade routes.

In a defense bill in April 2015, the Swedish government concluded that air and sea lines of communication in the Baltic Sea were of strategic importance for

Northern Europe and for the ability to provide and receive military support in a time of conflict.[12] Advanced air-defense systems, including ground-based air defense and fighter aircraft, were important for conducting military operations in the Baltic Sea. Gotland was considered to be of strategic importance in this context. Control of Gotland and basing of antiair and antisurface capabilities on the island were expected to increase the ability to control activities on and over the Baltic Sea and would thus be important for supporting the Baltic states in a conflict with Russia. As during the Cold War, it was assumed that armed aggression against Sweden would be part of a larger conflict and that Russia would only be able to use parts of its resources in such an operation. Russian control of parts of Swedish territory would in such a conflict not be an end in itself but a means to support other objectives. This could be achieved through the basing of military capabilities on Swedish territory or through applying political pressure in an effort to influence Swedish decision making.

The defense budget was increased, thus breaking the trend that had started in the early 1990s. A military presence on Gotland was considered a Swedish strategic interest and would have a stabilizing effect on the security situation in the region. A standing force in the form of a mechanized battle group, consisting of a mechanized company and a tank company, was to be based on the island from 2018. The command-and-control capability and the home guard on Gotland were to be increased, as were the training and exercise activities on the island.

Gotland's Role Today . . .

Further developments in Russia's military capabilities are obvious through the military intervention in Syria. Its increased ability to project power and sustain an operation far from its own territory also changes the calculus for security in the Baltic Sea region and for the defense of Sweden. Together with the deteriorating Russian relations with the West, this means that Russian security interests in the Baltic Sea region are more extensive than before. They include maintaining strategic depth in the defense of the nuclear assets on the Kola Peninsula, defending sea lines of communications for Russian trade,[13] and protecting land, sea, and air access to the Kaliningrad enclave, as well as maintaining a strategic depth for the air defenses of western Russia.

New Russian weapon systems such as the S-400 Triumf air-defense system, the Iskander ballistic missile, the Kalibr cruise missile, and the Oniks antiship missile, together with the development of a new generation of fighter and attack aircraft and modern command-and-control systems, can be seen to constitute parts of a Russian "reconnaissance-strike complex," similar to concepts of the US "second offset strategy." The fielding of these systems has significantly increased Russia's ability to restrict the freedom of movement of an opponent in the vicinity of Russian territory. It has also given Russia an increased ability to attack targets on

Gotland directly from Russian territory. This developing antiaccess/area-denial (A2/AD) capability changes the balance of power in the region. A continued development would further increase Russia's ability to attack targets on and over Gotland without having to deploy ground forces on the island. Russia's interest in attacking Gotland preemptively might thus decrease, and the use of Gotland and its airspace for support to forces defending the Baltic states would become more difficult.

A NATO operation to deploy reinforcements to the Baltic states would be dependent on open sea and air lines of communication. In a time of crisis, Russia might have an interest in decreasing NATO's ability to do so or to decrease its capability to conduct operations in and over the Baltic Sea. Within the A2/AD "bubble"—the area within which the Russian potential to deny NATO the ability to operate is high—NATO units would run an increased risk of being attacked should Russia choose to enter into an open armed conflict with NATO. As long as Russia chooses not to do so, the consequences of NATO's ability to reinforce the Baltic states would be limited to the constraints NATO puts on itself. In case NATO considers such risks to be unacceptable, alternative routes with a lower level of risk might be sought. Such routes could involve the use of Swedish airspace and territorial waters, including over and around Gotland. Maintaining control of this space would be central to Sweden's ability to provide support to this kind of an operation. Russia's interest in denying any opponent such control is equally clear.

Sweden's decision to enter into a host-nation support agreement with NATO, combined with the decision to increase its military presence and exercise activities on Gotland, facilitates a closer cooperation in addressing crises and challenges in connection with supporting the Baltic states.[14] By building on the high level of interoperability that has developed over more than two decades and by using existing training and exercise activities, a common ability to maintain control of the air and sea around Gotland can be achieved. Such exercises could include elements such as deployment to the island of advanced air-defense systems and antiship missiles, as well as deploying forces to the Baltic states through its airspace. This would increase Sweden's ability to provide and receive support in connection with operations in the Baltic Sea region. The Swedish exercise Aurora-17 contained such elements.

Russian exercises such as the Zapad series are apparently conducted to prepare for a war with NATO. In such a conflict, Russia's aim would seem to be to push forward the defense perimeter of western and northwestern Russia, thus denying NATO the use of the Baltic states and the Scandinavian Peninsula as bases for offensive operations, while projecting Russian military power into the North Atlantic and threatening NATO naval assets there.[15] In such a scenario, the Russian interest with regard to Gotland would simply be to deny anyone the ability to interfere with these objectives. There would be no immediate reason in that stage of a conflict to try to defeat any ground forces stationed there, as long as they lack the ability to negatively influence Russian military operations.

Establishing a Russian military presence on Gotland in order to enlarge the A2/AD bubble or to deny an adversary the ability to project power out of Gotland could also fit into a strategy coupled to a larger conflict. In doing so in an opening phase, Russia would cross the threshold to open military conflict and would have to balance this diversion of resources against other operations that might be pursued elsewhere. If Russia, after a military conflict with Sweden, were in control of Gotland without having entered into an armed conflict with NATO, that would greatly enhance Russia's military strategic position in the Baltic Sea region. The consequences for NATO's ability in a subsequent conflict to reinforce the Baltic states would be significant.[16]

In a military conflict with Russia, Gotland still would provide Sweden with strategic depth for the defense of the Swedish mainland. Swedish forces on Gotland would have to include capable ground forces to protect, together with the Swedish air force, a military presence that could have an impact on such a Russian operation. For the immediate future, the more advanced offensive capabilities needed to influence Russian operations would, however, have to be provided by a third party. Swedish security policy is open to such a possibility, but there are no guarantees that such support would be provided. Given that the range of Russian weapon systems increasingly makes targets on Gotland vulnerable to attack, an international deployment to Gotland might not be the best option for third parties to project power into the Baltic Sea region, provided they have a sufficient capability to operate from outside of an established Russian A2/AD bubble. Should this bubble be degraded, it would change both the risks involved in basing assets on Gotland and the need to deploy them there in the first place.

...and Tomorrow

The current situation, with heightened Russian aggressiveness and emphasis on military power, is expected to remain for the foreseeable future.[17] As a consequence, Russia's interest in denying its main adversary the ability to deploy advanced capabilities to Gotland in a time of crisis or conflict is likely to remain. Gotland's importance for Swedish deterrence, given its potential role in a defense in depth of Sweden, is also still relevant. The Swedish acquisition of advanced medium-range ground-based air-defense systems would, should such assets be deployed on Gotland, increase the deterrence against an attack on Sweden. It would also increase Sweden's ability to control the airspace around the island. A deployment of antiship missiles would have a similar effect.

The NATO summit in Wales in September 2014 resulted in decisions to develop NATO's rapid reaction capabilities and the US decision in June 2014 to increase its efforts to reassure and provide military support to its Eastern European Allies have been followed by commitments from NATO's European members at the summit meeting in Warsaw in July 2016. Should NATO's presence in the Baltic states in the form of multinational formations be substantially increased, the threshold for conflict would be raised. At the same time, the need for rapid reinforcements to the Baltic states would decrease, NATO's possible need for Gotland's airspace would be reduced, and the time available to NATO to degrade Russian A2/AD capabilities in the region would increase.

The role of Gotland would also be affected. Sweden would gain from an increased deterrence through stronger defenses in the Baltic states. In a time of conflict, Russia's interest in controlling the airspace over Gotland in order to cut off NATO's access to the Baltic states might remain. Russia would, however, still need to balance any operation against Gotland and Sweden with the needs it would have elsewhere.

The ongoing defense reform in the United States and the development of new methods to achieve conventional deterrence have the potential to substantively change the military balance in the Baltic Sea region. A central challenge for that reform to address is how to defeat the type of systems that constitute the A2/AD capabilities—in effect, reconnaissance-strike complexes—of advanced military powers such as China and Russia. If the strategy is successful, the conventional deterrence of NATO and the US would increase significantly, and Russia's ability to deny NATO access to, or the ability to operate within, the Baltic states and their surroundings would be severely degraded. NATO's ability to defend the Baltic states would increase accordingly, and the need for rapid reinforcements would not be as pressing. This would, in turn, affect the importance attached to Gotland.

Today Gotland's importance for deterrence, for the defense of Sweden, and for the stability of the region as a whole is again increasingly acknowledged. Gotland's military importance must, however, as was true already in the Crimean War in the 1850s, continue to be measured in a wider context, where the need to balance the power of Russia, the different interests of the powers around the Baltic Sea and beyond, and the continued developments in military technology and capabilities are all taken into account.

Notes

1. Swedish Government's Bill on Defense, "Försvarspolitisk inriktning, Sveriges försvar 2016–2020" [Defense political directive, Sweden's defense 2016–2012), prop. 2014/15:109 (2015), 55, www.riksdagen.se.

2. Official Report of the Swedish Government, "Om kriget kommit. Förberedelser för mottagande av militärt bistånd 1949–1969" [If war had come. Preparations for receiving military support 1949–1969), SOU 1994:11 (1994), 103–15.

3. Swedish Government's Bill on Defense, "Kungl. Maj:ts prop. angående försvarets fortsatta inriktning m.m." [Concerning the continued direction of the defense, etc.] prop. 1972:75 (1972), 67, www.riksdagen.se; and Swedish Government's Bill on Defense, "Om säkerhets- och

försvarspolitiken samt totalförsvarets fortsatta utveckling" [On the security and defense policy and the continued development of the total defense], prop. 1981/82:102 (1982), 25. www.riks dagen.se.

4. Swedish Government's Bill on Defense, "Totalförsvarets fortsatta utveckling" [The continued development of the total defense], prop. 1986/87:95 (1987), 5. www.riksdagen.se.

5. Swedish Government's Bill on Defense, "Totalförsvarets utveckling till och med bud-getåret 1996/97 samt anslag för budgetåret 1992/93" [The development of the total defense up until fiscal year 1996/97 and appropriations for fiscal year 1992/93], prop. 1991/92:102 (1992), 27. www.riksdagen.se.

6. Swedish Government's Bill on Defense, "Totalförsvar i förnyelse, etapp 2" [Total defense in renewal], prop. 1996/97:4 (1996), 90–93. www.riksdagen.se.

7. Swedish Government's Bill on Defense, "Förändrad omvärld—omdanat försvar" [A transformed world—an altered defense], prop. 1998/99:74 (1999), 14, www.riksdagen.se.

8. Swedish Government's Bill on Defense, "Det nya försvaret" [The new defense], prop.1999/2000:30 (1999), 75, www.riksdagen.se.

9. Swedish Government's Bill on Defense, "Fortsatt förnyelse av totalförsvaret" [Contin-ued renewal of the total defense], prop. 2001/02:10 (2001), 129, www.riksdagen.se.

10. Swedish Government's Bill on Defense, "Vårt framtida försvar—försvarspolitisk inrikt-ning 2005–2007" [Our future defense—defense political directive 2005–2007], prop. 2004 /05:5 (2004), 25, www.riksdagen.se.

11. Swedish Government's Bill on Defense, "Ett användbart försvar" [A usable defense], prop. 2008/09:140 (2009), 64, www.riksdagen.se.

12. Swedish Government's Bill on Defense, "Försvarspolitisk inriktning, Sveriges försvar 2016–2020" [Defense political directive, Sweden's defense 2016–2012], prop. 2014/15:109 (2015), 8–9, www.riksdagen.se.

13. Tomas Malmlöf and Johan Tejpar, Ett skepp kommer lastat: Ryska handelsflöden via Östersjön i ett tjugoårsperspektiv [A loaded ship is arriving: Russian trade via the Baltic Sea in a twenty-year perspective], FOI-R--3586--SE (Stockholm, February 2013): 56.

14. Official Report of the Swedish Government, "Samförståndsavtal med Nato om värd-landsstöd" [Agreement with NATO on host nation support], Ds 2015:39 (2015), www .regeringen.se.

15. Johan Norberg, Training to Fight: Russia's Major Military Exercises, 2011–2014, FOI-R--4128--SE (Stockholm, December 2015): 38.

16. Bo Hugemark, ed., Friends in Need: Towards a Swedish Strategy of Solidarity with Her Neighbours (Stockholm: Swedish Royal Academy of War Sciences, 2011), 191.

17. Gudrun Persson, ed., Russian Military Capability in a Ten-Year Perspective: 2016, FOI-R--4326--SE (Stockholm, December 2016): 187–93.

11

Sweden and Finland

*Partnership in Lieu
of NATO Membership*

ANN-SOFIE DAHL

In a NATO that now encompasses twenty-nine members, with European Allies from every corner of the continent, two countries are conspicuously missing. In spite of more than twenty years of ever-closer military and political cooperation as partners with NATO and in spite of a dramatically deteriorated situation in the Baltic Sea region in the course of the last few years, Sweden and Finland seem intent on staying just that: partners only, for the foreseeable future.

Observers generally agree that a change of security doctrine by the two non-aligned Nordics would significantly enhance the level of security in the region and greatly facilitate the deterrence measures currently undertaken by NATO in support of its frontline Allies on the eastern flank. In addition, popular support for NATO membership has gone up in the two countries, with even a majority in favor in Sweden, ever since the Russian-instigated conflict in Ukraine erupted in early 2014 and even before, with Russian aggression already targeting the two Nordic nonaligned countries from 2013 on.

However, rather than take what might seem as the next logical step for two of NATO's top partners and contributors and abandon their partnership policies in favor of membership in the Alliance, Sweden and Finland have both embarked on parallel tracks with policies that actually *circumvent* NATO membership. What is the logic behind this policy, and what does the future look like for the two non-aligned Nordic countries?

Russian Aggression in the Baltic Sea Region

The Russian intervention in Ukraine and the illegal annexation of Crimea further accelerated the process of finding a new modus operandi with the NATO partners in the Baltic Sea region. Tension in the Baltic Sea had noticeably risen already in the years prior to February 2014, with Russian military aggression at sea and in the air turning into a regular feature for the countries in the region, while leaving the already vulnerable Baltic states in an ever more exposed position. Security in the Baltic Sea had entered into "a new normal," as famously declared by the defense ministers of the region in a joint op-ed.[1]

For the defense of NATO's Allies in the region, in particular the Baltic states and Poland, the two Nordic partners—which occupy a substantial part of the Baltic Sea coastline—are key actors. History has indeed shown that "most military operations in the Baltic region require access to what is today Swedish and Finnish air, sea, and land."[2] The Danish island of Bornholm, the Finnish Åland Islands, and the Swedish island of Gotland—the latter being in the midst of the Baltic Sea a short distance from Kaliningrad and until recently without any military presence (and still with primarily a symbolic one)—are strategic gems for any power aiming for control of the sea. As concluded by Edward Lucas in his report on Baltic security, "if carried out successfully, control of those territories would make it all but impossible for NATO allies to reinforce the Baltic States."[3] With the heavy Russian buildup of nuclear and other capabilities, Stockholm, Helsinki, and Copenhagen are now all conceivably within reach from Kaliningrad, as are, of course, the capitals of the vulnerable Baltic states.

Already prior to events in Ukraine in early 2014, the dramatic events on Good Friday on March 29, 2013, were a major wake-up call to the region in general and the Swedes in particular. That night, four Russian strategic Tu-22 bombers escorted by two Su-27 fighter jets simulated nuclear-bombing attacks on targets in "southern Sweden"—assumed to be a military base in the province of Småland—and "outside Stockholm," which has been interpreted by experts as the headquarters of Försvarets Radioanstalt, the National Defense Radio Establishment, located only a short distance from the home of the Swedish royal family.[4] Apart from causing a major scare, it was also a highly embarrassing event for the Swedish military, since all of its pilots were off duty to celebrate Easter with their families. Danish F-16s instead scrambled from the Šiauliai base in Lithuania, where they were stationed as part of NATO's Baltic Sea air-policing mission.

Similar attacks took place that fall when Russian bombers targeted the Swedish island of Öland and in the early summer of 2014 with a simulated attack on the Danish island of Bornholm, in the midst of a political gathering with thousands of politicians and others assembled. In August the same year, Finnish airspace was breached three times in a single week by Russian aircraft and twice in one day in October 2016 by Russian jets escorting a transfer of military matériel and missiles to Kaliningrad. In the summer of 2017, a Russian Su-27 flew dangerously close to a Swedish military plane over international waters outside of Kaliningrad, only hours after a similar incident with an American plane.[5] Russia has also repeatedly warned Sweden that membership in NATO would be considered a "threat" that Moscow would "need to eliminate" (similar warnings having been issued warning Denmark not to join NATO's missile system).[6]

These are only a handful of the many incidents that have occurred in a short period of time in the Baltic Sea region, including innumerable incidents of cyber-attacks emanating from Russian sources. In the course of only a few years, the Baltic Sea moved from a generally peaceful sea dominated by trade and commerce to one characterized by high-tension, large-scale exercises and Russian military provocations, of which many were directed at nonaligned Sweden and Finland. It is clear that from Moscow's perspective the two nonaligned countries, without the protection of any security guarantees, are seen as something of the region's weakest link.

Special Special Partners

Since it is generally recognized that Sweden and Finland are not in a position to defend themselves on their own against outside aggression, and NATO would have difficulty protecting its Baltic Allies without the full cooperation of the two Nordic partners, other forms and venues of cooperation thus have to be turned to in lieu of a forthcoming change of doctrine. The security policies of both Sweden and Finland could be described as resting on several legs—increasingly so ever since the dramatic events in Ukraine in February and March 2014.

The first leg consists of Swedish and Finnish participation in the Enhanced Opportunities Partnership program (EOP), embarked on by NATO as of the Wales Summit in September 2014 with a select group of partner countries. The EOP is an extension and continuation of the previous partnership models and departs from two basic conclusions. One is the need to further deepen military cooperation and fine-tune interoperability, create improved mechanisms for political consultations, and facilitate participation in NATO exercises and training—and much more— with a number of NATO's outstanding partners in regions of major strategic significance for the Alliance.

The five countries included in the program have been NATO's main operational partners, with an extensive record of contributions over the last decade and more. The focus on regional partners also reflects the main strategic hot spots of today's world. These range from the Asian-Pacific region, where Australia is NATO's prime partner, to Jordan—in the Middle Eastern turmoil next door to Syria—to Georgia, one of two countries with an individualized NATO commission[7]—and on to the two partner countries in the strategically sensitive Baltic Sea, Sweden and Finland.

In addition, the group of five reflects the different categories of partnership that NATO has organized over the past two decades.[8] Though profoundly different in many ways and confronted with a wide range of security concerns, all five EOP countries represent strategically important regions where NATO needs to be able to rely on local partners that can be trusted to make solid contributions to enhancing security. To put it simply, these are partners that NATO needs to handle regional security—and vice versa.

The EOP also departs from a sober realization on both sides that these are partners that for various reasons would or could not join the Alliance as full members in the foreseeable future. As for the two Nordic EOP partners, it is reported that Sweden and Finland would be warmly welcomed into the group of Allies the minute they decide to take this step, for which they are militarily, but not yet politically, ready. The fact that the EOP countries are presently not on the path toward applying for membership, and therefore not likely to be included in NATO's collective-defense measures in the foreseeable future, has necessitated a process of creative thinking in order to find other ways to further involve these partners in the joint efforts to maximize security in the various regions. The result—the EOP—is a pragmatic and flexible model based on individual, tailor-made arrangements with each of the five partners, often jokingly referred to as NATO's "gold card holders."

That nickname is only one of many that have been used to describe the Nordic partners over the years, as they have consistently been found in the vanguard in the partner community. Other nicknames over the years include "partner number one"—an honorary title that has alternated between Sweden and Finland, depending on which was found at the operational forefront at a specific time— and "special special partners." In addition, Sweden was also jokingly referred to at NATO headquarters in Brussels as the organization's "seventeenth member" because of its far-reaching cooperation with a number of Allies during the Cold War, when Sweden was officially neutral and the Alliance still consisted of only sixteen members.[9]

Both Sweden and Finland have played exceptionally active and constructive roles throughout the existence of NATO's partnership programs. Sweden and Finland were actually the very first two countries to sign up for the first partnership model introduced by NATO, the Partnership for Peace (PfP), in the summer of 1994. In the two decades since the invention of NATO partnership, they have taken advantage of every opportunity granted them to cooperate with NATO, through missions at headquarters in Brussels and in Mons and in operations and missions worldwide, from the Stabilization Force in Bosnia and Herzegovina (SFOR) through the International Security Assistance Force (ISAF) in Afghanistan, including the Operation Unified Protector in Libya in the Swedish case.

Contrary to the majority of the countries in the rapidly expanding group of partners in the mid-1990s, the two Nordics, however, never saw the PfP as a first step toward membership in NATO. Rather, partnership was looked upon in mainly practical terms, as a means to politically and militarily strengthen transatlantic ties and for developing and improving military interoperability with NATO after the many years of (official) neutrality between the two blocs.[10] With several rounds of enlargement—and especially after the 2004 "Big Bang" when seven countries transferred from partner status to full membership, including the three Baltic states in the Nordic "near abroad"—Sweden and Finland found themselves in the company of an extremely heterogeneous group of partners, consisting of the European nonaligned countries plus basically the faraway partners in "the stans" (among them Tajikistan, Uzbekistan, and Turkmenistan).

At that point, it was obvious that the PfP had become both obsolete and impractical. The need for a new model became even more urgent with the termination of ISAF, which had allowed the contributing partners to enter into a close and confidential relationship based on practical, day-to-day cooperation with NATO, with little distinction on the Afghanistan ground between full Ally and partner.[11] A new format was clearly needed to maintain the high level of close cooperation with those partners that had made significant contributions to ISAF and elsewhere, thus the launch of the EOP.

Again, the Nordic partners were as previously mentioned actively involved already from the start—and even before. It was actually Sweden that came up with the original idea of comparing the EOP to a gold card arrangement, whereby participants are rewarded for their contributions and given special privileges, but that involves obligations as well as rights and may be taken away from the "card holders" should they fail to deliver. The concept was coordinated and fine-tuned with Finland and presented as a joint idea to NATO by the two Nordics, which by then were often referred to at NATO headquarters as the Alliance's "special special partners."

In Lieu of Membership

The EOP was thus a much-needed solution to a number of quite unexpected problems that occurred in the last few years, not least as a result of the dramatically deteriorated situation in the Baltic Sea region. However, partnership cooperation within the EOP is, as mentioned, only one of a number of instruments utilized by the two nonaligned countries to effectively respond to an increasingly assertive and aggressive Russia. Another, obvious step was to strengthen their national defense posture, which in the Swedish case was in rather desperate shape after many years and several rounds of severe cuts in the military by governments across the ideological spectrum.[12] In particular, the strategically significant—to the entire region—island of Gotland was in a highly vulnerable position without any military presence. In September 2016, the Swedish supreme commander, Micael Bydén, announced that the 150 mechanized-infantry troops that were on the island for the purpose of training would remain as a permanent military presence. For Finland, though some increases had been announced, the need was much less urgent than in Swe-den. As Karoliina Honkanen says, Finland "has always taken good care of its own defense capability and will continue to do so."[13]

Parallel with the EOP and the increases in military spending, both countries have embarked on another track, or leg, of signing bilateral defense agreements with a number of neighbors and NATO Allies. First and foremost of these—and always presented in such terms in official statements by both governments—is the bilateral Swedish-Finnish defense agreement that was unveiled by the defense min-isters of the two countries in February 2015 after the presentation at the end of January of a joint report by the armed forces of the two countries that explored the possibilities for deepening the bilateral defense cooperation.[14] Sweden and Finland have for many years engaged in close military cooperation, but what made this agreement special—even extraordinary—was the stated ambition that the cooper-ative venture could now also extend "beyond peacetime." As a completely new relationship between Sweden and Finland, the agreement departs from "the assumption that challenges in the region will be addressed together" and "include[s] combined operations to handle contingencies up to and including war."[15]

Apart from this bilateral agreement and the cooperation that takes place within the framework of the EOP, the two countries also work closely together in the Nordic Defence Cooperation (mostly referred to as NORDEFCO), which to a large extent is a Swedish and Finnish project, with participation by one or both countries in most if not all its different programs.[16] Furthermore, a number of additional defense agreements have been signed in the last few years. Sweden has entered into such formal military cooperation on a bilateral basis with, apart from Finland, regional NATO Allies Denmark and Poland, as well as with the United Kingdom and—of particular significance—the United States. This is in many ways reminiscent of the above-mentioned military cooperation that was pursued by Sweden throughout the Cold War with its Nordic NATO Allies, the UK, and the US—only nowadays it is not top secret and hidden from the Swedish people, as it was then.[17] Both Sweden and Finland have now also signed host-nation support agreements with NATO, which would enable them to give and receive military support in times of crisis and to host and support NATO exercises and operations in the Baltic Sea region. In addition to the above-mentioned countries, Sweden and Finland also both signed bilateral defense agreements with Germany in the sum-mer of 2017.[18] In addition, as of summer 2017, Sweden and Finland also actively participate in the Joint Expeditionary Force led by the United Kingdom.

Contrary to what could be expected, and to what has been argued, these various schemes of bilateral cooperation should not be seen as a first step toward NATO membership. Quite the opposite. Rather than moving the security doctrines of the two countries closer toward a formal membership in NATO, the defense agree-ments are in fact elaborate ways to *avoid* such a step—a sophisticated way of actu-ally circumventing NATO membership.

Members or Not Members

The odds for a Swedish and Finnish application for membership in NATO anytime soon are as a matter of fact quite slim, in spite of some overly optimistic conclusions to the contrary. Speculations on whether a Swedish and Finnish membership in NATO has been on the verge of happening have popped up at irregular intervals ever since they first joined the PfP in the mid-1990s. Over the past two decades and perhaps more, the two Nordics have alternated in the role as the country perceived to be slightly ahead of the other in the national debate and most likely to be the first to join NATO. The two neighbors are carefully studying each other and cautiously coordinating their security policies and defense moves to avoid a repeat performance of the unpleasant surprise that hit Finland in the 1990s when Sweden overnight decided to change its stance on the EU and file a membership application, without first having informed Helsinki.

When Sweden in a short span of time participated both in the Libyan operation, Operation Unified Protector (OUP)—sending its air force abroad for the first time since the 1960s—and made an impressive performance in NATO's 2011 Crisis Management Exercise (CMX), there were intense speculations about the motives behind the Swedish activities. The Swedish delegation surprised everybody involved in the CMX by offering direct support to NATO, primarily maritime assets with ships and air capabilities, with the intention that these be placed under NATO command and control—indeed an exceptional step for a partner country in an exercise with the aim of practicing an Article 5 situation with the Allies.[19] This move led many in NATO headquarters to—mistakenly—conclude that a Swedish application for NATO membership was in the making. Similarly, Swedish participation in the OUP mission was not a step toward NATO but rather seen as a golden opportunity to exercise interoperability—and, some argued, a golden chance to showcase the JAS Gripen fighter jets to an international audience.

Finland has "a NATO option" as part of its security doctrine, and membership advocates had great hopes that Sauli Niinistö, once a prominent figure in the Finnish pro-NATO camp, would help bring the country into the NATO fold as president of the republic. Once his predecessor, Tarja Halonen—who was vehemently against Finnish membership—had moved out of the presidential residence, things would start to happen, according to this (also mistaken) conclusion. Contrary to many expectations, President Niinistö has instead chosen to engage in dialogue with Russia rather than pursue the membership track.

In both countries, the pro-NATO camps have been joined in the last few years by high-ranking officials. A group of former Swedish ambassadors has been forcefully arguing the NATO membership case ever since the Russian intervention in Ukraine. Events in Ukraine and the aggressive behavior in the Baltic Sea region by Russia since 2013 resulted in a new and vital debate in Sweden and quite a sharp increase in support for membership in opinion polls. The change of government in the fall of 2014 also led a small number of activists to conclude that Swedish membership was now right around the corner and that the Social Democrats would make another political U-turn, just as they had on the EU in the early 1990s. That too has proven wrong and severely underestimated the support that still exists for the nonaligned policy. Prime Minister Stefan Löfven—who leads a government coalition with the Green Party, with roots in the pacifist movement—has consistently refused to even discuss the NATO issue, even after the publication of an official report concluding that a Swedish NATO membership would clearly benefit and enhance security in the Baltic Sea.[20] Also found in the anti-NATO camp—apart from the Social Democrats, the Green Party, and the former Communists—is the populist and anti-immigration party the Sweden Democrats, which departs from a nostalgic perspective on Swedish politics.

All four parties in the center-right opposition are now fully in favor of NATO membership but suffer from a lack of credibility after eight years in power (2006–14) when the membership issue was off the table and when, in addition, the government made historically deep cuts in the military. This was a highly unexpected move by a government lead by the Moderate Party, which has traditionally been the main promilitary party in the Swedish Parliament.[21]

While Sweden produced its first NATO study in the summer of 2016, Finland has had several over the years, the latest of which was presented in the summer of 2016. Former Finnish president Martti Ahtisaari has for quite some time been a prominent advocate for a change of doctrine and makes the point in a coauthored book that there is no need for Finland to wait for Sweden to join.[22] Whether Sweden will join first and Finland will follow along, or the reverse, has been hotly debated for years. The case could certainly be made that it would be best for all, and in particular for security in the Baltic Sea region, if both would join and simultaneously.

Enhancing Baltic Sea Security

Security could thus, most observers agree, be enhanced basically overnight in the Baltic Sea region with Swedish and Finnish membership in NATO. That these two countries, which occupy a substantial part of the territory of the region and the shoreline bordering on the sea, still remain outside of NATO as nonaligned partners is a complicating factor and adds an element of uncertainty to the joint Western efforts to meet Russian aggression. By finally joining their neighbors in the Alliance, Sweden and Finland would be in a position to make major contributions to regional security. It would allow them to significantly upgrade their ability to provide their share of reassurance to the Baltic countries by participating in the deterrence measures undertaken by NATO, as agreed on at the Warsaw Summit and previously in Wales, foremost among these the Enhanced Forward Presence and the Very High Readiness Task Force.

Also, Swedish and Finnish membership in the Alliance would instantaneously block any attempts by Russia to use their territory, or part thereof, in an A2/AD move to stop NATO from entering the sea to provide assistance to its Baltic Allies. The positive impact of Swedish and Finnish membership in NATO would consequently be substantial for the entire Nordic and Baltic region. The impact would actually extend even further than that, considering that aggressive Russian behavior in the Baltic Sea is part of a major strategy to challenge and undermine the entire Western security system.

Former president of Estonia Toomas Hendrik Ilves has, however, repeatedly emphasized that Sweden and Finland need to recognize the fact that an application for NATO membership takes time and that not all Allies would be enthusiastic about an application by the Nordic partners but instead see an enlargement of the Alliance in the Baltic Sea as provocative toward Russia—whose president, also repeatedly, has warned Sweden of the consequences of joining NATO.[23] And although the Swedish and Finnish membership in NATO would clearly benefit regional security, no such decisions should be expected in the foreseeable future in the two capitals. Instead, the governments of the two countries have, as we have seen, chosen to rely on alternative models for security, combining enhanced partnership with NATO with intensified defense cooperation on a bilateral basis with a number of key countries, foremost of these the United States (apart from the extensive Swedish-Finnish bilateral cooperation).

The wisdom of relying on such bilateral agreements has been questioned at a time when the American president may embark on a new and positive US relationship with Vladimir Putin's Russia, as has, for that matter, the wisdom of joining the Alliance under such US leadership. During the visit to Washington in the spring of 2017 by the Swedish defense minister, Peter Hultqvist, his American counterpart, James Mattis, went surprisingly far in his statements. Mattis even promised US support to Sweden in the event of a Russian attack and referred to the nonaligned country as not only a friend but an "ally."[24]

Nevertheless, it is important for Sweden and Finland to appreciate that partnership can take a country only so far and that a very clear line excludes partners from the collective defense of Article 5. By far the best way for Sweden and Finland to enhance security in the Baltic Sea region would thus be by joining NATO as proper members.

Notes

1. The op-ed was, as previously mentioned in the introduction, simultaneously published in *Dagens Nyheter*, *Aftenposten*, *Jyllands-Posten*, and *Hufvudstadsbladet* on April 10, 2015. The

Swedish title in *Dagens Nyheter* was "Vi fördjupar det nordiska försvarssamarbetet" [We are deepening Nordic defense cooperation].

2. Luke Coffey and Daniel Kochis, "The Baltic States: The United States Must Be Prepared to Fulfill Its NATO Treaty Obligations," *Backgrounder*, no. 3039, Heritage Foundation, September 29, 2015.

3. Edward Lucas, "The Coming Storm: Baltic Sea Security Report," *Center for European Policy Analysis*, June 2015, 9.

4. "Ryssland övade kärnvapenanfall mot Sverige" [Russia practiced nuclear attack on Sweden], *Dagen Nyheter*, February 2, 2016, http://www.dn.se/nyheter/sverige/ryssland-ovade-karnvapenanfall-mot-sverige/.

5. "Ryska planet tvingade svenska planet att vända" [The Russian plane forced the Swedish plane to turn around], *Dagens Nyheter*, June 27, 2017.

6. For instance, in June 2017: "Russia Vows Military Response to 'Eliminate NATO Threat' if Sweden Joins US-led Alliance," Newsweek.com, June 2, 2017, http://www.newsweek.com/vladimir-putin-vows-eliminate-nato-threat-sweden-joins-619486.

7. Three, if counting the NATO-Russia Council, which was, however, suspended after Russia's illegal intervention in Ukraine. The other one is the NATO-Ukraine Commission.

8. For an extensive presentation of the different categories and forms of NATO partnership, see Trine Lockhardt, "Introduction: Changing Partnerships in a Changing World," in *Cooperative Security: NATO's Partnership Policy in a Changing World*, ed. Trine Lockhardt (Copenhagen: DIIS, 2014).

9. Ann-Sofie Dahl, "Partner Number One or NATO Ally Twenty-Nine? Sweden and NATO Post-Libya," Research Paper 82, NATO Defense College, September 2012; and Ann-Sofie Dahl, *Svenskarna och NATO* [The Swedes and NATO] (Stockholm: Timbro, 1999). See also Magnus Petersson, "The Allied Partner: Sweden and NATO through the Realist-Idealist Lens," in *The European Neutrals and NATO: Non-alignment, Partnership, Membership?*, ed. Andrew Coffey (London: Palgrave Macmillan, 2017).

10. Please note that "neutrality" has not been a correct term to describe the official security doctrines of the two countries since 1995, when they both joined the EU and changed the vocabulary in their doctrines to "nonalignment."

11. Ann-Sofie Dahl, "Operational Partners or Allies-to-Be?," in *Trends and Threats: NATO in the 21st Century*, ed. Ann-Sofie Dahl (Copenhagen: Centre for Military Studies, 2014).

12. Claes Arvidsson presents an exposé of this in his book *Fritt fall: Nedslag i debatten om försvar och säkerhet i Sverige* [Free falling: On the debate on defense and security in Sweden] (Stockholm: Penna till papper bokförlag, 2017).

13. Karoliina Honkanen, "Finnish Views on Partnership Cooperation," in *Baltic Sea Security: How Can Allies and Partners Meet the New Challenges in the Region?*, ed. Ann-Sofie Dahl (Copenhagen: Centre for Military Studies, 2016).

14. "Final Reports on Deepened Defence Cooperation between Finland and Sweden," http://www.government.se/globalassets/government/dokument/forsvarsdepartementet/final-reports-on-deepened-defence-cooperation-between-finland-och-sweden.pdf. For an extensive analysis of the Swedish-Finnish defense cooperation, see Johan Raeder, *Enhanced Defense Cooperation: New Opportunities for US Engagement in the Baltic Sea Region* (Washington, DC: Atlantic Council, February 2016).

15. Raeder, *Enhanced Defense Cooperation*, 2.

16. For an analysis of the Nordic defense cooperation, see Ann-Sofie Dahl, "NORDEFCO and NATO: 'Smart Defence' in the North?," Research Paper 101, NATO Defense College, May 2014.

17. Mikael Holmström, *Den dolda alliansen: Sveriges hemliga NATO-förbindelser* [The hidden alliance: Sweden's secret relationship with NATO] (Stockholm: Atlantis, 2011).

18. "Svensk-tyskt avtal om försvarssamarbete" [Swedish-German agreement of defense cooperation], *Dagens Nyheter*, June 29, 2017.

19. Dahl, "Partner Number One," 7.

20. Government of Sweden, *Säkerhet i en ny tid* [Security in a new age], SOU 2016:57 (Stockholm: September 2016).

21. For a study of the foreign and security policies of the Moderate Party, see Ann-Sofie Dahl, *Du gamla, du fria: Moderat utrikespolitik från Högerparti till Alliansregering* [You old, you free: Moderate foreign policy from Högerparti to the Alliance Government] (Stockholm: Medströms, 2014).

22. Yrsa Grüne, "Ahtisaari: 'Finland behöver inte vänta på Sverige' för att gå med i NATO" [Ahtisaari: "Finland does not need to wait for Sweden to join NATO"], *Svenska Dagbladet*, October 5, 2016.

23. "NATO Membership Not Automatic for Nordic States, Officials Warn," Defense News, April 28, 2016, http://www.defensenews.com/story/defense/international/europe /2016/04/28/nato-membership-not-automatic-nordic-states-officials-warn/83649744/; and "Ryskt hot om Sverige skulle gå med i NATO" [Russian threat if Sweden were to join NATO], *Expressen*, September 10, 2015. See also "Putin: svenskt medlemskap i NATO ett hot mot Ryssland" [Putin: Swedish membership in NATO a threat to Russia], *Aftonbladet*, June 1, 2017.

24. Mikael Holmström, "USA lovar stöd vid väpnad konflikt" [US promise of support in case of an armed conflict], *Dagens Nyheter*, May 19, 2017.

12

Finland and NATO's Renewed Focus on Collective Defense

KAROLIINA HONKANEN

In just a few years, the security environment "has changed to the most complex, unpredictable, and challenging security situation Europe has seen in decades and this is unlikely to change in the near future."[1] In Warsaw, NATO confirmed its "360 degrees" approach and readiness to combat threats from any direction.

NATO's change has implications also for its partners, including Finland and Sweden, which are close and active partners and located in a strategically important region for the Alliance. NATO's change has already shaped and will continue to shape Finnish and Swedish partnership cooperation with the Alliance. Both countries have long cooperated with the Alliance in crisis-management operations and other activities. Now—for the first time during the two decades of their partnership cooperation with NATO—these countries are engaged in cooperation with an Alliance whose focus is back on the northern flank and on collective deterrence and defense.

The increased importance of Finland and Sweden to NATO was recognized at the Warsaw Summit. Its communiqué notes that the Alliance has developed mutually beneficial partnership relations with Finland and Sweden and promises to further strengthen cooperation with these countries, "including through regular political consultations, shared situational awareness, and joint exercises, in order to respond to common challenges in a timely and effective manner."[2]

As a result of NATO's renewed focus on deterrence and defense, Finland and Sweden perceive cooperation with NATO more and more from the perspective of strengthening their own defense capabilities. NATO's change has already opened up new mutually beneficial areas for cooperation, such as demanding exercises and joint assessments of Baltic Sea security. Conversely, NATO's change also poses certain restrictions or preconditions that need to be taken into account by these countries when formulating their future partnership policies. Moreover, NATO's change may affect the ongoing NATO debates in both countries.

Adaptation of Partnerships

It is useful to keep in mind how NATO's partnership cooperation started and how much it has evolved since the beginning. In the early 1990s, time was not ripe for accepting new members to the Alliance. Instead, NATO invented partnerships as a way of reaching out to the former socialist countries that were eager to join the Alliance. In addition to those countries, the Partnership for Peace mechanism also became useful for the (then) neutral countries, including Finland and Sweden, which were not seeking membership in NATO.

Partnerships soon proved their value for the Alliance's key activities. Partners became important contributors to the NATO-led crisis-management operations in the Balkans, providing not only troops but additional political legitimacy to NATO's operations. Today NATO has an extensive partnership network consisting of more than forty countries. The growing importance of partners to the Alliance was recognized in the 2010 Strategic Concept. According to it, partnerships "make a concrete and valued contribution to the success of NATO's fundamental tasks." NATO's partnership policy was reformed in the Berlin Foreign Ministerial in 2011, with its tools and programs, such as the Planning and Review Process, now becoming available in principle to all partners.[3] The Chicago Summit (2012) confirmed the importance of partnerships to NATO but did not present any specific new initiatives. The Wales Summit (2014) launched the Partnership Interoperability Initiative (PII), which consists of two elements: (1) the Interoperability Platform, which currently includes twenty-five countries, and (2) the Enhanced Opportunities Partnership (EOP), which as mentioned in the previous chapter was granted to five countries (Australia, Finland, Georgia, Jordan, and Sweden).[4]

It is noteworthy that the PII was not created as a direct consequence of the changed security environment; the need to develop partnerships had been on the Alliance's agenda long before the events in Ukraine. However, the PII—and especially the EOP—has turned out to be a functional way of working with partners also in the changed security environment. It enables NATO to tailor partnership cooperation to support the primary aim of strengthening collective defense. NATO is likely to look at partners more and more through the lenses of collective defense, while still accommodating the wishes of individual partners as long as they do not jeopardize the priority task of collective defense. This approach may take different forms, depending on where it is applied.

The biggest achievement of the EOP so far has been the establishment in 2014 of the Baltic Sea Security Assessment Process, which enables a joint assessment of the region among the Allies, Finland, and Sweden on both the political and military levels. The process benefits not only Finland and Sweden but also the Alliance, by increasing the common situational awareness and understanding of the region. According to one study, the main drivers leading to the establishment of this process include (1) the enhanced Russian military activity and aggression in the region, (2) the increasing understanding that the area must be viewed as one military strategic area, and (3) the estimation that NATO membership of Finland and Sweden did not appear likely.[5]

The Finnish Approach to Partnership Cooperation

The Finnish approach to partnership cooperation with NATO can be characterized as substance-driven and pragmatic.[6] Finland has taken full advantage of the partnership tools and programs available. The main goal has always been to maintain and develop the capabilities and interoperability of the Finnish Defence Forces, and this purpose will remain valid also in the future.[7] The Finnish foreign and security policy report of 2016 confirms the EOP as a useful instrument for Finland in maintaining and developing its NATO partnership. It states that "the continual development of military cooperation with NATO is one of the key elements through which Finland maintains and develops its national defense and the capabilities for defending its territory. Finland continues to extensively participate in NATO exercises and training activities."[8] According to the government's Defence Report of February 2017, Finland has strengthened its national defense and intensified international defense cooperation. Finland promotes the deepening of cooperation with NATO under the auspices of the EOP and the "29 (NATO) +2 (Finland and Sweden)" format.[9] Finland and Sweden share the same goals and objectives in their cooperation with NATO, to a large extent. Therefore, cooperation between the countries also within NATO has been natural and beneficial.[10]

The scope of the Finnish cooperation with NATO has been wide—ranging from operations, training and exercises, and capabilities cooperation to civil emergency planning and involvement in NATO's activities to reinforce stability and security and defense sector reform in third countries. Finland also closely cooperates with NATO's agencies and contributes personnel to NATO's command structure and force structure. In February 2017, Finland—as the first partner nation—signed a bilateral political framework arrangement on cyber defense with NATO. In addition to pragmatic cooperation, Finland considers political dialogue of utmost importance. In the Finnish view, this dialogue should take place regularly and on all levels, including the highest political one. The EOP is the priority framework for Finland's cooperation with NATO, enabling the capable and willing partners to go even deeper in the existing areas of cooperation and also to identify new opportunities for cooperation. In the Finnish view, the EOP should be mutually beneficial and thus provide added value not only to the EO partners but to the Allies as well. On the national level, the efforts have very much focused on the practical and systematic implementation of the EOP. To this end, the Finnish Defence Forces prepared a road map for the EOP cooperation just a few months after the Wales Summit. The key cooperation areas listed in the road map include participation in demanding exercises and in the enhanced NATO Response Force as well as cyber-defense cooperation. NATO's focus on demanding large-scale exercises also benefits Finland because these kinds of exercises give the biggest value for the development of national defense. At the same time, Finland has opened up some of its national exercises to NATO and NATO nations.

To put it simply, Finland's cooperation with NATO is no longer about participation in distant operations but more and more about the development of national defense. Predictability and ensured access to NATO's training activities, exercises, and other forms of cooperation are necessary for the maintenance and further development of interoperability and capabilities.

Moving from practical cooperation to the policy level, Finland adheres to the same understanding of the Baltic Sea security situation as the Allies. From the Finnish perspective, NATO's role in the Baltic Sea region is a stabilizing factor, which has been noted in the key government reports on foreign and security policy as well as on defense. It is important that there is no doubt about NATO's commitment to fulfill its Article 5 obligations, should the need arise. It is also essential that all the measures that NATO takes are defensive, proportionate, and in line with NATO's international commitments. It is important for Finland that NATO keep its partners in the region informed of its actions and engage in dialogue with them on topics of mutual interest.

Prospects for Future Cooperation

The Finnish partnership cooperation in the coming years will be shaped by a number of parameters deriving from NATO's change. First, collective defense and deterrence is the priority task of the Alliance, and everything else is secondary to that. This does not mean that NATO would forget partners and abstain from further development of partnerships. However, when it comes to prioritization of meetings, functions, or resources, Allies come first. This is a fully logical and understandable development for a collective-defense organization responding to a deteriorating security environment.

Second, NATO is likely to look at the partnership policies more from the perspective of collective defense—not so much from the angle of what it can offer to partners. In other words, partnership cooperation will need to support or even add to NATO's primary task of strengthening collective defense. This may mean different things to different partners. For example, when it comes to partners in the south, NATO's efforts are likely to focus on preventing destabilization—or, in other words, projecting stability—through the various partnership tools and programs. The activities of the Defense and Related Security Capacity Building (DCB) Initiative that support the development of the partner and third countries' own capabilities will play a key role.

In the north, Finland and Sweden are already security producers. What they need is pragmatic work to keep up their high level of interoperability and increase joint situational awareness, as well as political dialogue to discuss developments in the security environment. It is essential to understand that if a crisis occurs in the region, Finland and Sweden would be involved in one way or another. While it is clear that Allies and partners have different responsibilities and commitments, it is necessary to enhance information exchange and situational awareness and also to coordinate the respective operational efforts of NATO and the partners in the region.

Furthermore, these mechanisms for coordination should be prepared during "normal" times; if started only when the crises emerge, it will be too late. It goes without saying that NATO's Article 5 does not apply to partners. Finland would make an independent, case-by-case decision in a possible crisis situation on whether and to what extent to cooperate with NATO. However, the decision makers can have this choice only if the mechanisms for cooperation are built and put into place in normal times. In this context, it is also worth remembering that Finland is bound by the EU's Mutual Assistance Obligation (Lisbon Treaty 42.7) and takes its EU commitments in a very serious manner. Finland has amended its legislation so that provision and reception of international assistance is one of the main tasks of the Finnish Defence Forces.

Third, the Alliance's internal cohesion and solidarity will be more important than ever and the key ingredient in strengthening deterrence. NATO also needs to manage partnerships in a way that does not cause division in the Alliance and keeps all partners motivated to continued cooperation.

Finally, even though NATO has been reforming partnerships and listening to the wishes of partners, the difference between partners and members is real. It became even more evident after the events in Ukraine. The distinction between an Ally and a partner was also stated clearly by NATO secretary-general Jens Stoltenberg when he visited Sweden in November 2015.[11] It is important to communicate the Finnish and Swedish understanding of this fact both to NATO and to the domestic audiences in both countries.

Partners will never have their relationship with NATO under their own control, as was aptly pointed out in the report by the Swedish diplomat Tomas Bertelman.[12] However, by basing their policies on the realistic understanding of the above-mentioned parameters, they increase the likelihood of succeeding in their goals. Actually, these parameters have already, to a large extent, been taken into account in the Finnish and Swedish partnership policies, which have aimed at making partnerships a two-way street and have identified activities that benefit not only Finland and Sweden but also NATO.

While recognizing this, there are many pragmatic ways in which NATO, Finland, and Sweden can work together both in the Baltic Sea region and beyond. Examples of the first include sharing information and exchanging views on the strategic situation in the region, increasing Finland's and Sweden's connectivity to NATO, participating in NATO's exercises and opening up some of their own national exercises to NATO, and encouraging Russia to adhere to common tools to increase military transparency and predictability (e.g., modernization of the Vienna Document and discussions in the International Civil Aviation Organization related to Baltic Sea flight safety).

Regarding the latter, NATO's efforts beyond the Baltic Sea region, Finland and Sweden are also contributors. They support NATO's activities in the south, including participation in crisis-management operations, DCB, and other efforts to project stability beyond the Alliance borders. The European Centre of Excellence on Countering Hybrid Threats in Helsinki includes countries from both the north and the south and from both sides of the Atlantic. The center has potential to intensify EU-NATO cooperation in many ways.

It is also of importance that the countries' national activities in the changed security environment support NATO's efforts. The Finnish focus on strengthening the national defense capability and boosting resilience through the comprehensive security model contribute to regional security. Also, bilateral Finnish-Swedish cooperation and Nordic Defence Cooperation (NORDEFCO) activities all support NATO's efforts in the Baltic Sea region.[13] In sum, Finland considers itself a partner that not only benefits from NATO but also makes a meaningful contribution to the Alliance.

NATO's Change and the Finnish NATO Debate

For over a decade—since the government's Security and Defense Policy Review 2004—the official Finnish policy has included an explicit reference to keeping open the possibility for applying for membership in NATO. The current government program states that "Finland is a militarily non-allied state which is engaged in a practical partnership with NATO and it maintains the option to seek NATO membership."[14] According to the Foreign and Security Policy Report, "while carefully monitoring the developments in its security environment, Finland maintains

the option to seek NATO membership." The same lines have also been incorpo-
rated into the government's Defence Report.

The question of membership in NATO has been discussed in Finland since the
mid-1990s. The debate has popped up every now and then, either as a response to
external events or when provoked by the Finnish media or researchers. Public support for membership has been quite solid, with roughly one-fifth of the population
in favor of membership. While the majority of the Finns are still opposed to membership, the polls indicate that the number of undecideds has been increasing.[15]

With the aim of adding facts to the debate, the government has earlier (in 2004
and 2007) prepared two assessments on the impacts of possible membership in
NATO.[16] In April 2016, it published yet another study on this topic, which was
prepared by an independent group of assessors.[17]

The arguments in the Finnish NATO debate have remained basically the same
since the mid-1990s. Both proponents and opponents have formulated their arguments along the dimensions of security, influence, identity, and resources.[18] From
the security perspective, it has been debated whether the security guarantees would
strengthen national defense and add to regional stability or alternatively provoke
Russia and destabilize the region. Proponents of membership have emphasized the
deterrent value as the most important benefit to be gained by joining NATO.
Opponents of NATO membership have tended to view the EU, NORDEFCO,
and the bilateral cooperation with Sweden as sufficient guarantees for Finland's
security, while the proponents have emphasized that NATO will be the only
collective-defense organization in the foreseeable future.

When it comes to the second dimension of the debate, the political influence,
those in favor of joining have pointed out that only the NATO member states have
a seat at the North Atlantic Council table where key decisions on European security are made. The opponents have argued that NATO membership would decrease
the freedom of action in foreign policy and constrain the possibilities to serve as a
mediator in international disputes.

Also, identity and the question of Finland's proper reference group have been
brought up in the debate. Proponents of membership have noted that NATO constitutes a value community of like-minded North American and European democracies and pointed out that almost 95 percent of the population living in the EU
countries belongs also to NATO. From this perspective, it does not make sense
that while Finland has engaged in tight political and economic collaboration in the
EU, it has chosen not to enter into full-scale cooperation in defense issues with, in
many cases, the very same countries. Those opposing NATO membership on the
basis of identity-related considerations often have reservations concerning Finnish
participation in a US-led Alliance.

In times of economic austerity, resources are a critical dimension in any debate.
Opponents of membership have worried that, as a NATO member, Finland would
have to significantly increase its defense budget. Many of the price tags presented in

the debate have been proved inaccurate but nevertheless continue to circulate in the debate. Proponents of membership have recognized that membership cannot be seen as a way of saving money, because it does not remove the need to take care of one's own defense. It has been estimated that—with approximately the same level of defense spending—NATO membership would increase the options available in the development of the Finnish defense system. Long-term savings could be possible by doing more together and by sharing capabilities.

In the current security environment, the arguments related to security carry the heaviest weight. One can no longer argue that NATO would not take its collective defense task seriously. In light of the decisions taken in Wales and Warsaw, it is clear that the Alliance continues to strengthen its deterrence and defense.

The reactions to the Russian aggression can be divided into two camps in the Finnish debate: There are those who say that Russia is bullying Finland and Sweden into the Alliance,[19] and there those who say that Russia is scaring the countries from doing so.[20] It could be argued that—as a result of the deteriorating security environment—the debate has centered on two themes: the increased relevance of Finland and Sweden to NATO in a crisis situation due to their geographic positions and the perceived interdependence of the Finnish and Swedish NATO decisions.

With regard to the first point, it has been pointed out by several analysts that geography makes the defense of NATO's most vulnerable members, the Baltic states, difficult, or even impossible, without the full cooperation of non-NATO Sweden and Finland. The Bertelman Report notes that the defense of the Baltic states against an attacker with powerful resources could be expected to involve the entire Baltic Sea and most of the Scandinavian Peninsula as a potential theater of operations.[21] With Finland and Sweden in NATO, it would be easier for NATO to defend the Baltic countries. As another analyst puts it, "Instead of having forces trek across the narrow Polish border, or risk sailing in hostile Russian-controlled waters, it would be fairly easy, and almost safe, to reach the Baltic States before things got out of control."[22] Analysts have also pointed out that Finland and Sweden hold sovereignty over two island territories in the Baltic Sea—the Åland Islands and Gotland, respectively—both of which are of potentially high strategic importance not just for these states themselves but also for the collective defense surrounding the Baltic Sea rim.[23]

In the same vein, some reports have pointed to the perceived lack of clarity that could be exploited by Moscow.[24] According to a report by the Finnish Institute of International Affairs, it is plausible that NATO membership for both states would close a potential "grey zone" concerning the defense of Europe's northeastern flank while removing some of the current obstacles to strengthening NORDEFCO, as well as Nordic-Baltic defense cooperation.[25]

The second new factor is thus the increasing linkage to Sweden. While Sweden has always played a central part in the Finnish NATO debate, this dimension is becoming even more important as a result of the deteriorating security environment as well as the deepening bilateral defense cooperation between the two countries. On one hand, it has been emphasized in both countries that a decision to join NATO would always be made on the basis of a national assessment. However, both countries agree on the need to keep each other informed. On the other hand, many observers in both countries have recognized that it would be a very difficult position for one of the countries to stay outside of NATO if the other joined.[26] No changes in the current policies are, however, to be expected in the near future. In January 2016, the Finnish and Swedish prime ministers wrote a joint article to the Finnish and Swedish media in which they stated that the current policy of staying outside military alliances serves both countries well.[27]

Moreover, time is emerging as a critical factor to be taken into account in the NATO debate of both countries. NATO has been very clear that its door remains open, and the membership of Montenegro, which entered into force in June 2017, is an important proof of this. However, one cannot rule out the possibility that NATO's door may not be—now or in the future—as wide open as earlier. It takes only one hesitant Ally to prevent enlargement or delay an already started accession process of a would-be member. Moreover, as has been noted in several Finnish publications, NATO would not want to accept new members during an escalating crisis.[28]

The Way Forward

The answer to the Finnish NATO question belongs to Finnish politicians, which has been explicitly recognized by the Alliance on several occasions.[29] Due to the changes in the security environment and in NATO, there is a clear need to update the previous NATO studies and engage in a serious, objective, and calm analysis of all defense options available to Finland. The Juha Sipilä government stated in the program that listed its key goals and areas that it would assess the effects of Finland's possible NATO membership. An assessment by a group of experts was completed in the spring of 2016 and may contribute to a better and more rational discussion on NATO.[30]

Regardless of how the Finnish NATO debate develops, there is a continuous need to keep up Finland's strong national defense capability and to continue to develop the Finnish Defence Forces in such a way that there would be no practical obstacles for a NATO membership. Maintaining the high level of interoperability is crucial, as it facilitates common actions with the Alliance whenever the political leadership so desires.

The necessity of international defense cooperation is widely recognized by Finnish politicians. As the minister of defense, Jussi Niinistö, has put it, "the development of strong national defense capabilities is secured only in combination with active defense cooperation. It is an essential part of our defense, both in peacetime and war."[31]

Notes

The views expressed in this article are those of the author and do not necessarily reflect the official views of the Finnish Ministry for Foreign Affairs or the Finnish Ministry of Defence.

1. See, e.g., the speech delivered by the chairman of the NATO Military Committee, Gen. Petr Pavel, at the European Parliament, October 20, 2015, http://www.nato.int/cps/en/natohq /news_124125.htm.

2. "Warsaw Summit Communiqué: Issued by the Heads of State and Government participating in the meeting of the North Atlantic Council in Warsaw 8–9 July 2016," http://www .nato.int/cps/en/natohq/official_texts_133169.htm.

3. *Active Engagement in Cooperative Security: A More Efficient and Flexible Partnership Policy*, http://www.nato.int/nato_static/assets/pdf/pdf_2011_04/20110415_110415-Partner ship-Policy.pdf. Earlier these tools had been reserved only for the countries of the Euro-Atlantic Partnership Council, but they also became available to the countries of the Mediterranean Dialogue and the Istanbul Cooperation Initiative, as well as to the global partners, pending case-by-case approval by the North Atlantic Council.

4. "Wales Summit Declaration: Issued by the Heads of State and Government Participating in the Meeting of the North Atlantic Council in Wales from 4 to 5 September 2014," http:// www.nato.int/cps/en/natohq/official_texts_112964.htm.

5. Anna Wieslander, "A 'New Normal' for NATO and Baltic Sea Security," US Atlantic Council, October 5, 2015, http://www.atlanticcouncil.org/blogs/natosource/a-new-normal -for-nato-and-baltic-sea-security.

6. Ann-Sofie Dahl and Pauli Järvenpää, "Sweden, Finland and NATO: Security Partners and Security Producers," in *Northern Security and Global Politics: Nordic-Baltic Strategic Influence in a Post-Unipolar World*, ed. Ann-Sofie Dahl and Pauli Järvenpää (Milton Park, UK: Routledge Global Security Studies: 2013).

7. Karoliina Honkanen, "Finland and NATO: Pragmatic Partners," in *Perspectives on European Security: STETE / The Finnish Committee for European Security Yearbook 2011*, http://www.stete.org/perspectives-on-european-security.html; and Ministry of Defence, http://www.defmin.fi/en/tasks_and_activities/defence_policy/nato.

8. *Government Report on Finnish Foreign and Security Policy*, June 17, 2016, http:// formin.finland.fi/public/download.aspx?ID=159273&GUID={BE1F0734-B715 -4C7F-94AA-CBFD3AF7EA5A} (emphasis mine).

9. *Government Defence Report*, February 16, 2017, http://www.defmin.fi/files/3688 /J07_2017_Governments_Defence_Report_Eng_PLM_160217.pdf.

10. Juha Pyykönen: *Nordic Partners of NATO: How Similar Are Finland and Sweden within NATO Cooperation?* (Helsinki: Finnish Institute of International Affairs, 2016), http:// www.fiia.fi/fi/publication/616/nordic_partners_of_nato/.

11. "Natochefen: Sverige så nära det går" [NATO secretary-general: Sweden is as close as possible (without being a member)], *Dagens Nyheter*, November 10, 2015, www.dn.se. http:// www.dn.se/nyheter/sverige/natochefen-sverige-sa-nara-det-gar/.

12. Tomas Bertelman, "International Defence Cooperation Efficiency, Solidarity, Sovereignty," Report from the Inquiry on Sweden's International Defence Cooperation Fö 2013:B, http://www.government.se/49b72f/contentassets/5c39a5fe2c2745f18c8e42322af4fbc4 /international-defence-cooperation—efficiency-solidarity-sovereignty.

13. Efforts are ongoing to deepen Finnish-Swedish bilateral defense cooperation. In January 2015, the defense forces of both countries put forward a report with recommendations on practical steps for closer bilateral cooperation, which will cover all services and joint capability areas. *Final Reports on Deepened Defence Cooperation between Finland and Sweden*, February 17, 2015, http://www.government.se/globalassets/government/dokument/forsvarsdeparte mentet/final-reports-on-deepened-defence-cooperation-between-finland-och-sweden.pdf; and *Joint Statement Regarding Deepened Defence Cooperation between Finland and Sweden*, May 22, 2015. http://www.regeringen.se/4aa8af/globalassets/regeringen/dokument/forsvars departementet/2015-05-22-joint-statement—signed.pdf.

14. *Strategic Programme of Prime Minister Juha Sipilä's Government*, May 29, 2015, http:// valtioneuvosto.fi/en/sipila/government-programme.

15. See, e.g., an opinion poll conducted by Yle/Taloustutkimus in October 2015. https:// yle.fi/uutiset/3-8408558.

16. Antti Sierla, *Effects of Finland's Possible NATO Membership* (Helsinki: Ministry for Foreign Affairs, December 21, 2007); and Pauli Järvenpää (with working group), *Effects of a Possible Membership in a Military Alliance to the Development of the Finnish Defence System and to the Defence Administration* (Helsinki: Ministry of Defence, February 27, 2004).

17. François Heisbourg, René Nyberg, Mats Bergqvist, and Teija Tiilikainen, *The Effects of Finland's Possible NATO Membership: An Assessment*, April 29, 2016, http://formin.fi/public /default.aspx?contentid=345685&nodeid=49298&contentlan=2&culture=en-US.

18. See, e.g., Max Jakobson, "Nato, Finland och Sverige" [NATO, Finland and Sweden] *Internationella Studier*, no. 2, 1996; Tomas Ries: *Finland and NATO*, Department of Strategic Studies Report no. 15 (Helsinki: National Defence College, 1999); Karoliina Honkanen, "Small States in NATO Decision-Making: Influence or Accommodation?," in *Activism and (Non-) Alignment*, ed. Ann Sofie-Dahl and Norman Hillmer (Stockholm: Swedish Institute of International Affairs, 2002); Tuomas Forsberg: *Nato-kirja* [NATO-book] (Helsinki: Ajatus, 2002); Fred Blombergs: "Suomen Nato-jäsenyys realismin näkökulmasta tarkasteltuna" [Finland's membership in NATO from the perspective of realism], *Sotilasaikakauslehti* no. 12 (2015); Pauli Järvenpää, "Argumentteja Suomen Nato-jäsenyyden puolesta" [Arguments in favor of Finland's NATO membership], in *Suomen turvallisuuspoliittinen ratkaisu* [Finland's security political solution], ed. Fred Blombergs (Helsinki: Finnish Defence Forces Research Establishment, National Defence University, 2016), https://www.doria.fi/bitstream/handle/10024/124431 /Blombergs_verkkoversio_2016-2.pdf?sequence=2; and Janne Kuusela: "Naton muutos ja tulevaisuus" [NATO's change and future] in Blombergs, *Suomen turvallisuuspoliittinen ratkaisu*.

19. See, e.g., Mark Seip, "Fearful of Putin, Finland Explores NATO Membership," *Newsweek*, April 6, 2015.

20. See, e.g., Jorge Benitez, "The Bully to the East: Russia Is Trying to Scare Sweden and Finland away from Joining NATO," *US News and World Report*, August 6, 2015.

21. Edward Lucas, *The Coming Storm: Baltic Sea Security Report* (Brussels: Center for European Policy Analysis, June 2015); and Bertelman, "International Defence Cooperation."

22. Ezra Kaplan, "NATO Is Two Properties away from a Baltic Monopoly, and Russia Is Freaking Out," Vice News, September 11, 2015.

23. Eoin Micheál McNamara, Magnus Nordenman, and Charly Salonius-Pasternak, "Nordic-Baltic Security and US Foreign Policy: A Durable Transatlantic Link?," FIIA Working Paper 87, June 2015.

24. Mark Seip, "Finland's Exploration of NATO Membership: The Benefits of Joining the Alliance," *NATOSource*, June 3, 2015, http://www.atlanticcouncil.org/blogs/natosource/finland-s-exploration-of-nato-membership-the-benefits-of-joining-the-alliance.

25. McNamara, Nordenman, and Salonius-Pasternak, "Nordic-Baltic Security."

26. Regarding Finland, see, e.g., the interview with Tuomas Forsberg (University of Tampere) and Charly Salonius-Pasternak (Finnish Institute of International Affairs) in "Tutkijat: Ruotsin Nato-jäsenyys pakottaisi Suomenkin mukaan" [Researchers: Sweden's membership in NATO would force also Finland to join], *Ilta-Sanomat*, January 12, 2014.

27. Stefan Löfven and Juha Sipilä, "Pitkäjänteinen ulko-ja turvallisuuspolitiikka luo vakautta" [Long-term foreign and security policy creates stability]. Several Finnish and Swedish newspapers published this article on January 10, 2016. In Finland, see, e.g., *Lännen media*.

28. See, e.g., Heisbourg et al., *Effects of Finland's Possible NATO Membership*.

29. See, e.g., the reports of Secretary-General Jens Stoltenberg's visit to Finland in March 2015 in *Uusi Suomi*, March 5, 2015.

30. Interview of the Finnish minister of defence, Jussi Niinistö, *Maaseudun tulevaisuus*, July 25, 2015.

31. Speech by Minister of Defence Jussi Niinistö at the briefing of defense attachés in Helsinki on November 26, 2015, http://www.defmin.fi/en/topical/speeches/minister_of_defence_jussi_niinisto_at_the_defence_attache_briefing_in_helsinki.7545.news.

Conclusion

ANN-SOFIE DAHL

The Baltic Sea region has been at the strategic center of attention for the past few years, ever since Russia shocked the West by openly seizing a sizable part of a neighboring country in early 2014. That year is by now forever down in the history books as one that marked a profound change in the relations between Russia and the West. Russia's military aggression in Ukraine and the blatant disregard of international legal norms and the established world order demonstrated by the illegal annexation of the Crimean Peninsula represent a major game changer. The arrival of little green men on Ukrainian ground triggered a series of responses, as NATO made something of a strategic U-turn back to its original core task of collective defense after decades of out-of-area operations with a focus on collective security and crisis management. It was clear that geography, as Christopher Coker noted in his chapter in this volume, still mattered. Indeed, it always had mattered for Russia, though, Coker said, the West—busy at work reducing its national armed forces—had convinced itself that the 230 percent increase in the Russian defense budget over ten years' time was not cause for alarm. Even more alarming, Coker warned, is the fact that NATO is not doctrinally prepared for the ambiguous security challenges that come with hybrid warfare. In its present form, Article 5 might actually be NATO's greatest weakness.

By the time of the Russian annexation of Crimea, the countries in the Baltic Sea region had, however, already been exposed to various forms of Russian military aggression for some time. Not everyone was equally surprised by the complete disrespect of the sovereign borders of its neighboring countries that Russia displayed in attacking Ukraine. Gudrun Persson reminded us in her chapter that already in his speech in Munich in 2007—that is, a year before the war in Georgia—President Vladimir Putin had openly stated that his goal was a new world order, one where the great powers divide the world into spheres of interests. The Congress of Vienna

153

in 1812 and Yalta in 1945—or even the Westphalian world order of the mid-seventeenth century—serve as sources for inspiration for the Russian president. The latest Russian Military Doctrine puts a great deal of emphasis on increased tensions and rivalry between different values and models of development. The West therefore needs to work out a long-term response and understand that Russia, Persson explains, is ready to defend its own interests with all means, nonmilitary and military—and nuclear.

The Baltic Sea is a convenient region for Russia to test its geopolitical ambitions, as Justyna Gotkowska wrote, to divide and weaken the West, to undermine NATO's credibility and the US commitment to Article 5. Poland is one of NATO's traditional "Article 5ers," the group of Allies geographically close to Russia that have consistently advocated—and keep advocating—the preeminence of collective defense, also during the decades when collective security and crisis management in out-of-area operations were given priority. Though already one of only a handful of countries to meet the 2 percent defense spending goal, Poland plans to further increase its military expenditure to continue modernizing its armed forces and, ever since the summit in its capital in 2016, has served as something of a hub for the US military presence on the eastern flank. However, more needs to be done, Gotkowska emphasized, such as the full implementation of reforms of the NATO Response Force (NRF) and of NATO's command structure, to meet the new realities on the eastern flank.

Norway, next door to Russia in the High North, is another of the steadfast Article 5ers in the Alliance, though the country actually only recently discovered the vital security interests that it has in the Baltic Sea—where it does not itself have a border—as a result of the Russian aggression in Ukraine. Nevertheless, Håkon Lunde Saxi wrote, the main security priority for Norway still remains its maritime High North and Arctic regions. As a result of the combined efforts of Norway, France, the United Kingdom, and Iceland, the 2016 Warsaw Summit agreed to strengthen NATO's activities and force posture in the North Atlantic, which was added to the list of strategically important areas with "evolving challenges," especially with regard to protecting the vital sea lines of communication. A main goal was thus achieved as a result of active Norwegian efforts to make NATO look northward more often.

Protection of the sea lines of communication is key in the antiaccess/area-denial (A2/AD) challenge that is of particular relevance in the Baltic Sea. In order for the Allies to provide a credible deterrence, Mikkel Vedby Rasmussen explained in his chapter, NATO must have the capabilities necessary to increase the costs of a Russian intervention in the Baltic countries. As a matter of fact, A2/AD capabilities can also be used the other way around, as an effective countermeasure to Russian incursions, in a similar fashion as during the Napoleonic Wars when Denmark was able to deny the British Royal Navy easy access to the Baltic Sea and dramatically increased the costs for operating there.

With its location in the middle of the Baltic Sea, the Swedish island of Gotland would be central to any such A2/AD operations and, thus, to security in the entire region. It is obvious that for Russia, Johan Raeder argued, an attack on, or occupation of, Gotland would be of enormous political and strategic value. As was the case already during the Crimean War in the 1850s, the different interests of the powers around the Baltic Sea and beyond need to be considered when analyzing the role of Gotland today. In the event of an attack, Sweden would, Raeder wrote, make a determined effort to defend the island with the forces now deployed there and elsewhere. The country's decision to enter into a host-nation support agreement with NATO and the increased military presence and exercise activities on the island and in the sea are all important factors in this respect.

While the deteriorated security environment in the Baltic Sea has resulted in political decisions to increase the national levels of preparedness in a number of countries in the region, others have come around more slowly, with Germany as a prime example. Though Germany is a major country in the Baltic Sea region and a European economic great power, its positions, as Claudia Major and Alicia von Voss explained, are somewhat puzzling, with still no clear Nordic or Nordic-Baltic focus in its security and defense policies. The traditional role as a broker between East and West has resulted in Germany's advocating a double posture for NATO of both deterrence and détente in the Baltic Sea, thus bringing back the old leitmotif of the 1967 Harmel Report.

Having a border of 1,340 kilometers (approximately 833 miles) with Russia and a long history of wars with its eastern neighbor, Finland is known for taking its defense very seriously and is one of NATO's top partner countries and respected security producers, jointly with Sweden. As Karoliina Honkanen showed in her chapter, Finland has taken full advantage of all the programs and tools offered by NATO, but its partnership cooperation has more and more become a matter of developing the country's national defense rather than for participation in distant operations. In the event of a crisis in the Baltic Sea region, Finland would, Honkanen concluded, become involved in one way or the other, which makes military interoperability with NATO absolutely crucial.

The same would obviously be true for Sweden. Contrary to Finland—which has also maintained a high level of military preparedness during more peaceful times—Sweden has quite a bit of catching up to do after decades of severe cuts in its national defense budget. However, neither nonaligned country, I explained in my chapter, is likely to hand in an application for NATO membership in the foreseeable future. In the Swedish case, the optimistic predictions in the last few years that such a change of doctrine was about to happen were based on wishful thinking rather than of sober analysis of the facts and on the position that "neutrality"—as the nonaligned policy is still sometimes referred to—still holds in politically significant segments of society. Instead of membership in NATO, Sweden has invested heavily in other formats—apart from its partnership with NATO—such as NORDEFCO but also in a number of bilateral defense agreements with key NATO allies: the United States, the United Kingdom, Denmark, Poland, and Norway. In addition, Swedish-Finnish military cooperation is exceptional in the sense that it extends also "beyond peacetime."

Though outside of Article 5 guarantees, the two partner countries still contribute to NATO's reassurance and deterrence measures through active participation in the exercises and training programs, political dialogue, joint assessment of security in the Baltic Sea, and much more offered to them as "gold card holders" in the partner community. These measures were also outlined by Jamie Shea in his chapter. Shea took a close look at NATO's work in reestablishing deterrence and projecting stability thus far, from the Wales Summit in 2014 to "the year of decision" in 2016 to the "the year of implementation" in 2017. The long list includes the implementation of the Readiness Action Plan, with four battalions in the Baltic states and Poland; the Very High Readiness Joint Task Force, which is now deployable within forty-eight hours; the NRF, which has tripled in size; the former German-Polish-Danish headquarters in Szczecin, which has been upgraded to a Multinational Corps Headquarters Northeast; and so forth. Nevertheless, Shea concluded, more is needed to further enhance deterrence, such as a review of the command structure (also mentioned by Gotkowska), greater focus on follow-on forces and logistics to increase NATO's strength in depth, and more maritime forces for the NRF and NATO's maritime standing groups. What is, however, also of great significance is a robust public-opinion effort to rebrand NATO, in particular in the United States where the Donald Trump administration has to make clear its firm commitment to NATO's treaty obligations.

The list of NATO's measures in response to Russia's aggression is indeed impressive. But is it enough to deter Russia from continuing its provocative behavior in the region? Or is Narva next, as Andres Kasekamp put it in his chapter? The Estonian border town only eighty miles from St. Petersburg and, with a 95 percent Russian-speaking population, has become a symbol of the vulnerability of the Baltic states. His conclusion is a decisive no. Though Estonia is, as are the other Baltic states, by now very familiar with Russian hybrid warfare, no little green men will likely appear on the streets of Narva.

For one thing, the Baltic states, though small, are all members of both NATO and the European Union, and the consequences of a Russian intervention there would thus be so much graver than was the case in Ukraine. If asked, the Russian population of Narva would also much prefer the euro to the ruble and the healthcare systems of the Baltic countries to that offered on the other side of the border. Most important, Kasekamp argued, is the huge increase in the US defense spending for Europe, including the European Reassurance Initiative, which was extended by President Trump in the budget for fiscal year 2018. Though the president himself has cast doubts about the US commitment to NATO, one should look at deeds rather than words when analyzing US policy.

With that conclusion Robert Lieber wholeheartedly agreed in his chapter on the US and Baltic Sea security, which opened this volume. The United States remains, he states, the "indispensable power" for Europe's defense and in NATO, with no other country coming even close to the overall capabilities that the US possesses. The ambiguous statements by President Trump with regard to the relevance of NATO and Article 5 have, however, caused a lot of uncertainty and confusion on the European side of the Atlantic. Lieber characterizes Trump's "America First" agenda as basically Jacksonian, as defined by Walter Russell Mead—that is, nationalist and populist—but argues that it is nevertheless way too soon to write off NATO and the transatlantic link in US policy. The relevance of both is demonstrated by the extensive deterrence measures and the increased US defense spending in Europe, after decades of a dramatic drawdown of the American military presence in Europe. Without NATO, Lieber emphasized, core US interests and values would be at risk as well—not to mention, one might add, the severe consequences this would have for security in the Baltic Sea region.

CONTRIBUTORS

Christopher Coker, PhD, is professor of international relations at the London School of Economics. He is the author of *The Improbable War* (2015) and *Future War* (2016), among many other books. Previously a NATO fellow, he is a visiting fellow at the Swedish Defence College.

Ann-Sofie Dahl, PhD, is associate professor (docent) of international relations and nonresident senior fellow at the Atlantic Council. In recent years, she has been an adjunct fellow at the Center for Strategic and International Studies in Washington, senior research fellow at the Centre for Military Studies in Copenhagen, and a visiting fellow at the NATO Defense College in Rome. Previous to that, she has been affiliated with a number of other research institutions and universities in the United States and Scandinavia. She has published extensively on Nordic-Baltic security, NATO, and the transatlantic link.

Justyna Gotkowska coordinates the project Security and Defence in Northern Europe at the Warsaw-based analytical institute Centre for Eastern Studies, where she has worked since 2008. In her work she has focused on security and defense issues in Northern and Central Europe. She has followed defense policies and armed forces' developments in Germany, Poland, and the Nordic and Baltic states and has written extensively on bi- and multilateral military cooperation in both regions and on developments and adjustments to the new security environment within NATO and the European Union (EU).

Karoliina Honkanen works as ministerial adviser in the Finnish Ministry of Defence. From 2014 to 2017, she served as defense counselor at the Mission of Finland to NATO in Brussels. Earlier she worked in various functions in the Finnish Ministry of Defence, the Finnish Defence Command, and the Finnish Institute of International Affairs.

Andres Kasekamp, PhD, is a professor at the Munk School of Global Affairs and chair of Estonian studies at the University of Toronto. He holds a PhD in modern history from University College London. From 2004 to 2017, he was professor of Baltic politics at the University of Tartu. He served as the director of the Estonian Foreign Policy Institute—a think tank affiliated with the Estonian Ministry of Foreign Affairs—from 2000 to 2013. His book *A History of the Baltic States* (Palgrave Macmillan, 2010) has won several awards and been translated into nine languages. He is president-elect of the Association for the Advancement of Baltic Studies.

Robert J. Lieber, PhD, is professor of government and international affairs at Georgetown University. He is author or editor of seventeen books on international relations and US foreign policy. In addition to his latest book, *Retreat and Its Consequences: American Foreign Policy and the Problem of World Order* (Cambridge University Press, 2016), his recent books include *Power and Willpower in the American Future: Why the United States Is Not Destined to Decline* (Cambridge University Press, 2012) and *The American Era: Power and Strategy for the 21st Century* (Cambridge University Press, 2007).

Claudia Major, PhD, is senior associate in the International Security Division at the German Institute for International and Security Affairs (SWP) Berlin. Her research, advisory work, and publications focus on security and defense policy in Europe (the EU, NATO, Germany, and France). Previous placements include the EU Institute for Security Studies (Paris), the Center for Security Studies of ETH Zurich, the German Foreign Office, and Sciences Po Paris. Major graduated from the Free University Berlin and Sciences Po Paris and holds a PhD from the University of Birmingham.

Gudrun Persson, PhD, is associate professor at the Slavic Department of Stockholm University and works at the Swedish National Defence Establishment, where she focuses on Russian security policy and Russian military strategic thought. She holds a PhD in government from the London School of Economics. Among her publications are *Russian Military Capability in a Ten-Year Perspective 2016* (edited, FOI, 2016); *Military Thinking in the 21st Century* (coedited with Carolina Vendil Pallin and Tommy Jeppsson (FOI, 2015); and *Learning from Foreign Wars: Russian Military Thinking, 1859–1873* (Helion, 2010). She has published widely on Russian affairs and is a member of the Royal Swedish Academy of War Sciences.

Johan Raeder is the defense adviser at the Embassy of Sweden in Washington, DC. He served at the Ministry of Defence in Stockholm as director-general for international affairs (2013–14), as director-general for political affairs (2008–13), and as head of the Department for Security Policy and International Affairs

(2001–8). He joined the ministry in 1996 from the National Defence Research Establishment, where he served as an operations analyst working on matters related to air defense, operational planning, and chemical, biological, and nuclear defense. He has been stationed in the Armed Forces Headquarters and at the Swedish Mission to the Conference on Disarmament in Geneva.

Mikkel Vedby Rasmussen, PhD, is professor of political science at the University of Copenhagen. He has served as the head of policy development in the Danish Ministry of Defence and founded the Centre for Military Studies, a university think tank focusing on defense and security policy. His latest book is *The Military's Business* (Cambridge University Press, 2014).

Håkon Lunde Saxi, PhD, is a senior fellow with the Norwegian Defence University College and the Norwegian Institute for Defence Studies. He received his PhD in political science from the University of Oslo in 2016. His research focuses on Norwegian, Nordic, and European security as well as multinational defense cooperation. He has previously published articles in the *Journal of Strategic Studies* and *Defense and Security Analysis*. Among his most recent publications in English is "British and German Initiatives for Defence Cooperation: The Joint Expeditionary Force and the Framework Nations Concept," in *Defence Studies*, vol. 17, no. 2.

Jamie Shea, PhD, is NATO deputy assistant secretary-general for emerging security challenges. Previous positions at NATO include director of policy planning in the private office of the secretary-general, deputy assistant secretary-general for external relations in the public diplomacy division, director of information and press, spokesman of NATO, and deputy director of information and press. He holds a DPhil in modern history from Oxford University and is a regular lecturer and conference speaker on NATO, European security affairs, and public diplomacy. Dr. Shea is a professor at the Collège d'Europe, Bruges, and is involved with several other prominent academic institutions.

Alicia von Voss coordinates a research project on northern security issues at the German Council on Foreign Relations in Berlin. She previously worked as a research assistant in the International Security Division at the SWP in Berlin. From 2013 to 2017, she worked with Claudia Major on the research project Security and Defence in Northern Europe. Her current research focuses on European defense cooperation, particularly in Northern and central Eastern Europe. She holds an MA in European studies from the European University Viadrina, Frankfurt (Oder), and a BA from University College Maastricht.

INDEX

CPSIA information can be obtained
at www.ICGtesting.com
Printed in the USA
LVHW111155020323
740769LV00009B/71